THE
American Connection
TO

THE SINKING OF HMS *DASHER*

JOHN STEELE & NOREEN STEELE

Introduction

HMS *Dasher* seems to have been a fairly constant part of our lives for almost 20 years. It has become like an old friend who keeps remembering exciting stories of yesteryear and whispers quietly in the ear that these stories should be revealed to the folk of today, if only to ensure that government secrecy will never again result in a mother not being told about the circumstances of the passing of a dear son.

Unearthing information about the sinking of HMS *Dasher* proved quite shocking, particularly as it happened just a few miles offshore in almost a straight line from our home in Ardrossan, on the beautiful Clyde coast, with the backdrop of the stunning Arran Mountains.

Later on as we had the privilege of meeting *Dasher* survivors and next of kin, it became clear that a major injustice had taken place in relation to not informing relatives of the disaster. The more stories we recorded, the angrier we became. It seemed heartlessly cruel to have sailors buried with their ship or placed in a mass grave without telling wives, mothers, sweethearts and other relatives the known facts and allow them some closure. Today such an action would be inconceivable. Sadly, many of *Dasher's* next of kin went to their graves without ever learning the truth, a cruel act beyond belief.

We are extremely grateful to so many people for their kind and willing assistance over the years of our research. We have been exhilarated at the stories of *Dasher's* crew members, some showing immense personal bravery at the height of the unfolding tragedy. We have also joined in a tear as the personal stories were told by next of kin with heart-rending sadness.

This is the latest and final edition of the *Dasher* story and it unravels the mysteries surrounding the sudden, catastrophic explosion that resulted in the sinking of HMS *Dasher* on 27th March, 1943, in home waters on the Clyde without any enemy involvement. The casualties were high, 379 lives were lost within sight of land. Strict silence was imposed. Prior to the 149 survivors being dispersed to different ships they were warned:

Don't ever talk about this!

Conflict and blame began immediately between the Royal Navy and their American counterparts. The British blamed the Americans for the loss of the ship and the Americans blamed the British. Who would be held responsible? Even more mystery was to surface from the deep! A connection has been established with a World War II plan to deceive the Germans as to where the planned allied invasion would take place. The plan, described as the most fiendish plot ever conceived, involved the use of a body carrying false invasion documents and became known as *The Man Who Never Was*.

Strong evidence points to a body from HMS *Dasher* being used in this highly successful operation which saved the lives of almost 30,000 Allied troops.

But what of *Dasher's* crew and their kin? Up to the present time the bereaved relatives have only been given meagre information regarding the loss of their loved ones. Why were the rules contravened regarding the Admiralty directive which clearly states:

> *Relatives of casualties should be given as much information as possible.*

The 379 victims of this disaster deserve to be remembered and a memorial on Ardrossan seafront helps to do just that and nowadays there is an annual service of remembrance.

It is our hope that this book will also keep alive the memory of the *Dasher* crew. Most of the sailors and airmen would never have dreamt that *Dasher* would sink in home waters of the Clyde with such devastating loss of life. We salute them all and fondly tell part of their story with pride.

The American Connection To

**The Sinking of
HMS *Dasher***

ISBN: 978-0-9532637-1-4

John & Noreen Steele
Authors of
*They Were Never Told
The Secrets of HMS Dasher
Whispers of Horse Island
Welcome to Wee Cumbrae
The Tragedy of HMS Dasher
Burning Ships*

First published 2010   Editor Donald L. Reid.
John & Noreen Steele
j.steele2@talktalk.net

The authors have asserted their moral rights.

British Library Cataloguing-in-Publication Data.

A catalogue record of this book is available from
the British Library.

ISBN: 978-0-9532637-1-4

Artwork by
Delta Mac Artwork
(deltamacartwork@btinternet.com)

Printed by
Kestrel Press
25 Whittle Place
Irvine,
Ayrshire
KA11 4HR
01294 222 222

Front cover photographs
Top: HMS Dasher
Bottom left: Celebrating the handover "A toast to HMS Dasher and all who sail in her"
Bottom right: One of the first planes to land on, crash lands on the flight deck

Sea on fire

Dasher
A song
by Dusty Millar

Dusty Millar is an extremely talented and popular folk singer who resides in Saltcoats, North Ayrshire. He is untiring in giving of his time and talents to raising funds for worthy charitable causes. Dusty has always felt concern over the loss and subsequent cover-up relating to HMS *Dasher*. After reading the book 'They Were Never Told' by John & Noreen Steele, Dusty felt compelled to put his thoughts into words and the result is this very emotional song. This song is dedicated to all who suffered when HMS *Dasher* blew up and sank on the 27th March 1943

On the 27th day of March 1943
Dasher left Lochranza, she'd come round from Dundee
She was heading for an anchorage just north at Greenock town
When a bloody great explosion took the Dasher down
In the middle of the channel known as the Firth of Clyde
The spot the Dasher sank in is as deep as it is wide
She lies there, still a war grave, in the water deep and cold
And yet, for years, the families were never ever told
They were not told; never told.

A cargo ship, converted to carry aeroplanes
She escorted allied shipping during Hitler's bloody games
But she had a reputation; they said she was a jinx
In hindsight, from the stories told, she was sure someday to sink
Well the captain's name was Boswell and the poor man never knew
How quickly he would lose his ship and almost all his crew
As she turned her head for Greenock the day was calm and bright
Eight minutes later she' gone down just south of Cumbrae light
But they were not told; never told.

Those of the crew who did not drown, their fate was worse of all
For burning fuel had turned the sea into a fireball
And the cries of stricken sailors as they struggled to survive
Soon faded into silence as one by one they died
Yet it was not German action that ended Dasher's days
It seems a simple accident sent her beneath the waves
Almost 400 young men lost the chance of growing old
And yet for years the families were never ever told
They were not told, never told.

A government decision was taken right away
No one should ever talk about what happened on that day
"We are at war with Germany;" was their excuse, and so
They kept the story secret that Hitler would not know
But I find I can't help thinking that somewhere along the way
Those deadheads down in Whitehall should have had the guts to say
But they did not have the decency; their hearts were hard and cold
And so for years the families were never ever told
They were not told, never told.

And then the rumours started, someone was heard to say
That the body of a sailor lad who lost his life that day
Had been taken by the government to further Britain's cause
To fool Hitler they invented "The Man Who Never Was"
Did this sailor from the Dasher help the Allies win the war?
The answer still lies hidden in some secret Whitehall drawer
And still the nation's waiting for the whole truth to unfold
Some day they'll have to tell us what the families were not told.

John Melville, the man who never was

Acknowledgements

For their assistance in compiling this book we are extremely grateful to the following: Special thanks to Tony Atherton (Manchester), Frank Brand (Ardrossan) and Terry Whippy (Eastbourne) for the countless hours they have devoted to research; The HMS *Dasher* survivors who shared their personal accounts; The bereaved families for sharing their precious memories of loved ones; Alan Boswell and Robin Boswell, sons of Captain L A K Boswell; Duncan Bridge, Former R.N. Minewarfare and Clearance Diving Officer Paul Chadwick; CGMS Consulting, Morley House, 26 Holborn Viaduct, London; Cabinet Office London; Caledonian MacBrayne (Cal Mac), Gourock; Councillor Ian Clarkson, Deputy Provost, North Ayrshire Council; Commonwealth War Graves Commission, Maidenhead; Sue Goddard, Deddington, Oxon; Herbert Geoffrey Cameron, Spain; The late Colin Gibbon, Pontypridd, for first putting forward the connection between HMS *Dasher* and *The Man Who Never Was* and for access to his copious research papers; Jesus Copeiro, Huelva, Spain; Katy Clark MP; Pupils of Corrie Primary School Arran. John Cowan, CDM Ayr.

Ian Douglas, Racks Village; Fleet Air Arm Museum, Yeovilton; General Register Office for Scotland, Edinburgh; Kenneth Gibson, MSP; Bill Haggerty, Ayr; Neil Hamilton Bulger, Arran; Phil Hammond, former Royal Navy Leading Diver; David Hendry, Largs; United Kingdom Hydrographic Office, Taunton, Somerset; Robert Jack, former General Foreman, Ardrossan Harbour; The Mine Warfare and Clearance Diving Officers Association; John McGraa, Rhaytader, Powys, Wales; Jim Macaulay, Area Librarian, Saltcoats Library; Staff at the McLean Museum, Greenock; Canon Mathew F McManus, St Peter's Church, Ardrossan; Rev Jim Smith, EU Church, Ardrossan; James Murray, Tealby, Lincs; Billy McMurray, Gorokan, NSW, Australia; Bob McSherry, Local Historian.

Bill Miller, Isle of Stronsay, Orkney; 'Dusty' Miller, Saltcoats; Ministry of Defence, Naval Historical Branch, Portsmouth; Ministry of Defence, Secretariat (Naval Branch), London; North Ayrshire Heritage Centre, Saltcoats; The National Archives, Kew, Surrey; Councillor David O'Neill, Leader, North Ayrshire Council; Royal British Legion Scotland (Irvine Branch); Denise Richardson MA, California; Mark Reeves SMC (Tech) Optical Laboraty. Burray Orkney. John Linton Steele, Denver, USA; Sea Cadets, Ardrossan (TS Gannet); Paul Stevenson, Funeral Director, Saltcoats; David Stewart, Skelmorlie; Scottish Maritime Museum, Irvine; Jessie Taylar, Lamlash Arran.

John Urquart, West Kilbride

Colin Whitelaw, Co-operative Monumental Services, Ardrossan; staff at Watt Library Greenock; U-boat Archives, Germany.

Kathleen Reid, Beith for proof reading.

891 Squadron Fly-past at Dasher memorial service Ardrossan 1993. Each of the five Sea King helicopters proceeded to fly over Dasher to drop floral wreaths.

Contents

John & Noreen Steele
Authors

Foreword

by
Donald L Reid BA FSA Scot
Local Author & Journalist

The sinking of HMS *Dasher* and the tragic loss of 379 lives on 27 March, 1943, in the Firth of Clyde between Ardrossan and Arran should have been heart-stopping, jaw-dropping headline news in the United Kingdom and abroad, followed by a formal period of national mourning, such was the scope of this war-time Naval disaster in Scottish waters.

However, with the secrecy of war - inexplicable in the circumstances of this tragedy - it was quietly hushed up and remained relatively unknown until John and Noreen Steele began their research some 20 years ago, publishing *The Tragedy of HMS Dasher* (1995) followed by *They Were Never Told: The Tragedy of HMS Dasher* (1997) and *The Secrets of HMS Dasher* (2002).

Through meticulous and time-consuming research and interviewing many folk across the globe, whose lives were touched by this catastrophe, they have carefully pieced together a story that is both revealing and shocking. It is to the great credit of the authors, a quiet unassuming couple, who realised the shocking scale of the *Dasher* tragedy and steadfastly set about unearthing the secrets officialdom hoped would never see the light of day.

This is an important social history, telling as it does of an unfolding tragedy at sea and government secrecy which extended to denying next of kin information about their loved ones, who were the victims of the second worst Naval disaster in British waters. However, the highlight for me was learning so much about the ordinary people connected to HMS *Dasher*. This book is revealing, shocking, soul-searching and touches the heart.

The Ardrossan based authors can be justly proud that they determinedly stuck with their task despite stormy seas, and against all the odds, sailed home with the evidence on the demise of HMS *Dasher*.

Top: Two Dasher officers on top of the Empire State Building, whilst waiting the completion of the conversion the officers visited the popular tourist attractions. Bottom: Free Tickets. The crew were given free tickets to cinemas, theatres and dance halls.

Chapter 1

Cargo Boat Converted to Aircraft Carrier

During the early years of the Second World War Britain was losing the battle of the Atlantic. Convoys bringing vital food and war supplies from America and Canada were under constant attack from the dreaded German U-boats.

The loss of merchant shipping was an ever increasing problem due to Germany intensifying production of their U-boats. By the beginning of 1942 more than 300 U-boats were roaming the high seas seeking out and attacking British convoys.

During the month of January 1942 the U-boats had sunk 62 allied merchant ships. The following month 85 ships were lost and during March a further 95 ships were sunk. The enemy had their FW Condor long-range reconnaissance aircraft seeking out the convoys then reporting back their exact positions.

To give added protection to the convoys more aircraft carriers were urgently required. The strategy was that the aircraft carriers would sail in the middle of the convoy while their aircraft flew on almost constant patrol.

On the 29th April 1942 the Admiralty ordered six escort carriers from America under the Lend-Lease agreement. This would allow six existing American merchant ships to be converted into aircraft carriers for the Royal Navy.

One of the ships converted was the *Rio de Janeiro* which had been built and launched the previous year by the Sun Shipbuilding Company, Chester, Pennsylvania. It was destined to have a very different future to that envisaged by her Naval architects and builders.

The *Rio de Janeiro* entered Tietjen and Lang's dry dock, Hoboken, New York. There extensive work was carried out to convert her into a fighting aircraft carrier. Hundreds of men and women worked in shifts round the clock. Within a few months the converted ship had acquired a flight deck, a hangar and an aircraft lift. On the flight deck there was a single structure referred to as "The Island." This comprised of the bridge and wheelhouse also the flying operations office.

Below deck were the living quarters, sleeping accommodation, mess decks, toilets and kitchens to cater for more than 500 crewmen. While the finishing touches were being added, Royal Navy officers and crew arrived in New York in preparation for the official hand-over. During their stay in New York the officers resided in the luxurious Barbizon Plaza Hotel. The crew were based at Flushing Barracks, New York. The officers and crew were overwhelmed by the American hospitality. They were treated to tickets for free admission to cinemas, theatres and dance halls.

During the last few days of the ship's conversion, a handful of the crew went on board to familiarise themselves with the ship. Whilst below deck they stopped to watch a welder working on the last of the plates. As sparks flew the welder turned round to see who was there. On seeing the prospective crew he smiled and welded the letters R.I.P. onto a plate.

The conversion was completed on the 1st July, 1942 and the ship was officially "handed-over" to the Royal Navy and re-named HMS *Dasher*. At the hand-over ceremony the ship was welcomed with these words:

"A toast to HMS Dasher and all who sail in her."

The dignitaries raised their silver goblets to toast the ship.

The former merchant ship was now a Royal Navy Archer class escort carrier. She was the fifth of these American built carriers. Her sister ships were *Avenger, Charger, Archer* and *Biter.*

After the official hand-over, Captain Richard Bell-Davies took command of the ship. During at-sea exercises to "work-up" the ship a number of faults were found. The smaller of the defects were soon rectified; however there was a constant smell of petrol in the hangar area where the petrol pumps for refuelling the aircraft were located. The ship's engines were also presenting problems which required constant attention. Three weeks after the hand-over the engines were still unreliable. With many problems still unresolved, on 25th July, 1942 four aircraft of 837 Squadron landed safely in time to allow *Dasher* to join a convoy bound for the UK.

Unfortunately all did not go according to plan. Due to persistent engine defects *Dasher* was unable to join the convoy. The chief engineer had no faith in the design of the Sun Doxford engines and his low opinion was fully justified. The seriousness of the engine problems became evident when the ship was on her trials in the Hudson River.

Every time the 8 cylinder engines were started up they backfired and on many occasions this was followed by an explosion through the side venting exhaust pipes. This in turn would damage one or more of the 2 feet diameter cylinders. With the cylinder timing now "out" the ship would shudder violently until the faulty engine was stopped and repairs carried out.

During further sea trials the serious engine problems persisted and the ship was taken to the US Navy Shipyard, Brooklyn. Whilst in the yard attempts were made to rectify the engine problems and other defects. As Captain Bell-Davies was required for other duties he was replaced by Captain C.N. Lentaignes on 6th August, 1942.

Dasher departed from the Hudson River on route to Halifax, Nova Scotia where she joined convoy HX 205 bound for the UK. Prior to departure a group of young boys, aged from 8 to 14, were ushered onboard. The previous year they had been evacuated from blitz-torn Britain to Canada. It had been decided it was now safe for them to return home.

The convoy departed for the UK on 24th August. During the voyage *Dasher's* aircraft made constant searches for enemy submarines and reconnaissance aircraft. On one occasion a number of the evacuees were with the Captain on the bridge when an alert was raised by one of the airborne pilots reporting a possible U-boat sighting, and consequently the crew on all of the ships went to "Action Stations" immediately.

Onboard *Dasher* the excited boys in the bridge were hastily escorted below. As tension throughout the convoy rose, the waiting began. Fortunately the "All Clear" was sounded within a short time. The possible sighting had actually been a false alarm. Despite the evacuees being told the incident had been a false alarm, it did not diminish their excitement.

The remainder of the 17 day voyage was uneventful, however, it was recorded that *Dasher's* stability and her electrical system fell below Royal Navy standards. As for the engine, it was still giving concern to the chief engineer. On arrival in the Firth of Clyde it was arranged that the aircraft carrier would be examined by a Clyde shipyard, to have all the serious faults rectified.

When the convoy arrived safely on 10th September 1942, *Dasher* was manoeuvred into the shipyard of James Lamont & Company, East India Harbour, Greenock. Like the other American converted aircraft carriers *Dasher* required modifications to meet Royal Navy standards. Most of the crew who had sailed from America were given shore leave and made their way home.

Unfortunately prior to the rectification work being completed, *Dasher* was urgently required for operational convoy duty. On departure from Lamont's shipyard the Admiralty were advised the ship required between 1,200 tons and 2,000 tons of additional ballast. This work was contracted to Ross & Marshall, Greenock, who specialised in the loading and unloading of ships. It took them three days to load more that 1,200 tons of pig iron into the bowels of the ship. This vast extra tonnage added to the ship's engine problems.

During the loading of the extra ballast telegrams were sent to all the crew, who were home on shore leave, ordering them to return as soon as possible. Many of the crew expressed much surprise to their families that the ship had apparently been brought up to standard in such a short time. After collecting their travel warrants the off duty crew travelled from all over the U.K. to Greenock.

On arrival and boarding the aircraft carrier they met up with new crew members who had been drafted to the ship. On 16th October after the completion of rigorous sea trials, to work-up the ship, six Sea Hurricanes of 891 Squadron landed on. Ten days later they were joined by six Sea Hurricane aircraft from 804 Squadron. With the sea trials now complete and a crew in excess of 500 and with two squadrons of aircraft HMS *Dasher* was ready for convoy duty.

Top: U.S. Hand-over. The official hand-over ceremony took place on July 2nd 1942. The ceremony was scheduled to take place on Dasher's flight deck, however, due to a torrential downpour of rain the ceremony took place in Dasher's hanger. Bottom: One of the first swordfish aircraft to arrive on Dasher. On landing the handlers folded the wings over then pushed the aircraft to the lift, it was then lowered down to the hanger. The lift was then raised back to the flight deck for the next aircraft to land on.

Chapter 2

Invasion of North Africa 1942

An armada of Royal Navy ships was increasing steadily beside *Dasher* in the Firth of Clyde. The chatter onboard *Dasher* was:

"Something big is going to happen!"

Little did the crew know that other Royal Navy ships were also gathering at Scapa Flow, Liverpool and Loch Ewe. During late October 1942 the Royal Navy convoys started to depart. On 27th October the Clyde Convoy comprising of fifty-one Royal Navy ships including *Dasher* departed. The convoy's operational name was "Force LX" part of "Operation Torch" the allied invasion of North Africa.

Dasher was one of seven Royal Navy aircraft carriers providing air cover for the convoys. The other carriers were *Biter, Avenger, Argus, Furious, Formidable and Victorious.* Also involved in the invasion force were 106 United States Navy ships which had sailed from America.

More than 360 allied warships and in excess of 370 merchant ships were now sailing to North Africa. This was the greatest amphibious operation in history up to that time. Success was so vital that each convoy received added air cover and special U-boat surveillance.

Thanks to Alan Turing, a brilliant mathematician, the German Enigma secret codes had been broken. Unknown to the enemy the British could track the position of their U-boats. Now when a U-boat was tracked in the vicinity of the invasion force the convoy could be re-routed successfully.

At 1.20am on Friday 30th October *Dasher's* port-side engine broke down resulting in the ship reducing speed. It took the engineers 4 hours to successfully carry out the repair. During that time the convoy also had to reduce speed. At 5.29 am the convoy increased speed.

During the 10 day voyage the armada encountered treacherous weather. The conditions were so bad that the fighter pilots could only participate in flying exercises on 2 days out of the 10 days at sea. On one of the worst weather days one of *Dasher's* aircraft was washed overboard. Another two were damaged beyond repair.

Midway into the 1000 mile voyage a radar operator on board HMS *Zetland* detected an enemy submarine. "Action Stations" were sounded throughout the convoy and all gunners quickly made their way to their gun stations. On board

Dasher Lieutenant F. E. Price, the ships gunnery officer, reported:

"Guns ready."

As the convoy made an emergency turn to port then changed course into a zigzag pattern, the escort destroyers commenced a sustained depth charge attack. When no further contact was made with the U-boat, the destroyers returned to the convoy.

Later that same day a German reconnaissance aircraft was detected. To deceive the enemy pilot and his observer the convoy commander ordered the convoy to change course and a short time later the long range reconnaissance plane flew away. When the enemy aircraft could no longer be seen, the convoy returned to their planned course. During the rest of the voyage no further contact was made with the enemy. Before arriving at their destination the aircraft on board *Dasher* and *Biter* had their red, white and blue roundels over-painted with the five pointed white American star!

As the ships approached Africa they altered course and divided into three groups. Each group had a different target: Oran, Casablanca or Algiers. *Dasher* was delegated to be part of the Central Naval Task Force, the invasion of Oran. By the evening of 7th November all ships were in their appointed positions.

Dasher, accompanied by more than 67 Naval ships, was one mile offshore from Oran, which was a strategic harbour town with two airports. The assault ships were a formidable force which comprised of two escort carriers, two anti-aircraft ships, two submarines, eighteen supply ships, thirteen destroyers, eight mine sweepers, six corvettes and a flotilla of landing craft to shuttle forty thousand troops ashore. All ships were ordered to maintain radio silence.

Late into evening the fighter pilots from 804 and 891 squadrons on *Dasher* and also the pilots on her sister ship *Biter* waited to receive their orders. The order when issued was:

"Provide air cover for the Allied landings at Oran and the bombing of La Senia Airfield."

On Sunday 8th November during the early hours of the morning a horrendous bombardment on the coast of Oran commenced from the Royal Navy ships, including *Dasher, Rodney, Furious, Biter, and Delhi*. At the harbour entrance a heroic effort by two British battleships was thwarted by severe enemy cross fire causing one of the ships to sink and the other blowing up resulting in heavy loss of life.

At 5.30am *Dasher* and *Biter's* Hurricane aircraft were catapulted into the air prior to the landing craft heading for Oran Beach carrying 40,000 troops. When Pilot Jimmy Crossman was launched off *Dasher*, the tail of his aircraft touched the sea, but he managed to remain airborne.

The fighter pilots of the aircraft from 804 Squadron were Commanding Officer A. J. Sewell DSC, Sub-lieutenants J. Hancock, N. Goodfellow, J. Crossman,

J. McEvoy and A. C. McLennan. Unfortunately Allied Military Intelligence was unaware that the enemy aircraft outnumbered the Allies by four to one!

Dasher fighter pilot Sub-lieutenant Lionel Godfrey, of 891 Squadron, was completing an aerial reconnaissance of Oran Harbour when he was pounced upon by four enemy aircraft. As he had just expended all his ammunition he attempted to out-manoeuvre his attackers. Unfortunately one the enemy pilots managed to fire a burst from his guns which damaged Lionel's engine.

With thick black smoke pouring from his engine and his speed reducing Sub-lieutenant Godfrey had no option but to immediately lower his aircraft's landing wheels which signalled that he was surrendering. The four enemy aircraft then escorted the "captured" pilot to Oran's main airport at La Senia. On landing Lionel was taken prisoner and locked up in the town jail. The following day he successfully escaped and hid in the mountains.

The bombing of La Senia airport, five miles inland, proved to be very successful with sixty-seven enemy planes destroyed or badly damaged with the loss of only one Hurricane from *Dasher* and one Albacore aircraft. After an intense air battle for supremacy the airport surrendered. When the assault troops entered La Senia airport all the destroyed or damaged enemy aircraft were found to be fully armed and prepared for action!

At sea the Commodore in charge was alerted to U-boat activity at Oran Harbour. To give added protection to his valuable aircraft carriers he ordered them to a position further out to sea. The message also contained co-ordinates advising the new position. *Dasher* and *Biter* took immediate action and moved further offshore.

By now the fighter planes from 804 and 891 Squadrons had successfully completed their first tour of battle duty and were returning to the aircraft carrier to refuel. Unfortunately as radio silence had to be maintained the aircraft carrier could not contact the pilots to alert them to the ship's new position. To compound matters a heavy mist had descended making it impossible for the pilots to visually locate *Dasher*. They then searched, without success, for the other aircraft carrier HMS *Biter*.

Without a carrier to land on they desperately headed back to Oran in an attempt to make a landing before completely running out of fuel. One of the aircraft, piloted by Sub-lieutenant McLennan, was so dangerously low in fuel he had to bale out. When his parachute opened it brought his fast descent to a sudden arrest resulting in his flying boots falling from his feet and unceremoniously dropping into the Mediterranean Sea. Fortunately the pilot's landing in the sea was successful and he was quickly picked up, minus his boots, by a Royal Navy destroyer.

One of the other aircraft, piloted by Sub-lieutenant Goodfellow, landed intact on a dried-up lake. The following afternoon, after refuelling, he flew back to *Dasher*. The other *Dasher* fighter pilots, now down to their last drop of fuel, crash - landed at an area covered with rocks where the pilots were helped out of their damaged planes by some of the allied invasion force. The aircraft were so badly damaged they were "write offs."

On day three of the operation the enemy surrendered. The following day *Dasher* sailed to Gibraltar to have her recurring engine problems repaired. For reasons unexplained four of *Dasher's* pilots now joined the aircraft carrier HMS *Avenger*. The captured pilot Lionel Godfrey who had escaped from jail was returned safely to *Dasher*. The War diary regarding the invasion of Oran read:

> **"Day one**. *Landings successful and airport captured.* **Day two**. *Serious fighting due to enemy counter attack.* **Day three**. *Noon, enemy surrendered."*

The crew of HMS *Dasher* and the pilots of Squadrons 804 and 891 had successfully played their part in this massive operation. Unfortunately the cost was high as some of *Dasher's* aviators had lost their lives. As for her aircraft, of the 14 that had flown off *Dasher*, only 5 landed back on. The loss of life and aircraft was high.

On board *Dasher* a signal was received advising the captain that four of his "missing" pilots were now onboard the aircraft carrier HMS *Avenger* and it was decided they would remain there. They were officially classified in Royal Navy records as "Passengers."

On 14th November 1942 convoy MKF1Y sailed for the Clyde. HMS *Avenger* sailed with this convoy to afford protection. The convoy was additionally protected by a flotilla of escort ships under the command of the renowned Captain Frederick John Walker. The captain had his own very successful method of locating and sinking U-boats that harried his convoys.

In the early hours of 15th November 1942 the convoy had reached 120 miles North West of Gibraltar. Unfortunately the convoy had been sighted by Kapitan Adolph C. Piening on U-boat 155. The Kapitan reported the convoy's position to Berlin. The response he received from U-boat Headquarters was:

> *"Aircraft Carriers Are Your Priority."*

The Kapitan carefully set his course. His calculations brought him to a position where he could attack convoy MKF1Y with his torpedoes. Suddenly an alert Royal Navy radar operator detected the German submarine and the convoy captains were alerted.

Onboard HMS *Starling* Captain Walker's escort defence plan swung into operation. His well trained Royal Navy Captains positioned their ships around the convoy and each man on every escort ship was on full alert. The plan also included three defence ships making their way at top speed to a position at least 5 miles away from the convoy. Once they were in position one of the ships would stop engines and fire a number of snow flake rockets which lit up the surrounding area as if it were daylight.

The firing of snow flake rockets during the hours of darkness indicated a ship was stopped and required assistance. This ruse had proved to be successful on a number of occasions and it was hoped the U-155 would "take the bait."

If it did and as soon as the U-boat was within firing distance of the stopped ship, the other two British war ships would launch a surprise attack. The "crippled" warship would also spring into life and join the other two Royal Navy ships in the hunt for the U-boat.

All went according to plan and as soon as Kapitan Piening saw the flares light up the "crippled" ship he decided to change course and depart from the convoy. After all it was much easier to fire a torpedo at a stationary ship than to try and calculate the speed and hit a moving target. Just as he was about to bark out orders to his crew, a convoy merchant ship captain, seeing emergency flares being fired 5 miles away, also fired snow flake rockets. Then another merchant ship captain also unfortunately fired snow flake rockets. On reaching a height the rockets exploded lighting up the convoy.

As the U-boat Kapitan looked through his periscope he could not believe his luck, there, directly in front of him was HMS *Avenger*, a prize aircraft carrier.

After quickly calculating the estimated speed and distance of his target he fired two torpedoes at HMS *Avenger*. The aircraft carrier's bomb room took a direct hit from the torpedoes. As the bomb room had no substantial protection, the ship was blasted completely apart.

Tragically very few of the crew had any chance of escaping the raging inferno. Within five minutes both the stern and the bow of the stricken ship sank beneath the waves. Only 12 men survived the sinking of HMS *Avenger*. Five hundred and thirty three of the ship's company including the four *Dasher* pilots had perished. Interestingly, during 1942 U boats sank eight million tons of allied shipping including another British aircraft carrier, HMS *Eagle*.

The day prior to the sinking of HMS *Avenger*, another convoy had departed from Gibraltar. *Dasher* was the air support ship and their destination was Liverpool. Thankfully this convoy arrived safely on 20th November 1942.

With the sinking of HMS *Avenger* lessons had been learned at the Admiralty. As soon as *Dasher* berthed at Liverpool's Alexandria Docks, work commenced on strengthening the ships bomb room. Due to the persistent problems with the ship's engines they were completely overhauled. The constant smell of petrol fumes was also fully investigated. A defence operations room was fitted to improve the ship's air defence. Due to the amount of repairs, maintenance and modifications being carried out throughout the ship the situation on board was one of severe overcrowding of the ship's personnel with the ever increasing shipyard work force.

With Christmas approaching a successful festive party for local school children was held on board *Dasher*. This was followed by an onboard "silver service" evening meal enjoyed by a number of visiting Wrens. As work progressed onboard more and more problems were found and rectified. To make the overcrowding situation worse, the maintenance party from 827 Squadron arrived with their many boxes of tools, spare wheels, spare engines and other parts. Due to the amount of modifications and repairs required the ship was in dock for a period of eight weeks!

With the completion of all the repairs and modifications the aircraft carrier departed from Liverpool on 22nd January, 1943, to carry out sea trials. On entering the Irish Sea the Hurricane aircraft from 827 Squadron landed on. At the completion of the successful sea trials the ship set a course for the Clyde and passed through the boom defence net at 1.35pm on 26th January, 1943. After entering the Firth of Clyde, all aircraft from 827 Squadron departed for Machrihanish, on the Mull of Kintyre. The squadron's maintenance party were advised by the captain's messenger that they could leave on the boat that was alongside, if they could board it within twenty minutes! They made it! It was recorded that they had never moved so fast in all their lives, but they were all very anxious to get away from the prevailing petrol fumes in the hangar.

On board *Dasher* signals were received to prepare for departure from the Clyde in three days time. The destination was Scapa Flow. At the same time telegrams were sent to all crew who were home on shore leave. The telegrams advised the crew to join the ship at Scapa Flow, Orkney Isles.

On arrival at Scapa Flow on 1st February 1943 in preparation for convoy duties, *Dasher* took part in sea trials and flying off exercises. After completing sea trials the aircraft carrier entered Loch Ewe to join Convoy JW53 with a destination of Murmansk, Russia.

After the official hand-over ceremony Dasher now flying the Union flag whilst six of the crew relax on the flight deck.

Chapter 3

Convoy JW 53

On 15th February, 1943, Convoy JW 53 departed from Loch Ewe, North West Scotland. The convoy comprised of twenty eight merchant ships and a strong Royal Navy escort fleet of five minesweepers, eleven destroyers, two corvettes and HMS *Dasher*.

Before sailing from Loch Ewe the vessels lined up in nine columns ready to take up their positions in the convoy formation. Their destination was Murmansk, North Russia. Thirty merchant ships should have been in the convoy, however, two ships were not ready at the appointed time of departure and were left behind in Loch Ewe. Those on board the Royal Navy escort ships were well aware of the extreme danger they faced as the enemy had already sunk well in excess of half a million tons of allied shipping in the North Atlantic. Convoy JW 53 experienced atrocious weather conditions as it headed straight into one of the worst recorded storms ever encountered by Atlantic convoys. A force twelve gale smashed waves of over 70 feet high into the ships. As the bitterly cold wind reached 75 miles per hour it sent temperatures plummeting down to 25 degrees Fahrenheit. The extreme cold and gale force winds resulted in treacherous blinding snow squalls and severe icy conditions. With no sign of the weather improving, six of the merchant ships left the convoy and headed back to the UK. As the rest of the convoy battled on through the appalling seas, HMS *Sheffield* sustained extensive structural damage with the gun turret on "A Deck" being rendered useless! Storm damage was also reported on one of the escort ships after the hull had been badly damaged.

Onboard HMS *Dasher* the storm force winds and heavy seas were proving lethal to the ship and her aircraft. The portside was taking the brunt of the extreme savage conditions. As the storm raged the ship's lifeboats and carley floats were being whipped from their stowage positions and smashed, before vanishing over the side of the ship. The ship's horrendous pitching and rolling in the storm force winds had strained the securing wires lashing the aircraft and the lifeboats beyond breaking point. Crew were attempting to lash ropes around the lifeboats that were still in position to make them as secure as possible.

On the flight-deck three of the aircraft, which had been secured, were washed overboard after breaking loose. The deck was covered in tangled wires and other lashings whipping about in the gale force wind. It became clear that the two crewmen, who were attempting to make the other four aircraft on the flight deck more secure, were fighting a losing battle and they were ordered "*Below Deck.*"

After having made their way to safety and about to close the water tight door, the remaining wire lashing on the aircraft broke. They looked in astonishment as another huge wave swept the four remaining aircraft, as if they were mere toys, over the side. The two crewmen realising how lucky they had been, lost no time in securing the heavy water-tight door, and reporting what they had just witnessed. At this point the situation became life threatening and the order was given:

"*All personnel leave the flight deck. The flight deck is out of bounds.*"

Two aircraft handlers hurriedly made their way to a ship's ladder which would take them from the open flight deck to the hangar below. Tragically, whilst on the ladder, the welding fixing the ladder onto the side of the ship came apart, flinging both men into the cold stormy water. They were seen for a few seconds being washed away from the ship before disappearing under the mountainous waves. The conditions were such that no attempt could be made to recover them.

The flight deck was an extremely dangerous place to be but the hangar deck was no better even though it was shielded from the worst of the gale force winds and the driving snow. With the frightful movement of the ship a Swordfish aircraft broke free and smashed into other aircraft in the hangar. No sooner was the aircraft tied down securely then a spare engine broke loose causing havoc as it smashed from side to side with the roll of the ship.

As crewmen fled in fear out of the path of the dangerous object a quick thinking crewman managed to lasso it. With the help of his shipmates and much shouting from others it was eventually firmly fixed in a safe position.

The wire lashings that held the aircraft to the hangar roof also became loose allowing one aircraft to fall on top of aircraft secured to the hangar floor. To add to this melee the air fitters and air mechanics tool boxes broke loose from their stowage compartments. The heavy tool boxes added to the danger as they crashed continually from port side to starboard side.

Just as the havoc in the aircraft hangar was being brought under control a torpedo broke loose and was rolling erratically around the torpedo room. Three of the crew eventually managed to bring this dangerous situation under control. The hangar deck was also declared out of bounds as it had become a danger to life and limb.

In the kitchens everything was a shambles. Pots, pans, crockery and cutlery had come loose and were being tossed around and smashing against anything that stood in their path. Tables, chairs and other furniture were toppling over and careering across the deck.

In the midst of this mayhem, *Dasher's* speed had to be maintained, to keep up with the convoy. The ship's motion was so chaotic that many of the crew, in particular air crew, speculated the ship was about to capsize. Conditions were now so extreme that very few of the crew were capable of performing their normal duties. As for meals food was of little or no interest to the vast majority of the crew.

With no let up in the atrocious weather the top heavy aircraft carrier took a severe buffeting as she rose to the peaks of the waves before plunging down into the troughs. With the bow low in the water the heavy waves washed dangerously over the flight deck. At the same time the gale force winds rocked the ship from side to side. By now everyone on board was clinging onto something solid trying to keep their balance. *Dasher* was now in mortal danger!

As the convoy plunged through the mountainous seas a giant wave was spotted heading directly towards the convoy. It appeared to be a wave riding on top of another wave. Evasive action was immediately taken by all ships in an effort to scatter out of the path of this monster wave. Unfortunately the mountainous wave smashed directly into the starboard side of *Dasher*. On impact, the aircraft carrier was tossed like a cork, onto its port side. Over it went until at the last moment the ship started to right itself.

One deck below the hangar deck a member of the ship's crew recoiled in sheer horror as a huge split sixty feet long opened up just above the water-line on *Dasher's* side. In sheer astonishment he could see the convoy through the huge gash on the ship's side. The American welding on the hastily converted aircraft carrier had torn apart!

When the extent of the storm damage was reported to the captain he sent the duty officer below deck to confirm the damage report. On receiving confirmation a signal was transmitted to the convoy commander reporting all the storm damage the aircraft carrier had sustained. The convoy commander immediately deemed the ship to be unseaworthy and unfit for active service. *Dasher* then received orders to sail, accompanied by two Royal Navy Destroyers, to Seydisfjordur in Iceland to wait out the storm before proceeding north/north west to Akureyri, north Iceland. On arrival on the 17th February temporary repairs were carried out. Aircraft were landed onboard to replace the ones that had been washed overboard and all the damaged equipment was replaced.

On 1st March 1943 the ship was then escorted by HMS *Newark* and HMS *Wells* from Iceland to Caledon Shipyard, Dundee. Whilst at the shipyard undergoing substantial weather damage repairs a fire broke out in the aircraft lift shaft. It was determined the fire had been caused by overloading the aircraft lift. This resulted in the resistors in the electronics becoming red hot and igniting a discarded oil rag in the lift shaft. Twelve days after arriving at Dundee, Captain G.N. Lentaigne DSO was replaced by Captain L.A.K. Boswell.

The Dundee shipyard took three weeks to make the ship seaworthy and to overhaul the unreliable Sun Doxford engines. On completion of the work the ship departed on 20th March bound for the Royal Navy Dockyard, Rosyth. Within one hour of arriving at Rosyth, *Dasher* entered the dry dock to allow her hull to be inspected. After a rigorous examination the ship's hull was found to be 100% sound.

On the next tide the aircraft carrier sailed for the Firth of Clyde via the Pentland Firth and the Minches escorted by HMS *Blankney*. On Friday 26th March, 1943, the aircraft carrier sailed into Lamlash Bay, Arran and dropped anchor.

Dasher's fighter pilots standing on the flight deck discussing tactics.

Chapter 4

Horrendous Explosion

Saturday 27th March, 1943
Lamlash Bay, Isle of Arran.

C aptain Boswell had been advised that his ship would join Western Command in four days time. This elite Royal Navy task force was dedicated to hunting and destroying the dreaded U-boats. The captain was determined that *Dasher* would have a thorough work-up to ensure that his ship and crew would be in peak condition. Immediately after departing from Lamlash Bay and entering the Firth of Clyde all *Dasher's* aircraft commenced flying-off and landing-on exercises. Crucially, HMS *Dasher's* fuel storage tanks were completely full with seventy five thousand gallons of fuel and the aviation tanks were filled to capacity.

After sailing north for approximately five miles *Dasher* altered course and proceeded south for five miles then once again sailed north. The aircraft carrier continued to sail back and forth all day with the aircraft practising flying off and landing on.

During the flying exercises the ship's crew went about their normal duties.

Sub-lieutenant John Ferrier from Greenock, with two of his mates, made his way from the engine room, to an open deck. Once up on deck they were enjoying the fresh air and admiring the beautiful view with the sun highlighting the snow-tipped Arran hills. One of the men, Trevor Buxton, said:

"When this is all over I will return to this lovely part of the country."

At 4.30pm Captain Boswell ordered a signal to be passed to the Flag Officer at Greenock. The signal read:

"Will arrive at Greenock 1800 hours. Open the gate."

The gate referred to a boom net which straddled from the Cloch Lighthouse near Greenock across the Clyde to Dunoon. This boom defence prevented enemy submarines from entering the upper reaches of the Clyde where more than 200 anchorages for allied shipping were positioned.

Captain Boswell then made the following announcement over the ship's loud speakers:

"Will arrive at Greenock 1800 hours. All non duty crew can go on shore leave."

(Sadly Trevor was never to return as he now lies in Ardrossan Cemetery)

All flying had been completed and the ship was making her way to Greenock. On board, Commander Lane, Captain Boswell and Sub-lieutenant Helps were on the bridge. All the aircraft except one had been secured. Two of the aircraft were being re-fuelled. A work party had just completed removing 24 depth charges from the depth charge magazine holding-area and stowing them in the hangar, twelve feet from the aircraft lift. Another 6 depth charges were stowed on each side of the lift shaft in preparation for lifting up to the flight deck for the aircraft. The work party also brought up 9 torpedoes complete with war heads and primers. Three torpedoes were stored on each side of the lift and 3 torpedoes were placed on a rack port-side. 68 depth charges were also stored in a large hatch under the Fleet Air Arm central stores. This depth charge storage hatch was in front of the aircraft lift one deck below.

The non duty crew quickly made their way below deck to the wash rooms and their lockers, as they hurriedly got themselves ready to leave the ship at Greenock. They were looking forward to having a great time ashore in the bar lounges then perhaps the local dance halls. Some of them were already in their number one uniform enjoying the first sitting for supper.

The time was now 4.40pm, when suddenly there was a horrendous explosion on board which made the ship shudder violently. Sub-lieutenant T. Helps was second officer of the watch. He was in the bridge looking over starboard-side when he saw the explosion come out of the ship's side. With it came pieces of metal, flames and smoke. He then looked in horror at the aircraft lift soaring level about 200 feet into the air. As flames started licking out of the lift shaft he heard small arms ammunition exploding in the hangar.

Bad luck was in store for 20 year old air mechanic, William MacDonald, who was below deck standing beside his locker holding his kit bag. The force of the explosion blew William violently through the hole in the ship's side. He was thrown about 400 yards from the ship. As he floundered in the water he still held onto his kit bag.

Royal Navy Motor Launch 528 was approximately 600 yards from the ship. The crew were on constant alert to recover any pilot who overshot *Dasher's* flight deck and careered into the sea. On hearing the massive explosion they saw the aircraft lift, weighing almost a ton, shooting into the air, helped no doubt by the 24 depth charges and 9 torpedoes that had been stored adjacent to it. After reaching a height of around 200 feet the lift plunged down into the sea narrowly missing *Dasher*.

At the same time a large tongue of bright red flame shot out from the flight deck, port-side followed by belching black smoke. As the crew of the motor launch were ordered to *"Crash Stations"* the launch sped through the water at high speed towards the stricken aircraft carrier. On seeing a man floating in the water they altered course and hauled the man, clutching a kit bag, onboard. His face, hands and chest were badly burned. The skin on his hands had been blown off. On being asked his name he replied:

"William MacDonald!"

When asked what had happened he said:

"I don't know, I remember looking in my locker and holding my kit bag under my arm."

Onboard *Dasher,* Lieutenant Commander Brian Paterson, the aircraft Batsman was standing on the flight deck quite close to the aircraft lift. His duty was to ensure all returning aircraft landed on safely. He was always extremely safety conscious and wore a Mae-West life jacket at all times.

The Batsman had just finished having a quick chat with Lieutenant Babington who had just landed-on. As Lieutenant Babington made his way to the Flying Officer's office there was a terrible explosion followed by huge flames shooting high into the air around the Batsman. Realising the ship had been mortally wounded he dived overboard. On surfacing, astern of the burning *Dasher*, he saw the ship rising by the bow and hundreds of men jumping overboard.

Sub-lieutenant D. Price was on the flight deck when he heard a deep rumbling followed by a violent explosion. Looking in disbelieve he saw the aircraft-lift soaring high into the air. When it started to fall back down the lieutenant ran for his life towards the bow fearing he would be crushed by the huge falling object.

In the hangar where the aircraft were being refuelled numerous fires fuelled by aviation petrol vapour were burning out of control and spreading rapidly.

Members of the Fleet Air Arm working in the hangar had taken the full brunt of the explosion. Amidst the ferocious fires air mechanics, aircraft handlers and pilots were all vainly attempting to reach an open deck.

Petty Officer Reginald Dickens was standing in the centre of the hangar when the explosion threw him down. He then saw the hangar was a burning inferno. The flames were very red with thick dense smoke billowing up. He managed to scramble clear of the debris lying about and made his way to the flight deck.

Petty Officer Mann was also in the hangar standing on a trestle carrying out maintenance on one of the aircraft. The explosion blasted him off the trestle. As he hit the deck he suffered a blackout for a few seconds. On opening his eyes he saw a sheet of flame between 4 and 6 feet high then the hangar quickly filled with very dark smoke. The petty officer managed to struggle to the open deck where he climbed up a ladder, as quickly as he could, to the flight deck. From there he could see dark smoke gushing out of the aircraft lift shaft.

The ship began to list to starboard. To rectify the list the "port wheel" order was given but by now *Dasher's* steering was out of action. Tom Dawson was at the wheel of the aircraft carrier for the voyage to Greenock. With him in the wheelhouse was Danny Mc Arthur. They heard a dull explosion then the alarm bell on the fire alarm board started to ring and a number of lights on the board indicated that there were numerous fires spreading throughout the ship.

The electric light bulbs and the lights on the fire alarm board started flashing for about 30 seconds before they all went off. The ship's power had failed.

Tom Dawson tried to contact the Captain via the voice-pipe but unfortunately there was no response. As the deck began to tilt the two men made their way quickly out of the wheelhouse and onto the open deck. They realised the ship was sinking and terrified as they were, jumped from a great height into the cold sea.

On surfacing they both swam clear of the ship then Tom turned to watch her dying moments. He watched the one remaining aircraft on deck break clear from its lashings and slither into the sea. At that moment the ship's navigator, who was about 40 yards away and supporting a man called out for assistance. Tom Dawson swam over to try to help them but it soon became obvious to him, that the man was beyond help.

In the engine room the engineers heard a long explosion then a blazing fire spread along the floor. At the same time flashes of flame shot along between the port and starboard engines bringing thick smoke which filled the engine room. As the bulkheads in the engine room began to buckle with the searing heat from the flames the engineers quickly evacuated through the escape hatch.

Petty Officer Frederick Lovell was about to enjoy a meal in the Petty Officer's mess deck when the explosion occurred. He was knocked off his feet and thrown the full length of the mess deck. He was left in complete darkness when the lights went out. He gathered his wits about him and managed to get back on his feet and scramble out to an open deck away from the suffocating fumes.

Members of the crew could feel the ship dipping towards the stern. Due to the electric power failing they did not hear the order "*Abandon Ship.*" As *Dasher* started to rise steadily at the bow the crew instinctively knew the ship was doomed. They ran as fast as possible to internal ladders that would lead to an open deck and hopefully escape with their lives.

As the ship's bow rose out of the water crockery slid off tables and smashed onto the floor. As the list of the ship increased chaos followed when furniture started to slide across the floors smashing into walls adding to the noise. Lockers toppled over clattering onto the floor. The stress on the metal plates caused the doors to buckle and jam. Below deck and throughout the ship it was now mayhem and terror for those still on board.

Petty Officer John Stamp and Petty Officer Cyril Terry showed great courage assisting many young Ratings to safety. Tragically both officers lost their lives in doing so.

Jack Verlaque was leading a group of men to safety. He kept shouting for them to follow him. He led them to a ladder he knew would take them up to an open deck where they might have a chance to board a lifeboat. On reaching the ladder Jack started to climb up. Immediately behind him, the group waited without panic for their turn to ascend the ladder.

When Jack popped his head into the hangar he stared in horror at a scene of utter carnage. The hangar was full of flames. Metal plates were red hot. Jack was horrified to see members of the Fleet Air Arm with their clothes on fire. One man was screaming as his clothes burned and his hair was on fire. It was a nightmare, but to make matters worse Jack could hear the sound of gunfire as bullets from the aircraft guns were now exploding due to the intense heat. Jack shouted as loud as possible for the men to go back down the ladder but they could not understand why he was preventing them from reaching the outside deck of the hangar. Once they realised the situation they started to make their way back down the ladder with Jack now behind them. They quickly regrouped and took an alternative route. As they made their way to an open deck through the choking smoke they ran past doors which had buckled with the heat.

On the bridge Lieutenant Commander Lane had been ordered by Captain Boswell to go below and appraise the situation. The Lieutenant Commander went along the port alleyway down to the 2nd deck. At this point the ship was in darkness, but he could hear water pouring in. Realising the ship was sinking he made his way to the upper deck. By now water was also coming on to this deck. With the ship rising steeply by the bow he crawled forward and went over the side of the ship, and dropped into the cold waters of the Firth of Clyde.

Daniel Gaffney had joined the ship just 3 weeks previously at Dundee. As he had no leave due, he was playing cards in the mess deck with six other ship mates. On hearing the terrible explosion they quickly made their way to the nearest open deck. However on reaching the first exit, the steel door was stuck fast. One of the lads in a state of panic shouted at the top of his voice:

"We're done for."

However four of them pulled with all their strength and managed to wrench the door open. As they were two decks down from an open deck they ran along an alley-way to a ladder. On reaching the next deck they climbed up a ladder to the open deck. As the ship was rising at the bow everyone was virtually walking uphill. Just as Daniel was about to jump off one of the lads with him screamed:

"I can't jump from this height."

Daniel looked at the lad, who was about the same age as himself, and replied:

"You'll have to - come on."

The young lad took another look at the water, about 60 feet below, and then he jumped quickly, immediately followed by Daniel.

When Daniel hit the water he plunged down very deep. He managed to get his back against the hull of the ship and pushed himself upwards. By the time he reached the surface he was gasping for breath. As he was afraid the ship would pull him under he pushed with his feet against the side of the ship and swam away as strongly as he could.

Prior to the explosion Able Seaman Tom Hunter from Leeds was in the mess deck watching some of the lads playing a game of cards. On hearing the terrible explosion the men tried to get out of the mess deck, but the exit they chose was blocked by fire. They then had to stand in line to climb up a ladder. They soon scattered when the first man to reach the top of the ladder shouted that the deck was on fire and bullets were exploding from the belts of the aircraft machine guns. In addition, a torpedo had broken loose and was sliding about. The men quickly changed tactics and ran to the cafeteria, but they found it a complete shambles and saw a hole in the side of the ship where flames were shooting out. The situation was getting worse by the minute.

It was imperative they reach an open deck. In fact their lives depended on it. They scrambled over debris through the smoke and flames. By now the deck was at such a steep angle they were crawling uphill. Eventually they reached a doorway where the door had been blown off. After getting through they were on an open deck. From there they jumped off the ship into the sea.

In another part of the ship a number of men were hastily making their escape when they were met with a few shipmates rushing towards them. The first lot of men shouted to the on comers:

"You're going the wrong way."

The reply they received was:

"We're going to our lockers for our belongings."

The men running to their lockers were never seen again.

Hundreds of men who were below deck at the time of the explosion had by now made it to an open deck. The next problem was to find a clear spot in the water to jump from the burning ship without landing on top of someone already in the water.

Peter Leach, an 18 year old fireman, had joined *Dasher* just three days before the disaster. He was sitting in the mess deck already dressed to go on shore leave when the ship reached Greenock. He was talking to two greasers, one of whom had given him a tot of rum. They were chatting away when there was a terrible explosion. The place became a maelstrom with objects flying everywhere then all the lights went out. The three of them managed to get out onto the middle deck without too much panic.

One of the greasers, Charlie Weedon, who had served for many years on merchant ships shouted:

"Follow Me."

Charlie then jumped overboard. As for Peter he remained on the ship. By now a number of the crew had gathered beside him. Just at that moment the ship lurched to one side throwing all of them off balance and onto the deck. One of them then screamed:

"That's it."

He got to his feet and immediately jumped overboard and the rest all followed him. Once in the water, Peter Leach was so frightened he prayerfully said goodbye to his mother, father, brothers and sisters before he blacked out.

On reaching an open deck Lieutenant "Pip" Culmer, (later Captain Culmer) secured a rope and threw it overboard. He then grabbed hold of it and started to lower himself down. As he passed one of the lower decks a frantic crew man jumped and grabbed hold of the Lieutenant. With the added weight Pip started to slither uncontrollably down the rope burning both his hands. The Lieutenant held onto the rope with one hand and used his other hand to push the crewman away. The man fell backwards into the water. Pip saw him surface and swim away from the ship.

With both his hands suffering from severe rope burns Lieutenant Culmer was relieved when he reached the water. He immediately started to swim as quickly as he could before he was pulled under when the ship went down.

Each survivor tried frantically to distance himself from the sinking ship to avoid being sucked under by the doomed aircraft carrier.

As the men in the water frantically struggled to survive, they watched anxiously for the sign of any rescue ships.

Dasher anchored in the Hudson River near New York awaiting the arrival of the two other aircraft. Four swordfish had departed from HMS Jamaica to join HMS Dasher. Prior to the arrival of the aircraft the lift was raised to flight deck level.

Chapter 5

Witnesses on Arran

Prior to hand-over hundreds of Royal Navy ships carried out sea trials and exercises in the Firth of Clyde. The measured mile was positioned on the east coast of the island of Arran. This was well used by newly built ships for their speed trials. Aircraft carriers were also heavily involved in deck landing training in this safe stretch of water.

During 1942 /1943 Royal Navy Signalman, Reg Summerscales, was stationed at Kings Cross Point on the Isle of Arran. Reg received signals from all Royal Navy ships in the vicinity. He would acknowledge them and pass the message to his signal headquarters based at Marine House Signal Station, Lamlash.

On Saturday 27th March 1943, Reg was on duty and noted HMS *Dasher* anchored nearby in Lamlash Bay. At 9am he watched the ship departing to carry out deck-landing-exercises in the Firth of Clyde.

At 4.40pm *Dasher* signalled Reg by lamp.

> "To Flag Officer in Command, Greenock, from HMS Dasher. All planes recovered. Returning to Tail-o'-Bank Greenock. Estimated time of arrival 18.00 hours."

This was to be the last signal sent from HMS *Dasher*.

Reg telephoned the signal to the Naval officer in command at Marine House, Lamlash, for onward teleprinter transmission to Greenock. On completing the call Reg looked out and noticed smoke coming from *Dasher's* stern below the flight deck. At first Reg thought an aircraft had crashed, but all aircraft had landed and flying was complete. He immediately tried to contact *Dasher* by Aldis lamp, but received no reply.

The signalman then telephoned Marine House signal station and told them what he had just witnessed, advising them that he had sent a signal to *Dasher*, and had not received a reply. The Naval signal officer said that he would instruct a taxi to pick up Reg and take him to Brodick with his hand-held signalling equipment. The purpose of this was so that Reg might receive a stronger signal at Brodick which would enable him to make contact with *Dasher*.

At Brodick he made several unsuccessful attempts to make contact with *Dasher*. The signalman was then ordered to board a tug which took him to sea. His attempts to contact *Dasher* once more proved to be unsuccessful. By now there were a number of Royal Navy rescue ships converging in the area.

For security reasons the Royal Navy had decided it was imperative that no civilian vessels should be involved in the rescue operation. As a result the tug's civilian crew were ordered to return to Brodick. This decision would undoubtedly have cost lives. In fact it was later known that two coastal vessels were very much involved in the rescue operation and indeed they rescued more than 50% of the survivors.

When Reg Summerscales stepped ashore at Brodick he was told to keep the *Dasher* disaster quiet and never repeat anything he had seen. A number of Arranites also witnessed the tragedy. Isobel Turner was on duty at Lamlash post office and on hearing a loud explosion, she looked out of the post office window. Offshore she saw the aircraft carrier sinking by the stern.

Isobel said:

"I could see the bow of the ship rising out of the water. I couldn't believe it. Men were jumping off the ship. They looked like match stick men. Then the bow shot up into the air, men were still jumping off. When the bow was pointing to the sky the aircraft carrier went under quickly. Although it happened all those years ago, I still see it today and I still can't believe it!"

Eleven Year old Alister McKelvie's parents owned Seaview Farm, Brodick. Alister was making his way through one of his father's fields when he heard his father shouting:

"Something dreadful has happened to that aircraft carrier."

Alister immediately looked seaward and saw a tremendous amount of black smoke. He ran over to a neighbour's house where he would get a better view. On reaching the house he saw the neighbour's two sons, Dougie and Archie Cook. They were standing outside their house. Dougie was looking through powerful binoculars. He turned to Alister and said:

"It's a terrible tragedy, the sea is on fire."

Dougie turned and handed the binoculars to Alister. When Alister looked though the binoculars he saw the sea was indeed on fire. The flames were about 20 feet high and there was colossal black smoke. Everything appeared to be so near and in fine detail.

Alister then looked in the direction of Brodick Pier, on seeing some activity he made his way towards it and on reaching it he saw *"The Two Boys"*, a Naval vessel not unlike a fishing boat, was quickly making its way out of Brodick harbour. On clearing the harbour the vessel then went at top speed, leaping through the water, onwards towards the area of the burning sea.

Alister waited at the pier until *"The Two Boys"* returned. There were no survivors or bodies aboard and the navy grey paint on the vessel was all blistered with the heat from the burning sea.

A few days later Alister made his way to Lamlash pier and enquired if any survivors or bodies had been recovered by the boats that had departed from

Lamlash. He was told that no bodies or survivors were brought to Lamlash. (Unknown to the residents of Arran, all small vessels involved in the rescue operation transferred survivors and bodies to the Royal Navy major ships.)

William John McRae was born on the island, one Saturday afternoon he was out gathering firewood with his brother and their friend, Jimmy Campbell. Jimmy and his family were evacuees from Glasgow. As the three of them made their way through a wood they emerged at a position between Corrie and Sannox.

Jimmy, the evacuee, looked out to sea and noticed smoke near to an aircraft carrier. He pointed it out to the 2 brothers and they could hardly believe what was happening. The ship appeared to be sinking and men were jumping off. The 3 boys were in a direct line with the ship and as it was a very clear day everything seemed to be so near to them.

As they looked at the ship they realised it was on fire, above the sinking ship they saw aircraft flying overhead. It was hard for the boys to take in what was happening before their very eyes. Men were swimming in the water, men jumping off the ship, the ship slowly sinking, thick black smoke and planes flying overhead. Everything was unfolding before their eyes.

As they stood mesmerised looking at the bow rising, John McLaughlin Milne, a local artist, approached the boys and told them to move away from their vantage point. He ushered them away, as he was endeavouring to spare the boys from witnessing the dreadful scene that he knew would haunt them in the coming years.

That morning two other local boys, teenagers Bill Dickie and his friend Bill Spence, both shipping enthusiasts, had made their way to the seafront to watch the shipping activity in the Firth of Clyde. There was always a lot happening and that morning they were quite excited watching two small coastal vessels as well as an aircraft carrier.

Circling the aircraft carrier was a small motor launch which the boys knew to be a crash boat, they also knew it would be on duty just in case an aircraft had a mishap on landing and went over the side of the ship. It was all very interesting to the boys, especially the aircraft flying off the aircraft carrier then landing back on. The flying exercises were of particular interest. They watched one plane flying off at a good speed then rising higher and higher in the air. It flew around at quite a high altitude then it approached the stern of the aircraft carrier making an approach to land on.

As it came in low it appeared to be lower than the flight deck, then it disappeared from view. The boys were expecting the plane to fly off again but it never came back into view. Little did the boys know that it was the last plane to land on and it was being tethered to the deck.

Suddenly there was deep rumble followed by an almighty explosion. Within seconds the boys saw smoke billowing from the stern. They could not believe what happened next. They saw the ship starting to go down at the stern then it slowly disappeared!

A few seconds later the boys looked in sheer amazement when they saw the sea on fire. They just could not believe what they were witnessing. At Brodick pier a Royal Navy vessel, *"The Two Boys,"* which was known locally as *"The Contraband Ship"* put to sea. The boys watched it approaching the disaster area to assist. They also saw the two small coastal vessels divert from their courses to also render assistance.

The boys watched spellbound as the two small vessels went as close as they could to the high flames and the thick black smoke. Due to the distance and the smoke the local boys could not see the men in the water, however by the activity of the various rescue vessels, the boys knew that a major rescue operation was in progress before their very eyes! Both of the boys firmly believed it was the low flying aircraft that had crashed into the ship, beneath the flight deck, which had been the cause of the sea disaster.

During March 1943 army officer Lieutenant David McNair was on leave. As usual he liked to spend his leisure time on the island of Arran. He was staying with friends in the village of Corrie till his leave expired on the 27th March.

Unfortunately the young Lieutenant missed the bus, which would take him to Brodick, where he would catch the ferry to Ardrossan. He hastily borrowed a bicycle to cycle speedily round the bay in the hope of reaching the ferry before it sailed. The ferry captain had received a phone call requesting that he delay departure till the army lieutenant arrived.

After hurrying onboard, Lieutenant McNair stood at the stern of the ferry, watching the shipping in the area. As he noticed a small aircraft carrier at a distance behind the ferry he heard a loud blast. The aircraft carrier had suddenly exploded in a pall of smoke and flames. The ferry continued on its course to Ardrossan, without hesitation.

On docking, all the passengers were ushered down to the lounge. Once there two gentlemen, in civilian suits, made themselves known as "security" and commanded that no one was ever to speak about what had just happened to the aircraft carrier.

The lieutenant put the incident from his mind and concentrated on furthering his army career, reaching the rank of captain. After a change of career in later years, he became Dean of Education at Manchester University. Over fifty years later, he discovered the name of the aircraft carrier after reading John Steele's book *"The Tragedy of HMS Dasher."*

Chapter 6

Dasher Has Sunk

(Not To Be Spoken About)

At HMS *Fortitude* (Ardrossan Harbour) a Royal Navy priority signal had been received stating:

"All vessels put to sea immediately. Major rescue operation involving Royal Navy Aircraft Carrier HMS Dasher. Ship reported sinking. Position 55 38 00 North. 04 57 00 West."

On receipt of the signal all ships within the harbour cast off immediately and made their way at full speed to the disaster area. One of the ships to speed out was Minesweeper *M23*. Even though two thirds of her crew were on shore leave the commanding officer had no hesitation in joining the rescue operation.

On the Isle of Arran two Royal Navy motor launches, one from Brodick, and the other from Lamlash, swiftly made their way to assist. In the Royal Navy Sick Bay at 8 South Crescent, Ardrossan the medical staff received a telephone call advising them to expect a large number of wounded personnel from a burning ship. The duty ambulance driver, Harry Judd, left at once to collect survivors being brought ashore at nearby Ardrossan Harbour.

The Sick Bay staff comprising of Lieutenant Surgeon Kennet, Lieutenant Surgeon Bulstrode, a young Wren, Barbara Kay and two other nurses quickly began moving patients who were recuperating into side rooms. This allowed them to admit up to 20 casualties from the burning ship.

The local cinemas were busy as usual on a Saturday. The cinema-goers had a choice of three cinemas in Saltcoats and one in Ardrossan. In all four cinemas the films were interrupted by a message flashed onto the screen stating:

"All First Aid and Civil Defence Personnel Report to their Posts Immediately!"

As the Royal Navy rescue operation swung into action and the ships closed in on the disaster area groups of *Dasher's* survivors could be seen in the water. The survivors were feeling the cold but they were heartened to see rescue ships approaching from north, east, south and west. If they could keep afloat they would soon be rescued.

While Wheelman Tom Dawson was swimming very slowly barely keeping himself afloat another crewman swam past him at speed. Tom recognised this chap from Newfoundland. He was a distance away from Tom and still swimming furiously when suddenly he stopped, put one hand into the air then disappeared under the water. Tom was losing his strength due to the cold. His brain was becoming dull and he was giving up hope. Luckily he was then hauled into a carley raft and promptly passed out.

Peter Leach the 18 year old fireman who had blacked out in the water after saying goodbye to his family was spotted by an RAF sergeant who grabbed hold of him and pulled him into the carley raft. Peter's watch had stopped at 4.50pm. Suddenly a shout went up:

"She's going!"

On hearing these words the men in the water turned to look at their ship. They were mesmerised to see the ship's bow rising higher and higher. Those still on board were screaming as they slid down the steeply sloping deck towards the stern. They now had little or no chance of survival. With the bow pointing directly to the sky, HMS *Dasher* slipped dramatically beneath the waves, her short but illustrious life as an escort carrier terminated in the most terrifying manner.

To add to the horror, *Dasher's* six diesel storage tanks ruptured when the stricken ship thudded on to the sea bed. The disaster area was now covered with 75,000 gallons of black diesel. The men knew there was diesel floating about as some of them were now black with the thick slimy fuel.

In the midst of this ongoing horror, crew members joked: *"You look like a black man!"* *"So do you,"* was the reply. Another smell became overpowering and shouting began *"What's that smell?"* It was from high octane aviation fuel. The aviation fuel tanks had also ruptured. The men were swimming in a lethal cocktail of diesel fuel and high octane aviation fuel. All the survivors were doing their utmost not to swallow the contaminated sea water, but it was difficult due to the choppy sea conditions.

Although the survivors could see the rescue ships, fate was about to play another cruel blow. As the rescue ships came closer there was a terrible whooshing noise. The aviation fuel and the diesel fuel had ignited. Searing flames were racing quickly across the water towards the survivors. The cries and screams of the men, who were caught in the path of the flames and were now being burnt to death, were terrifying to hear.

When 19 year old Ordinary Telegraphist, Fred Plank, jumped off *Dasher* and landed in the cold water all the breath was knocked out of him. He went down quite a depth then he kicked out and started to rise. As he approached the surface his head kept hitting against pieces of wood. Fortunately he avoided injury and swam towards a raft where he came upon one of the stokers that he knew by sight.

The stoker had injured his arm and was floundering about. Fred helped him over to a float-a-net and told him to hang onto it. An empty 50 gallon drum floated by and Fred managed to hang onto it. As the flames headed towards him, Fred quickly decided that his oil drum had lost its attraction. Discarding it he swam as fast as possible away from the flames.

After swimming clear of the flames he spotted a piece of wood about 12 feet long and found it a relief to hang onto it. As he floundered around he spotted Bob Powell and a Fleet Air Arm chap. Fred knew them both as they were also telegraphists. The three of them could feel the heat from the flames, and as it became more and more intense, they realised they were being carried towards the burning sea. They desperately swam in the opposite direction away from the intense heat. After swimming some distance they were greatly relieved to see a mast in the distance and swam towards it. The rescue ship was the *La Capricieuse*, a French sloop manned by a British crew.

The sloop's crew were in the process of lowering a lifeboat and when it hit the water Fred waved and yelled to attract their attention. The lifeboat crew rowed to them and heaved them onboard. They picked up more survivors and returned to the ship where willing hands helped them up the scrambling-net to safety.

The survivors were taken below to the mess deck where they saw the ship's crew doing their best to save four or five men laid out on the mess tables.

In the disaster area Daniel Gaffney was swimming slowly when suddenly he hit against a piece of wood and clung onto it. On looking around he saw a raft about 100 yards away and swam towards it. Halfway from the raft he saw a man floating in the water. The man was wearing a lifejacket, but his face was submerged in the water.

Daniel swam over to him and pulled his face out of the water. He then grabbed hold of the man and continued swimming towards a raft. After one of the men in the raft got hold of the injured man Daniel and an airman swam over to assist another survivor who was in trouble. Between them they managed to reach the raft with the injured crewman.

As they all held on to the raft they spotted the flames heading in their direction. Everyone on board immediately started to paddle with their hands whilst those in the water kicked with their feet. The frantic joint effort managed to propel them away from the flames. About 20 minutes later they were all manhandled onboard a rescue ship and taken to Ardrossan.

Harold (Nick) Carter had survived the explosion on board his ship. He also survived jumping from the ship into the water. On surfacing he swam towards a carley raft which was full of survivors. Nick and a few others in the water held onto the ropes dangling from the carley rafts.

On seeing a rescue ship heading in his direction, Nick said he was going to swim toward it. Petty Officer Gray and Signalman Cane both told Nick to remain where he was, but he let go of the rope and swam away. Unfortunately the wall of flame was sweeping towards him. As Nick made his way to the port-side of the rescue ship the inferno completely engulfed him. The survivors who witnessed Nick's fate believed had he remained with the carley raft, he might have survived.

As the flames spread they claimed another victim as they swept over Lieutenant Kenneth William Davies. Two of *Dasher's* carley rafts, each full of survivors and with men still in the water hanging on, were directly in the path of the rapidly moving fire. Both rafts and men were completely swamped by the flames.

Able Seaman George Lovegrove could hear the men screaming in agony then all was silent. As George frantically swam as fast as possible he could feel the heat from the searing flames. In the distance he saw two shipmates; George Harkness from Kilmarnock and the other man was called Ruggles. As George swam towards them he started to call out their names. Unfortunately they both drifted out of sight and he never saw them again.

By now George was feeling exhausted. Just then another man came into view. He was in a very bad way, his hair had been burned off and his face was bloated. George swam over and held him afloat but the man grabbed him with a vice like grip. As they both went under the water George managed to free himself, but on surfacing the man started to frantically climb on top of George, forcing him under the water. Once again George managed to free himself and the man slowly drifted away.

Shortly after a destroyer came alongside and a rope was thrown towards George. He grabbed it and was hauled onboard. Once safely onboard he passed out. On regaining consciousness one of the crew said:

"Thank goodness, we thought you were dead."

Whilst swimming in the water Able Seaman Fredrick Nunn swallowed some sea water which was contaminated with diesel. He was coughing badly when fortunately he was hauled onto a carley raft. His good luck nearly ran out when the sea suddenly caught fire and the flames were heading directly for the carley raft. The oarsmen frantically paddled to avoid the inferno. Just as the flames were almost upon them they managed to get themselves out of the fire's path.

Fredrick Nunn was still coughing and spluttering when a lifeboat from the radar training ship, *Isle of Sark,* came alongside and took them onboard. From the lifeboat they were transferred to the *Isle of Sark*. Frederick was ushered below deck where spoonfuls of rum were poured down his throat. The mixture of salt water and rum made him feel very ill. After being helped up to the open deck he was violently sick.

Lieutenant Culmer, *Dasher's* navigating officer was in a group of approximately 80 survivors. The devastating flames were coming straight for them. The men tried to escape the flames in a race for their lives. As the deadly flames came ever closer Lieutenant Culmer took a deep breath and dived under the water.

Down and down he went with his eyes open, the water was deep green in colour then everything went black. When Lieutenant Culmer could no longer hold his breath he shot up to the surface. The flames had passed over but sadly there was not one man in his group still alive. All the men had perished in less than three minutes. Tragically, young men who had survived the massive explosion and the sinking of their ship had lost their lives in the burning sea.

On seeing the spread of the flames and the speed at which they were travelling, the officer in command of the rescue operation signalled all ships:

"Keep clear. We cannot afford to lose another ship this day."

On receipt of the signal all Royal Navy rescue ships slowed down and stopped well clear of the rescue area. Lifeboats were then lowered from the rescue ships and the lifeboat crews rowed towards the disaster site which was almost a quarter of a mile away.

The rescue area was shrouded in thick black smoke and the overpowering smell of diesel and petrol. Shouts of commands from the various rescue lifeboats were being drowned out by the screams of those injured and burned. Officers onboard the Royal Navy ships were astonished to see the SS *Cragsman*, a small coastal vessel, sail directly towards the burning inferno. The vessel had been on passage from Stornoway to Glasgow loaded with fish. The chugging noise of the single diesel engine could be heard loud and clear as the *Cragsman* sailed straight into the dense black smoke and disappeared completely from view. It was feared that another ship had been lost.

Onboard the *Cragsman,* Captain James Templeton had no intention of losing his vessel or abandoning the men in the water. Amidst the smoke most of the crew were leaning over either side of the coaster, grasping hold of survivor's hands and hauling them onboard. Other crew members, in desperation, were throwing overboard anything that could float, anything that would help the men in the water. The skipper could not stop his vessel for fear of it catching fire. He maintained a slow speed whilst his crew did everything possible to save the lives of the men in the water.

It was heartbreaking for the crew of the *Cragsman*; they were simply unable to assist everyone as they sailed slowly through the searing heat and thick black smoke. They could only do their best to help. It was even more heart breaking when one of the crew took hold of a sailor's hand saying:

"I've got you."

Then as he tried to pull the man onboard, he couldn't hold his grip on the man's oily hand. The rescuer watched horrified as the man he had been holding slipped back into the water and was washed into the poisonous fumes.

Within minutes the small rescue vessel sailed clear of the intense heat and thick black smoke. On board were fourteen survivors! As skipper James Templeton navigated away from the fiery inferno, an I.C.I. coastal vessel, *SS Lithium,* with a cargo of 300 tons of sulphur, was heading straight into the flames and smoke to repeat the heroism of the *Cragsman.*

Captain J.F. Terretta on the *Lithium* did not hesitate in manoeuvring his vessel as close as possible to the survivors. Once more the survivors saw the chance of their lives being saved and made a frantic bid to swim towards their would-be rescuers. The stronger ones amongst them were able to fight against the strong current which was sweeping the weaker ones away. The crew of the *Lithium* were desperately reaching out, shouting words of encouragement as they hauled onboard as many as they could reach. Some were torn from their grasp as, like the *Cragsman* crew, their oil covered hands could not keep a hold and the poor souls slipped away.

The *Lithium* crew were devastated to have had so many within their grasp and then see them being swept away. As firm grips parted and the unfortunate men fell back into the sea their shouts for help as they drifted away would remain to haunt the brave *Lithium* crew for the rest of their lives.

As the *Dasher* survivors were brought onboard they were quickly ushered down to the warmth of the engine room. As the number being rescued increased the engine room became packed full and those rescued had to stay on the open deck. Had any more men been brought onboard, the vessel would have been in great danger of sinking.

The men still in the water watched as the *Lithium* crew were forced to cease their rescue efforts. No more could be taken onboard. The vessel, now overflowing with *Dasher* survivors, had to sail past them.

With a tear in his eye, Stan McKenzie recalled that frustrating event.

> *"Very soon we had so many onboard, we were taking in water as we were up to the gunnels. We were leaving so many behind, it was heart breaking. As there was a strong current flowing it was sweeping those poor souls past us. As they were being swept past, they were screaming for help.*
>
> *"In sheer desperation we threw overboard ladders, ropes, mops and brushes. Anything that would float and possibly help those we were leaving in the water. We threw overboard anything that they could hold onto until more help arrived. One of the survivors I helped onboard said that he was an engineer from the engine room. Unfortunately he died on board our vessel."*

The skipper and crew of the *Lithium* were grateful to find that they had been able to save 60 men from almost certain death. As the *Lithium* slowly left the disaster site some of the lifeboats from the major rescue ships arrived. Each lifeboat had eight men straining at the oars. Then more lifeboats arrived from the *Isle of Sark,* HMS *Sir Galahad,* HMS *Attacker* and a flotilla of Ardrossan based mine sweepers.

As soon as HMS *Attacker* arrived on the scene they launched two lifeboats to assist in the rescue. Onboard *Attacker "Action Stations"* was announced and everybody went immediately to their respective posts including the damage control teams. Many of the crew were in a position to see survivors struggling in the water. Everyone onboard *Attacker* was warily thinking that if such an unthinkable disaster could happen to *Dasher,* could it happen to us? Those below deck kept one eye on the nearest emergency door.

Later when the flames had subsided the Royal Navy ships sailed in closer to the survivors. The *Isle of Sark* took onboard thirty five, three of whom did not survive.

Approximately 5 miles from the disaster area the French vessel *La Capricieuse* had been engaged in exercises with two British submarines. On hearing the dreadful explosion the captain cancelled the exercise and headed towards *Dasher* at full speed. Although the captain was aware the sinking may have been the result of enemy action, *La Capricieuse* did not hesitate, but went straight to the scene where they saw men and debris in the water.

The captain positioned his ship as close to the flames as possible and had his boats lowered to pick up survivors. He watched the rescue operation from the bridge and could see survivors being pulled from the water. When the men in the water had no strength left lifeboat crews were jumping into the water to assist them. Once in the water they became thickly covered in oil. Every available member of the ship's company was involved and showed great bravery and genuine concern to the survivors. All possible help was given to them and every effort was made to revive and resuscitate others.

As they had injured survivors requiring urgent medical attention and there was by now many other ships searching and rescuing, the *La Capricieuse* was ordered to sail to Ardrossan with the 33 survivors. On arrival at Ardrossan sadly 7 of the survivors had died.

The Royal Navy motor launch ML 528 had plucked 17 men out of the water. They also transferred 22 men who had been huddled together in the two remaining carley rafts. All the men received medical attention from the crew of ML 528 prior to being taken to one of the major Royal Navy rescue ships.

Able Seaman Alex White from South Shields was a crewman onboard the *Isle of Sark.* He was ordered to join the lifeboat crew and row to the assistance of men in the water. They found some survivors and recovered a number of bodies. Some of the drowned were floating face down with their heads and feet submerged with the remainder of their bodies above the water. This was because their lifejackets were tied around their waist when the lifejacket should have been tied close to their chests.

With darkness falling and the rescuers not allowed to use torches or searchlights the rescue operation was called off. HMS *Attacker's* lifeboats returned to their ship and the oarsmen were immediately taken to the captain's office where they reported taking onboard many survivors and dead. Many of the rescuers reported a smell of petrol in the water.

The *Lithium* transferred her sixty survivors to the *Sir Galahad* and the *Cragsman* transferred her fourteen survivors to the *Isle of Sark*. The bodies they had recovered were also transferred. All rescue ships received a signal which read:

"This incident is not; repeat not, to be spoken about."

All personnel on board the Royal Navy rescue ships were ordered never to talk about the "incident."

All ships were then ordered to proceed to Ardrossan where a fleet of ambulances waited to take the wounded to the local Royal Navy sick bay. As the local sick bay could only contend with 20 casualties, the others were taken to Ballochmyle Hospital, Mauchline, 24 miles away.

As Ardrossan was finding it difficult to cope with the vast number of rescue ships the *Isle of Sark* was ordered to proceed to Greenock. As the ship neared Greenock the captain received a signal advising him that due to the possibility of a U-boat being in the vicinity the boom net would not be lowered until the following morning. All that night the *Isle of Sark* had to remain anchored, waiting for access to reach Greenock.

In Ardrossan the bedraggled sailors were taken to the Naval Base at the harbour. From there they were accommodated in a local dance hall known as The Castlecraigs. The Castlecraigs was a large prestigious building in the town centre surrounded by high walls. As there were no bedrooms or beds in the building the survivors slept on the floor.

Later the Women's Voluntary Service arrived at the Castlecraigs with sacks of clothes to kit out the bedraggled survivors. After being clothed and fed some of the men took a look around the town. The locals noticed the odd appearance of the survivors from "the big ship."

The officers were billeted in the Eglinton Hotel, Ardrossan, near the harbour.

Later that evening when the final count was made it transpired 379 young men had lost their lives. Only 149 of *Dasher's* crew survived! This information was withheld from the survivors. When they asked the question:

"Where are the rest of the crew?"

They were simply told:

"They have been taken to Brodick and Greenock."

The survivors in Ardrossan were never told that 379 of their ship mates had perished.

On the evening of the loss of HMS *Dasher*, and before any enquiry into the loss could possibly have taken place, the Admiralty in London recorded in the War Diary, at page number 1053.

War Diary.   27.3.1943.
                                              Saturday.

SITUATION REPORT.

Home Commands.

DASHER   1. The Escort Carrier DASHER sank at 1645 today
sunk.   when 5 miles south of Cumbrae Island as the
         result of an internal explosion believed not
         due to enemy action but to petrol.   Survivors,
         including the C.O., have been picked up.

After recording the sinking of the aircraft carrier the Admiralty received a signal
from the Flag Officer in Charge at Greenock. It was recorded on the 27th
March, 1943, in the War Diary.

MOST SECRET.

1063

27.3.1943.
Saturday.

HOME COMMANDS.

Casualties & Defects - Contd.

DASHER has sunk 5 miles south of Cumbrae
Island at 1645 today after explosion. Cause
not yet ascertained but probably not due to enemy
action.
Survivors being picked up. C.O. has been
picked up. A/S and minesweeping precautions
are being taken.
(F.O.I.C. Greenock 1858A/27 to Admty.)

(*The letters A/S signifies anti-submarine*)
(*The letters F.O.I.C.signifies Flag Officer in Command*))

When the *Lithium* arrived at Llanddulas in Wales, to discharge her cargo of sulphur, a voice from the jetty shouted out *"You're late."* In response Captain Terretta wrote out a report as to why he was "late."

Report made to NAVAL CONTROL SERVICE OFFICER, FLEETWOOD, by the

Master of s.s. "LITHIUM", owned by The Imperical Chemical Industries,

Fleetwood.

At 1642 on Saturday, 27th March, 1943, whilst on passage from Glasgow

to Llanddulas, when in a position S. by W. ½ W. (about 6 miles by log

from the Cumbrea Light, we passed Aircraft Carrier "DASHER".

¼ mile to Starboard.   CARRIER

At this time we observed the Aircraft blow up - a bright

flash appeared from after side amidships, and dense smoke issued from

under the Flight Deck.

We saw the ship was sinking rapidly by the stern - we

turned about to render what assistance we could, picking up

approximately 60 survivors.   These were placed on board the

M.s. "SIR GALAHAD".

At 1830 the ship proceeded on her voyage, after

disembarking survivors.

Signed   *J. Terretta Master*

Master s.s. "Lithium".

30/3/43.

50

Chapter 7

The Funerals Then Silence

A s the bodies were brought ashore they were cleaned and cared for by the local funeral director, Lawrie McLean. Due to the large number of bodies and the extent of the oil on them, the funeral director asked one of his friends, the local police sergeant, to assist him. Once the dreadful task was completed survivors had to undertake a grim task. They were led into the "temporary morgue" in an effort to identify approximately sixty bodies. Some were identified, others were not. There were two reasons for some of the dead being unidentifiable; either no one recognised the person or the person was simply too badly burned. After this ordeal the survivors were ordered to remain within the town of Ardrossan.

Sub-lieutenant John Ferrier's home town was in Greenock, 26 miles away. The young officer knew that with *Dasher's* non arrival at Greenock news of the disaster would become known within Royal Navy circles, and would swiftly spread. Concerned about his wife and family hearing bad news and possibly believing that he had died in the tragedy, the young officer disobeyed the order and stepped on the next bus for Greenock. He was very glad he had disobeyed orders, because when he arrived home his anxious wife already knew about the sinking of his ship and was so relieved to see him.

It transpired someone had telephoned the *Daily Record* newspaper, one of Scotland's national newspapers. The caller said he was phoning to tell the newspaper that HMS *Dasher* had sunk in the Firth of Clyde. Ironically the newspaper telephone receptionist who took the call was a cousin of John Ferrier. After connecting the call to a reporter, the receptionist immediately phoned her relatives in Greenock. As for the caller, when he spoke to a reporter, he was told that the government censor would not allow the story to be published.

John Ferrier arrived back in Ardrossan without being missed and was billeted with a Mr & Mrs McDonald in Ardrossan. Mr McDonald was a well respected businessman. He and his wife had an open door policy offering free bed and breakfast to military personnel. That first night John was asked to sign the visitor book. He duly wrote:

Sub/Lt John Ferrie?

sunk on HMS Dasher?

Sat 27/3/43

When John woke next morning he was embarrassed to see the black outline of his body on the clean bed sheet. Even although he had had a bath the previous evening and another bath on his second night ashore, the diesel impregnated salt water he had been swimming in was still in his body and was seeping out of his skin. As much as he enjoyed being in the company of the McDonalds, the young officer was pleased to be moved to join his shipmates at the Royal Navy Depot at Ardrossan Harbour. (HMS *Fortitude*)

On Sunday 28th March there was much activity outside the Castlecraigs, where many of the survivors were billeted. Situated on the right hand side was a tennis court. Across the main road, opposite the Castlecraigs was a two storey block of flats. It comprised of two flats on the ground floor and two on the upper floor. The residents on the upper floor had a clear view over the high wall and were astonished to see bodies from the *Dasher* being laid out on the tennis court.

Two local lads who were playing in the park behind the Castlecraigs heard loud voices. A large wall separated them from the Castlecraigs and they could not see who was speaking loudly and shouting. The inquisitive lads climbed up the wall and looked over the top. There in the tennis court they saw bodies laid out in rows. As they gawped a loud voice shouted at them, *"Get down off that wall."* The two lads quickly jumped down and ran home.

That same day after lunch the survivors were told that a Board of Enquiry would be held offshore from Greenock onboard HMS *Archer* on the 30th and 31st March. 25 names were then read out. These were the names of the survivors who were to be summoned as witnesses at the Board of Enquiry. Those not required to attend would be present at the funerals of their shipmates which were scheduled to take place on Wednesday 31st March.

Telegrams regarding the funeral arrangements at Ardrossan were received by the bereaved families on Monday 29th March. They read:

> *"Funeral will take place from Naval Base Ardrossan at 2pm on Wednesday 31st March. 1943."*

When the bereaved families received the dreaded telegram regarding the funeral arrangements five of the families immediately visited their local post office to send a telegram requesting a private burial for their loved ones.

Strangely four requests were granted and one was refused. The family who were refused permission were the bereaved relatives of John Melville. The four seamen whose families were allowed to take them home for private burial were:

> Sub-lieutenant John Lyle McFarlane, Greenock Cemetery; Leading Seaman Archibald Craig, Hawkhead Cemetery, Paisley; Sub-lieutenant John I.R. Walker, Mearns Cemetery, Glasgow; Able Seaman Sylvester Woolaghan, St. Joseph's Cemetery, Frizington, Cumberland, England.

The young widow of John Melville, whose request to take her husband home had been refused, had to attend the burial at Ardrossan Cemetery. On Tuesday 30th March, 1943, the day before the *Dasher* funerals, the grieving families arrived at Ardrossan and were escorted to the Naval base. When the Melville family requested a viewing of John in his coffin, this request was also denied.

The following day at 2.00 pm the cortège departed from the Naval Base headed by two highly polished lorries each carrying six coffins draped with the Union flag. Immediately behind were the bereaved relatives in cars provided by the Royal Navy. The cars were followed by the firing party then the Naval band. A large representation of the Royal Navy and the Women's Royal Navy services marched slowly behind the Navy band. The drums were muffled as the band played the *Death March* all along the route to the cemetery.

As a mark of respect shops along the funeral route were closed. Many locals lined the main street and stood in silence. Local man Roy Riddex recalls as the cortège passed the two local schools the children were waiting at the front and respectfully stood quietly as the procession passed. One lady whispered to her friends:

> "It's just like a royal funeral."

It was a very emotional occasion carried out with great dignity by all the immaculately turned out Royal Navy personnel.

After entering the cemetery gateway, the procession solemnly made its way to the rear of the walled cemetery, where the young men were to be laid to rest. As each coffin was slowly lowered into the grave a volley of six shots was fired overhead. At the conclusion of the ceremony the band quickly marched from the cemetery playing the tune *Colonel Bogey*, the drums no longer muffled. For the proud and sad band members, the funeral service was finished and they returned to normal duties. As the Royal Navy personnel returned to their base at Ardrossan, the bereaved made their way home.

Over 3 days the following burial services took place at Greenock.

1st April, 1943, Lieutenant Fleetwood Price; Leading Writer William Gillies; Leading Radio Mechanic Ronald Neath; Ordinary Seaman George H.M. Percival. On 3rd April, 1943, Ordinary Seaman Richard Liddle. On 4th April, 1943, Able seaman Henry Harper.

Ardrossan - Thursday 1st April, 1943

The day after the funerals in Ardrossan, the survivors were brought together and advised they were going home on 14 days survivors leave. They were each handed a train travel warrant to their home town. Prior to departing from HMS *Fortitude* they were all ordered in harsh terms:

"Don't ever talk about the sinking of HMS Dasher!"

The 149 survivors walked in groups from the Ardrossan Royal Navy base to the local railway station. From Ardrossan the trains took them to Glasgow where the groups split up to board trains departing to destinations all over the UK.

On reaching their home towns and walking homeward, each survivor experienced mixed feelings. Not one of them had received any form of counselling, they were on their own, never to talk about their personal traumatic ordeal and loss of their shipmates.

Seaman Reilly from Blackpool was glad to return to his family, however, he was no sooner home when someone knocked on the front door of his house. It was a bereaved mother who lived nearby. When the survivor opened the door the broken hearted mother asked him:

"What happened to my son?"

Reilly's reply was:

"I am sorry I cannot tell you anything. I am under orders never to talk about it."

The distraught mother implored him to tell her, but he steadfastly refused. He never spoke to the mother about the tragedy.

In the small town of Llandudno Junction, 3 miles from Llandudno, Charles and Gwladys Scragg had received a telegram intimating their son Francis (Frank) was missing presumed killed. They were waiting daily for more news, hoping upon hope that their missing son would be found alive. A few days after receiving the telegram Gwladys was in the local butcher shop being served. The butcher asked Gwladys if there was any news about her son. Sadly the mother replied:

"Not yet."

Unknown to the sorrowful mother, standing behind her in the butcher shop was a *Dasher* survivor from a nearby village. The survivor could have spoken to the mother but cruelly he said nothing.

The other bereaved families were in the same situation, they had all received the dreaded telegram stating their loved one had been killed or missing presumed killed on active service on 27th March 1943, as a result of an explosion onboard the ship on which they were serving.

All the families made contact with the War Office seeking more information. Their enquiries were passed on to "CW Casualties," the Royal Navy department responsible for contacting families to advise them their loved one had been killed or missing presumed killed in action.

When CW Casualties were inundated with enquiries from *Dasher* families they wrote to Captain J. Eccles, Director of Operations Division. The letter highlighted the fact that the meagre information they had been ordered to give the relatives broke Royal Navy rules. In particular rule C.A.F.O. 1477/42 which states:

> *"As much information as possible shall be given to the next of kin at the time they are informed of their loss."*

In the letter CW Casualties requested that they be allowed to divulge more information to the bereaved relatives. They also asked when the news of the sinking of HMS *Dasher* could be released.

Captain Eclles reply was short and specific:

> *"No additional information can be released at the moment and news of the sinking can be published as soon as the enemy is found to know or within one month of the date of sinking, whichever is earlier."*

Ironically the enemy recorded they were made aware of the sinking of HMS *Dasher* within days, from their agents (spies) who posed as Polish soldiers.

Max Groganski, a Polish soldier, had settled in Ardrossan and married a local woman. After hostilities Mrs Groganski returned home from work one day and found her husband packing a suitcase. When she asked him what was happening he replied that he was returning to the Fatherland. When Mrs Groganski asked her husband what he was talking about, he replied he was German and his name was Maximillian Von Baumann! The German then walked out of the house and was never seen again.

As for German Military Intelligence, not only were they aware of the loss of *Dasher* within days, they even knew the cause was due to an internal explosion. The Germans, however, did not make it known that they were aware of the fate of *Dasher*, but later confirmed that no U-boat was involved.

The bereaved relatives received no more information relating to the loss of their loved ones. Many of the mothers left the back door of their home unlocked at night. Having received no details from CW Casualties they were clinging to the hope that their son had perhaps lost his memory and would return home. As for the back door being left unlocked at night, the mothers believed it would be a terrible situation if their son arrived home and found the door locked.

Sub-lieutenant Lionel Godfrey was a fighter pilot with 891 Squadron. On the

26th March, 1943 four Hurricane aircraft from the Squadron and their maintenance personnel were attached to HMS *Dasher*. The remainder of 891 Squadron were based at Machrihanish in Kintyre. Lionel reported:

> *"On the 27th March 1943 I and three other pilots were in flying formation in the Firth of Clyde. Prior to flying back to our base at Machrihanish we witnessed HMS Dasher exploding and the aircraft lift being hurled between 200 and 300 feet into the air. There was nothing we could do but maintain radio silence and return to our base.*
>
> *891Squadron, left with only four aircraft, four pilots and less than a dozen maintenance personnel, was almost immediately disbanded. It was a sad ending to what had been a happy association with an efficient fighter squadron.*
>
> *Two days later with no appointment to another squadron I ended up taking compulsory leave in London. After four weeks without pay and without notice of an appointment I visited a branch of the Admiralty in Queen Ann's Mansions, London in an endeavour to learn what I should do with myself.*
>
> *From a Commander seated behind a desk in a depressing looking office I received a flat denial that anything untoward had happened to Dasher or to 891 Squadron.*
>
> *When I, a mere Sub-lieutenant protested that with my own eyes I'd seen Dasher go down and slip beneath the calm waters of the Firth of Clyde, the only response I got from the severe looking Commander was, 'Nonsense! You'd better get yourself a casual payment and remain on indefinite leave. You will be informed when you are needed.' At no time since the tragic end of HMS Dasher have I heard or seen an official acknowledgement of her sinking."*

Up to 4 months after the sinking the relatives who had received a telegram stating their loves one was missing presumed killed, received a letter that it has to be confirmed they had been killed. The bereaved families were completely unaware the cause of the sinking of HMS *Dasher* was creating intense embarrassment to the most senior Royal Navy officers, the Admiralty and their American counterparts. To prevent public embarrassment all information surrounding the cause of the sinking was subjected to total secrecy.

As the years passed the War Office became known as The Ministry of Defence. Many bereaved families persisted in writing, pleading for information regarding the loss of their loved ones. Sadly the MoD reaction was the same as the War Office reaction. No information was divulged!

John Clark resides in Luton, Bedfordshire. Sadly John's brother William lost his life on that fateful day. William, age 20, was a Leading Seaman. 43 years after *Dasher* blew up and sank, John Clark wrote a letter to *The Sunday Post*. John was seeking information regarding what happened to HMS *Dasher*. Surely, thought John, after 43 years someone would tell something. *The Sunday Post* published John's letter on 14th December, 1986 and as a result he received more than 200 letters from bereaved families. Shamefully everyone was still seeking information. Not one family was told any of the circumstances regarding the loss of their loved one or the sinking of the ship. Petty officers John Stamp and Cyril Terry, the two *Dasher* heroes who lost their lives whilst saving the lives of their shipmates, received no recognition. As for their families, they were never told any circumstances as to how the two men lost their lives. In the 1960's John Stamp's family went on their annual holiday to Butlins Holiday Camp in Ayr. Thereafter they returned every year. Midway through the two week holiday they always enjoyed a visit to the popular coastal town of Largs in North Ayrshire. As the bus passed through Ardrossan they enjoyed the sea view of the Firth of Clyde. Unknown to the family they were looking out to the position where *Dasher* sank! Fifty two years after John Stamp lost his life, his family found out his ship had sunk in the Firth of Clyde.

A Royal Navy rescue ship stopped well clear of the rescue area after the order was given when the sea caught fire:
Keep clear. We cannot afford to lose another ship this day.

Top: Dinner being served by the catering staff.
Bottom: Aircraft handlers on flight deck. Iceland February 1943.

Chapter 8

Board of Enquiry

On 30th March as Captain Boswell and Lieutenant Pip Culmer, *Dasher's* navigating officer, were enjoying breakfast in the Kilmacolm Hydro Hotel, 8 miles from Greenock, the Royal Navy lorries arrived at the Ardrossan Naval base to collect the 25 witnesses summoned to attend the Board of Enquiry.

One of *Dasher's* officers telephoned Captain Boswell from Ardrossan to report that seconds before the explosion, he was on the flight deck, directly above the hangar. The officer reported to the Captain that he saw a Rating smoking in a forbidden zone. The Rating must have been well aware he was in a 'No Smoking Area' as there were large signs stating:

'No Smoking.'

The officer reported that when the Rating turned round and saw him, he instantly threw the cigarette down a ventilating shaft which led to the hangar below. Immediately after the cigarette was thrown into the shaft the explosion occurred.

At the conclusion of making his statement the officer mentioned that he would meet up with Captain Boswell at the Board of Enquiry onboard HMS *Archer*.

When Captain Boswell telephoned Greenock to advise them he would arrive later that morning, he was astonished to be informed his presence was not required. Incredibly when Captain Boswell insisted that he would be in attendance, he was told in no uncertain fashion that his presence was not required! *Dasher's* navigator, Lieutenant "Pip" Culmer, was also told his presence was not deemed to be necessary. It was said that Royal Navy history was made that day because the Captain was not allowed to attend the Board of Enquiry into the sinking of his ship.

The road between Ardrossan and Greenock hugs the coastline. A few miles offshore is where *Dasher* blew up and sank, taking many of the survivors shipmates with her. The road was now closed to the public as bodies were being washed ashore onto the stretch of the beach.

After arriving at Greenock the 25 witnesses were taken out, by motor launches, to HMS *Archer* where the enquiry was to be held. One cannot begin to imagine the thoughts of the men from *Dasher* as they approached her sister ship, HMS *Archer*. After escaping from their sinking ship in the most horrendous circumstances, they were about to board an identical vessel.

In all 34 witnesses were called to give evidence at the enquiry. The witnesses in attendance comprised 25 personnel from *Dasher*, 4 from the *Isle of Sark*, 2 from *La Capricieuse* and 3 from the motor launch ML 528.

However, it is puzzling that only Royal Navy personnel were called to give evidence. No witnesses were called to give evidence from the *Lithium* or *Cragsman,* the small vessels that had heroically plucked so many desperate men from the burning sea, as the large Royal Navy ships stood by motionless. Nor were any civilians, who had witnessed the unfolding drama through binoculars, contacted and asked to give evidence.

Although there were many Naval shorthand writers at Ardrossan, Brodick, Greenock, Rothesay and other nearby Royal Navy land bases, a short hand writer was sent from London to record the minutes at the enquiry into the loss of HMS *Dasher.*

The Board of Enquiry committee comprised: Captain G Grantham C.B. DSO. R.N., HMS *Indominatable;* Captain J.I. Robertson R.N., HMS *Archer;* Captain J.G. Holt R.N., HMS *King George V;* Commander R. Cobb. O.B.E., R.N., HMS *Indomitable;* and Commander H.D. McMaster R.N.R., HMS *Archer.*

Their orders were marked*:*

"Most Secret."

Over the next two days the 34 witnesses were subjected to a total of 560 questions. The questions asked included:

Where were you standing? Could you see daylight? Where were the torpedoes? Could you smell petrol? What did the explosion sound like? Was there a lot of smoke? Did you see flames? What colour were the flames?

A number of questions related to the storage of petrol and to any smell of petrol.

Each question was fired at the witnesses in staccato fashion. At the conclusion of the enquiry a comprehensive report was forwarded to the Admiralty in London.

The findings of the Board of Enquiry were marked "Secret."

SECRET

BOARD OF ENQUIRY HELD ON BOARD H.M.S. "ARCHER"
ON TUESDAY AND WEDNESDAY, 30TH AND 31ST MARCH
1943 TO INVESTIGATE INTO THE CIRCUMSTANCES
ATTENDING

L O S S   O F   H. M. S.   " D A S H E R "
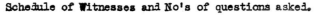

O N   2 7 T H   M A R C H,   1 9 4 3.

SCHEDULE OF CONTENTS.

Findings of the Board.

Memorandum convening the Board.

Schedule of Witnesses and No's of questions asked.

Minutes of proceedings.

Photographs and negatives of sinkings taken by
rating on board M.L. 528.

Original shorthand notes.

S E C R E T.

H.M.S. "ARCHER"

31st March, 1943.

Sir,

In accordance with your Memorandum dated 28th March, 1943, directing us to enquire into the loss of H.M.S. "DASHER" on the 27th March, 1943, we have the honour to submit the following report:-

2.   H.M.S. "DASHER" sank at approximately 1648A on 27th March in approximate position 205 degrees Cumbrae Island Light 5 miles. Commanding Officer and 148 of her ship's company survived out of a total of 527.

3.   <u>The following facts have been established:-</u>

(a) Explosion was not due to any external cause.

(b) It was muffled rumbling report and not an instantaneous detonation.

(c) It did not take place in the after 4" magazine; in the hangar; forward of the hangar area or in the engineroom.

4.   <u>The explosion vented itself:-</u>

(a) forward through the after bulkhead of the engineroom low down.

(b) upward through a large hatch just forward of the lift well.

(c) up and out through the ship's side to starboard via the Fleet Air Arm Messdeck.

(d) presumably through the ship's bottom in one or more places.

5.   The results of the explosion were:-

(a)   Immediate failure of all light and power; emergency
      dynamo cut in for about 20 seconds only.

(b)   Lift, at flight deck level, blown high in the air
      and after end of flight deck damaged.

(c)   Violent fire at after end of hangar.

(d)   Fire in the engineroom.

(e)   Rapid flooding of the ship extending from forward
      engineroom bulkhead to the stern.

(f)   A list to starboard of not more than 10 degrees
      which rapidly disappeared as the ship settled
      quickly by the stern.

(g)   The ship sank approximately eight minutes after
      the explosion.

SECRET.   Page 2.

6.   State of the ship was as follows:-

(a)   Flying had just been completed and all aircraft except
      one struck down.

(b)   In the hangar were 6 Swordfish and 2 Hurricanes.
      Two Swordfish were being fuelled.

(c)   Petrol control room was open with Greaser in attendance.

(d)   Access hatch from Fleet Air Arm messdeck to flat
      outside petrol control room was open.

(e)   Hatch in same flat at top of access trunk to shaft
      tunnel may also have been open, as this was in regular
      use for hourly visits to Plummer Blocks.

(f)   A hole, 1-inch in diameter between the shaft tunnel
      and main petrol compartment was known to exist.

(g)   It is uncertain whether a slow drip from a valve on
      one of the starboard tanks had been made good.

(h)   Some of Fleet Air Arm personnel, who had been working
      on aircraft and dismissed from hangar, were on their
      messdeck. "No smoking" notices were permanently
      in place above hatch to petrol control room. No
      sentry was placed.

(i)   Hands had been working in after depth charge stowage
      which is immediately abaft the petrol compartment
      during the forenoon. 68 depth charges were still in
      this magazine.

63

7.   We are of the opinion that:-

(I)   The original explosion took place either in the
after depth charge magazine or the main petrol stowage.
These two compartments are adjacent to one another.

(II)   There is no evidence that the explosion occurred in
the depth charge magazine beyond the fact that this is
located in the region of the explosion.

(III)   There is no direct proof that the explosion started in
the main petrol stowage. But evidence shows that
there may have been an accumulation of petrol vapour
in the main petrol compartment and that this could have
been ignited by a man smoking in the shaft tunnel, or
through someone dropping a cigarette end down from the
Fleet Air Arm Messdeck, to the petrol control
compartment or below.
   It is pointed out that the lighting system is
not up to magazine lighting specification, and that a
fault on the system could have ignited petrol vapour
when lights were switched on or off.

8.   We recommend that:-

(A)   Alterations detailed in Commander-in-Chief, Home Fleet's
telegram T.O.O.1339 of 15th February 1943 should be
applied to all Escort Carriers at the earliest
opportunity.

(B)   Access to petrol control compartments should be
trunked up to the deck of the hangar, as in "ARCHER"
and in no case to a crewspace.

(C)   Until B is carried out in existing carriers, the
trunk giving access to the forward end of the shaft
tunnel should not be used.

(D)   The watertight door giving access from the Engineroom
to the shaft tunnel should be permanently sealed, as
had already been done in "DASHER".

(E)   The shaft tunnel should be fitted with a ventilating
system.

(F)   All carriers to be supplied at the earliest possible
moment with portable petrol detector gauges.

(G)   All carriers be instructed to carry out rigidly
magazine and petrol regulations, and that all defects
in petrol systems are to be reported to the Commanding
Officer immediately they are discovered.

(H)   All carriers be instructed that life belts are to be
worn when ships are exercising in local areas as well
as at sea.

(I)   Calcium Flares should be withdrawn from Carriers, but
if carried should be stowed in a watertight container.

9.   The behaviour and bearing of the Officers and ratings was exemplary throughout. Petty Officer STAMP R.N.V.R., assisted many young ratings to safety, but lost his life in so doing. Petty Officer Telegraphist TERRY displayed a similar spirit and example and was also lost.

10.   Two small coasting vessels, the S.S. LILLIUM and S.S. CRAGSMAN gave valuable assistance in rescuing men from the sea, working close to the oil burning on the water.

We have the honour to be,

Sir,

Your obedient Servants,

(signature)

(PRESIDENT) H.M.S. "INDOMITABLE"

(signature)

H.M.S. "ARCHER"

ICE ADMIRAL, AIRCRAFT CARRIERS
   HOME FLEET.

(signature)

Staff of Commander-in-Chief,
       HOME FLEET.

(signature)

H.M.S. "INDOMITABLE"

(signature)

H.M.S. "ARCHER".

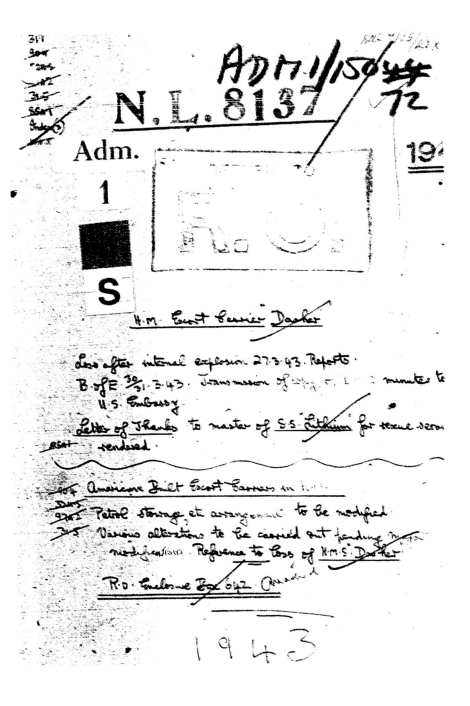

N.L. 8137

Adm.

1

S

<u>H·M· Escort Carrier "Dasher"</u>

Loss after internal explosion. 27·3·43. Reports.
B of E 30/31· 3·43. Transmission of ___ minutes to
U.S. Embassy.

<u>Letter of Thanks</u> to master of S.S. "Lithium" for rescue service
rendered.

American Built Escort Carriers in ___

Petrol storage etc arrangement to be modified.

Various alterations to be carried out pending
modifications. Reference to loss of H.M.S. "Dasher"

<u>R.O. Enclosure Box 642</u> Quadrid

1943

Chapter 9

Findings of the Board of Enquiry

When the Board of Enquiry's report was received in London it was immediately classified as "Most Secret." Copies were delivered by courier to the Admiralty, the British authority responsible for the command of the Royal Navy. Copies were delivered by special dispatch rider to the most senior Royal Navy officials including: The Director Operations Division, the Deputy Controller, the Director of Sea Transport, and also to Vice Admirals. After having been given time to study the top secret documents the Royal Navy Deputy Controller convened a meeting of all whom had studied the Board of Enquiry's report. On the 5th April, 1943, the officials compiled a file comprising 91 pages.

The contents of the report included: The findings of the Board of Enquiry; the Schedule of witnesses; questions asked; replies to each question; minutes of proceedings; photographs and negatives taken by a Rating on board Motor Launch 528 and original shorthand notes.

After a full discussion the Royal Navy's most senior officers agreed with the findings of the Board of Enquiry which included the probable cause of the disaster:

"There seemed little doubt the explosion was petrol vapour and that there may have been an accumulation of petrol vapour in the main petrol compartment which could have been ignited by a man smoking in the shaft tunnel, or through someone dropping a cigarette end down from the Fleet Air Arm Mess deck."

The Americans were anxious to be advised of the full outcome of the Board of Enquiry and on the 22nd April, 1943, the Naval Attaché at the American Embassy in London wrote to the British Admiralty. The contents were stamped *"Secret."*

Reply refer to
No. 5111

AMERICAN EMBASSY
OFFICE OF THE NAVAL ATTACHÉ
LONDON

WRM:HGA

U.S. CONFIDENTIAL
BRITISH   SECRET

April 22, 1943.

U.S. CONFIDENTIAL - BRITISH SECRET

My dear Sir Henry:

  It would be greatly appreciated if this office could be furnished with a copy of the report of the Board of Enquiry on H.M.S. DASHER, when same becomes available.

  It would further be appreciated if this office could be informed of any alterations, particularly to the petrol systems, which the Admiralty may authorize on this type of vessel.

    Yours sincerely,

    T. A. SOLBERG,
    Captain, U.S. Navy.

Sir Henry V. Markham, K.C.B.,
Permanent Secretary,
Board of Admiralty,
Admiralty,
London, S.W.1.

In response the Admiralty forwarded a diplomatic reply to the American Embassy. It read:

  "As a result of the experience of HMS Dasher the petrol system on sister ships require modification in accordance with normal British standards. Owing to the amount of work involved it may not be possible to carry out these alterations for some considerable time."

The following week the Royal Navy Deputy Controller wrote a damning report to the Admiralty:

I have held a departmental (i.e. D.N.C., E. in C., and D.E.E.) meeting to consider the report of Board of Enquiry on loss of HMS Dasher

2. The findings of the Board are concurred in generally and their picture of what happened so far as it goes is probably accurate.

3. There seems little doubt that the explosion was a petrol vapour one, the sustained "pouff" being consistent with such explosions. There was no evidence of a "detonation" type of explosion such as might be occasioned by depth charges or similar types of explosion.

4. From the damage sustained to the ship it is evident that the cause of the explosion was a large one consistent to a partial filling at least of the petrol compartment with vapour.

5. The causes of the presence and ignition of the vapour are not apparent but due to the inadequate safety arrangements in this class of ship may have been many.

6. As pointed out in my memo. D.N.E. 6321/43 of the 11th April, Safeguards against accidents of this nature are, by our standards, practically non existent, in the petrol arrangements and hangars of these American built escort ships. Steps have been taken to rectify this state of affairs in all classes so far as it is practicable, but this will take time and will mainly devolve on our resources. B.A.D. Washington has been kept fully informed, and asked to do what he can to get things rectified in new ships before delivery.

7. In spite of the fact that the safety standards of these ships was low compared with normal carriers standards, the personnel do not seem to have been particularly trained nor specific precautions taken. This has now been rectified in V.A. home fleet's signal of 011301/april, Para. 6 of A.M. 171657B and B.A.D. in his signal 162243 states that he is issuing a pamphlet describing the petrol system and sources of danger to all new ships of this type. No further action is considered necessary at this stage.

8. Action has already been taken to cover all the other points raised by this board of enquiry.

9 In his signal quoted above B.A.D. asks for "report of Dasher" enquiry at earliest possible moment. He has already had their recommendations and it is now proposed to send him by Air Mail the report (pp. 1-3), without the minutes of the evidence.

10. After action the report should be circulated to departments in the usual manner, except to the departments mentioned in para 1, who have already seen it.

DEPUTY CONTROLLER.
30th April, 1943

The Deputy Controller also recorded:

"Steps have been taken to rectify this state of affairs so far as is practical. The British Admiralty Delegation in Washington has been kept fully informed and asked to do what it can to get things rectified in new ships before delivery.

"In spite of the fact that safety of these ships was low, compared with normal standards, the personnel do not seem to have been particularly trained nor special precautions taken. This has now been rectified."

Now that the reports were finalised the Admiralty advised the American Embassy of the alterations that would be carried out to eliminate the dangerous situation posed to *Dasher's* sister ships.

61

M..8137/43.   19th May   3

SECRET.

Dear Captain Solberg,

With reference to your letter of the 22nd April No.5111 and mine of the 5th May, I enclose a copy of the report of the board of inquiry which investigated the loss of H.M.S. DASHER.

2.   As a result of the experience with DASHER, it has been approved as a long term policy to modify the petrol arrangements in these ships in accordance with normal British practice. Owing to the amount of work involved, it may not be possible to carry out these alterations for some considerable time, consequently the following alterations are being undertaken as an interim measure.

(1)   (a)   Reduce the amount of petrol carried to about 40,000 galls. The tanks not required for petrol to be filled with water and pipes blanked off.

(b)   Fit artifical exhaust ventilation to the hangar (inductor system).

(c)   Fit inductor ventilation to the petrol control compartment and cleavage gauge compartment.

(d)   Fit inductor ventilation to the petrol hold. (In ARCHER and BITER only).

(e)   Raise the general ship ventilation fans which are fitted in the hangar to positions as high as practicable above the 8' line. Fit spray shields to these fans.

(f)   Make doors leading to funnel uptake compartment, blower compartment etc. gastight.

(g)   Fit protective casing to exposed petrol piping on ships side outboard.

(h)   Remove existing wiring from the cleavage gauge compartment and magazine hand lamps pattern 8815.

Captain T.A. Solberg,
   Office of the Naval Attaché,
      American Embassy,
         Grosvenor Square,
            W.1.   /(1)

Six more safety alterations were programmed to be carried out at a later date. These were: Remove existing wiring from the petrol control compartment; fit exterior light box in petrol control department; fit asbestos fire curtains in the hangar; blank the door leading from engine room to shaft tunnel; fit protective casing to exposed petrol piping; remove existing wiring from the cleavage gauge compartment and use magazine hand lamp, pattern 8815.

The following ten safety observations were also to be implemented.

> *The trunk giving access to the shaft is not to be used; rigid observance of the magazine regulations to be enforced; rigid observance of the petrol regulations to be enforced; all defects in petrol systems are to be reported to the Commanding Officer immediately they are discovered; Commanding Officers are to ensure that the engineer officer in charge of the petrol system enforces rigid discipline in his organisation; smoking in the mess deck over the petrol hold is to be forbidden; particular attention is to be paid to keeping the bilges in the petrol compartment pumped dry so that the exhaust ventilating trunks are free from obstruction; lifebelts are invariably to be worn when ships are under way; calcium flares are not to be used on life floats, life buoys or life belts; any calcium flares which it is desired to retain on board are to be kept in watertight containers.*

The last precaution was included because a calcium flare may have been responsible for igniting the aviation fuel in the water. In total fourteen safety alterations and eleven safety precautions were identified on board *Dasher!*

All alterations and safety practises were to be in accordance with Royal Navy standards.

The Admiralty also forwarded a safety pamphlet to *Dasher's* sister ships alerting to the sources of danger in the bulk fuel storage system and the best way to handle them. With regard to the cause of the persistent petrol fumes, senior officials in the Royal Navy concluded that the American bulk storage of fuel had a design fault.

In response the Americans blamed the inexperience of the British officers in the handling of bulk petrol. The Royal Navy insisted there was an American design fault in the storage of fuel on *Dasher* and her sister ships. It is a fact that the Americans changed the design of the bulk fuel storage systems on all future escort carriers for the Royal Navy.

It is startling that Captain Boswell was not in attendance at the enquiry into the loss of his ship. It must be presumed that the Captain's concerns of the lack of safety on *Dasher* were unwelcome and clearly the Admiralty did not wish them to be officially noted.

Captain Boswell's son Robin writes:

> *"On several occasions my father spoke of the Dasher tragedy*

before he died in 1975. And since his death our mother has also referred to this event. My Mother's account is that my father was lucky to survive, after being dragged down to the bottom by an aerial wire. He apparently surfaced close to a raft, and managed to survive the ensuing fire.

"According to my mother he was hospitalised after swallowing oil. He was extremely upset by the Dasher explosion and loss, in part because he had vociferously voiced to his superiors his own strong concerns over the lack of safety on the Dasher, and had been ignored. The need to keep the ship operational, even if unsafe, to participate in convoy work, was paramount.

"After the sinking and loss my father demanded to be allowed to be present at the Board of Enquiry, but was not allowed to participate. He could have given extensive evidence regarding the official disregard of the known dangers on board. His protest at being silenced by his superiors, and his conflict with the Admiralty regarding the Dasher, later led to his being reassigned (in fact exiled) to an irrelevant backwater in Algiers for the rest of the war.

"My father was well aware of the Admiralty cover-up and demanded a full enquiry into the sinking. This was always refused and his uncooperative attitude was penalised.

"Perhaps it was the need to avoid a shocking scandal being exposed at the heart of the British Admiralty, the scandal being the callous way in which the Admiralty had knowingly insisted on Dasher being readied for sea when it was known that the ship was in a particularly dangerous condition for its crew of more than 500.

"My father was well known for his consideration of the welfare of the crews of his ships and his belief in keeping the crew as happy as possible in the circumstances."

Robin Boswell

Chapter 10

Possible Causes of Explosion

Although the Board of Enquiry had been held, the findings were classified as "Most Secret." The surviving crew of *Dasher* were never told what caused the ship to explode and sink within minutes. They were never told how many lives had been lost or how many had survived.

As the disaster had happened within sight of land many witnesses had their own theories as to the cause. As no official information was forthcoming, the rumours and speculation among the local population, inevitably gathered momentum.

To this day the mystery of the "big ship that sank" is still discussed with people having their own opinion of what did happen to cause this tragedy that affected the North Ayrshire town of Ardrossan so much. A few of the theories are briefly discussed below.

A Torpedo

When U-boat U33 entered the Firth of Clyde on the 12th February, 1940, it was quickly detected and sunk by the mine sweeper HMS *Gleaner*. General Admiral Erich Raeder then advised Hitler the Firth of Clyde was too dangerous for U-boats and that no further attempts should be made to enter that area. Records at the German U-boat archives in Cuxhaven records:

> *"The British escort carrier HMS Dasher is destroyed at 27th March 1943 on the River Clyde as a result of a petrol explosion and fire. No German U-boat was involved."*

Hence it is safe to affirm that HMS *Dasher* was not sunk by a torpedo from a U-boat. In summary this theory can be completely discounted.

An Enemy Mine

According to a radio report a few days before the disaster, it was suggested that German planes may have dropped mines in the Firth of Clyde. The night before the disaster some locals on the island of Arran were walking with an Army officer, Lieutenant D. McNair when, under cover of darkness, they heard an unfamiliar drone from planes overhead. They decided the aircraft were German possibly on a mine-dropping operation.

As HMS *Fortitude* (Ardrossan Harbour) was the biggest mine sweeping base in Scotland, an enemy mine was thought to be an unlikely cause of the sinking of HMS *Dasher*.

Stiftung Traditionsarchiv Unterseeboote
U-Boot-Archiv

Cuxhaven-Altenbruch, 27.09.1994

Mr. John Steele
104 Eglinton Road
Ardrossan
KA22 5NN
Scotland

Dear Mr. Steele,-

Thank you for your letter of 21st Sept.1994
and the enclosure of envelope for answer,- but no return-postage (see reverse side)

(I) To answer your request I enclose :
1. The british escort-carrier DASHER is destroyed at 27th March 1943 on the
2. River Clyde as a result of a petrol explosition and fire.
3. Ther was no German U-Boot near to that,- and no German U-Boot was involved.
4.
5.

Engine Crank Case Blowing Up

Six of *Dasher's* crew made observations at the Board of Enquiry. Lieutenant Commander Lane stated:

> *"I thought it was an engine crank case blowing up because it was similar to previous explosions of that nature."*

Lieutenant Commander E.A. Wootton was in the engine room at the time of the explosion. He told the board:

> *"It was a long explosion, similar to when the port engine crank case blew out."*

Able seaman Harold Martin said:

> *"It seemed like a boiler explosion."*

Able Seaman Tom Hunter stated:

"It seemed like a blow back from the engine."

Ordinary Seaman Michael Dury said:

> *"I thought the explosion was from the engine room."*

Able seaman George Reynolds reported he was in the engine room and saw *"a flash coming along between the port and starboard engines."*

A Plane Crashed Whilst Attempting To Land On *Dasher*

There are eye witnesses from Ardrossan, Seamill, Isle of Arran, West Kilbride and beyond who have stated they saw a plane crash-landing on *Dasher*.

However a number of *Dasher's* senior officers and crewmen were of the opinion the explosion could not have been caused by a plane crashing whilst landing.

They include Captain Boswell, the officer in command of the aircraft carrier. He and two of his officers were on the bridge at the time of the explosion. Each of them had a clear view of the ship including the whole flight deck.

Captain Boswell stated:

"I never believed a returning plane crashed on landing."

Commander Lane and Sub-lieutenant Helps were the two officers also on the bridge. Commander Lane gave evidence at the Board of Enquiry stating he saw flames and smoke coming from the lift shaft and the flight deck was buckled half the length of the hangar. As the three could not see what had caused the explosion below-deck Captain Boswell ordered Commander Lane to:

"Go below and find out what was happening."

Sub-lieutenant Helps told the Board of Enquiry that he was looking aft (to the stern of the ship) and saw an explosion coming out of the ship's side. He also stated he saw the aircraft lift soar about 200 feet in the air and smoke breaking out of the aircraft lift shaft. The officer was looking at the Flight deck and the stern of the ship. When asked if he saw any aeroplane parts he replied:

"I could not see any aeroplane parts."

Just prior to the explosion Lieutenant Commander Brian "Blinkers" Paterson, the aircraft batsman, was standing on the flight deck, at the stern of the ship. His duty was to ensure all returning aircraft landed on safely. As each aircraft approached to land the batsman stood on the flight deck with a small bat in each hand. The bats were not unlike a table tennis bat. It was of the utmost importance that each pilot obeyed the signals from the batsman.

If the aircraft was approaching too fast the signal was the batsman's right hand behind his back and the left hand extended to the front. It the approach was too low then the batsman's two hands would be outstretched high to the front and if the batsman decided the pilot should abort the landing he would circle both hands high above his head. This signal meant *"Do not land. Try again!"*

The batsman was always a high ranking Fleet Air Arm officer with a great deal of flying experience.

The batsman had just finished chatting with Sub-lieutenant Babington, who had just landed-on. If another plane was about to land-on Lieutenant Commander Paterson would have been watching, attentively, in readiness to land it safely.

The senior officer stated that he was standing on the flight deck when there was a terrible explosion followed by huge flames shooting high into the air around him. If a plane had crashed he would have seen the whole incident but he made no mention of being involved in a plane about to land-on or a plane crash.

Lieutenant D. Price was on the flight deck beside the lift shaft when he heard a deep rumbling followed by a violent explosion. Looking in disbelieve he saw the aircraft lift soaring high into the air. As it looked as if the lift would land on the flight deck he turned and ran towards the bow of the ship. Lieutenant D. Price made no mention of a plane crash-landing onto the deck or the stern of the ship.

Leading Airman Clifford Vines was also standing near to the lift shaft. All the witnesses who were standing on the flight deck beside the lift were in a prime position to see and hear an aircraft about to land-on. Not one of them reported hearing or seeing a plane about to land-on.

On hearing the explosion and feeling the ship listing, Able Seaman Reilly made his way to the flight deck. He immediately ran to the stern of the ship and jumped overboard. Had a plane crashed into the stern, it would have been impossible for Able Seaman Reilly to Jump overboard without seeing the aftermath of a plane crash.

Able Seaman William Walton was below deck at the time of the explosion. He frantically made his way to the flight deck and saw smoke and flames coming out of the aircraft lift shaft. However, he also speaks of their being no evidence of a plane crash.

Sub-lieutenant Babington DSC was an observer onboard the plane which had just landed on the aircraft carrier. After a quick chat with the batsman, the Sub-lieutenant made his way to the Flying Officer's office, to give his report. No sooner was he in the office when the explosion occurred. He later stated:

> "I believe that my aircraft was the last to land-on before the explosion."

(This witness later became a High Court Judge).

Motor launch 528 (ML 528) was known as a crash boat. When aircraft carriers were involved in flying-off exercises in the Clyde, crash boats accompanied the aircraft carrier. In the event of a plane careering off the flight deck and landing in the water, the crew of the motor launch were highly trained to render assistance to the pilot in the water.

Had an aircraft been approaching to land on *Dasher* the crew of Motor Launch 528 would have been watching it attentively in case their emergency services were required.

Personnel in the hangar stated all aircraft had landed-on and Lieutenant "Pip" Culmer, later Captain Culmer, stated:

> "Flying had ceased."

The Board of Enquiry report recorded:

> "Flying had completed prior to the explosion!"

Chapter 11

HMS *Dasher* - Roll of Honour

At the going down of the sun.
And in the morning.
We will remember them.

ODE OF REMEMBRANCE
From Laurence Binyon's poem "For the Fallen."

Ardrossan Cemetery, Ayrshire, Scotland

BUXTON, Sub-lieutenant (E), REVOR VICTOR, HMS *Dasher*, Royal Naval Volunteer Reserve. 27 March 1943. Age 25. Son of Hayward William and Eleanor Maud Buxton, of Ipswich, Suffolk. Grave Ref. Sec. D. Mid. West Div. Joint grave 125.

COSTAR, Able Seaman, ERNEST CHARLES, C/JX 190282, HMS *Dasher*, Royal Navy. 27 March 1943. Age 23. Son of Stephen Joseph Costar and Ada Florence Costar, of Burnt Oak, Middlesex. Grave Ref. Sec. D. Mid West. Div. Joint grave 124.

CRAWFORD, Greaser, JAMES, R/180150, HMS *Dasher*, Naval Auxiliary Personnel (Merchant Navy). 27 March 1943. Age 29. Grave Ref. Sec. D. Mid. West Div. Grave 120.

DAVIS, Ordinary Telegraphist, CECIL JOHN, C/JX 271890, HMS *Dasher*, Royal Navy. 27 March 1943. Age 21. Son of Frederick Thomas Davis and Charlotte Elizabeth Davis, of Leyton, Essex. Grave Ref. Sec. D. Mid. West Div. Joint grave 121.

GRIEVE, Flight Sergeant, ALEXANDER, 564019, 816 Squadron. Serving on HMS *Dasher*, Royal Air Force. 27 March 1943. Age 28. Son of James and Mary Taylor Grieve, of Edinburgh. Grave Ref. Sec. D. Mid. West Div. Grave 126.

HAUGHIE, Sub-lieutenant, WILLIAM PRATT, HMS *Dasher*, Royal Naval Volunteer Reserve. 27 March 1943. Age 25. Son of John and Margaret Pattison Haughie, of Glasgow; husband of Mary Granger Haughie, of Glasgow. Grave Ref. Sec. D. Mid. West Div. Joint grave 125.

KANE, Able Seaman, J, C/SSX 18806, HMS *Dasher*, Royal Navy. 27 March 1943. Grave Ref. Sec. D. Mid. West Div. Joint grave 123.

LAWRENCE, Greaser, ARTHUR CHARLES, R/191743, HMS *Dasher*, Naval Auxiliary Personnel (Merchant Navy). 27 March 1943. Age 23. Son of Vincent and Mary Ann Lawrence, of Burton-on-Trent; husband of Christina (Chrissie) Lawrence. Grave Ref. Sec. D. Mid. West Div. Joint grave 122.

MARTIN, Able Seaman, THOMAS JOSEPH, C/JX 168035, HMS *Dasher*, Royal Navy. 27 March 1943. Age 24. Son of Ernest Martin, and of Helen E. Martin, of Wandsworth Common, London. Grave Ref. Sec. D. Mid. West Div. Joint grave 123.

MELVILLE, Ordinary Coder, JOHN, C/JX 361352, HMS *Dasher*, Royal Navy. 27 March 1943. Age 37. Son of George and Bessie Dick Melville; husband of Euphemia Melville, of Galashiels, Selkirkshire. Grave Ref. Sec. D. Mid. West Div. Joint grave 121.

STALLARD-PENOYRE, Lieutenant, RALPH CARNAC BAKER, HMS *Dasher*, Royal Navy. 27 March 1943. Age 29. Son of Ralph Penoyre Baker Stallard-Penoyre and Dorothy Marion Baker Stallard-Penoyre; husband of Marjorie Jean Baker Stallard-Penoyre. Grave Ref. Sec. D Mid. West Div. Grave 127.

WRIGHT, Able Seaman, JACK STEPHEN, C/J 110766, HMS *Dasher*, Royal Navy. 27 March 1943. Age 34. Son of Charles Stephen and Olive Rose Wright, of Gillingham, Kent; husband of Constance Jane Wright, of Gillingham. Grave Ref. Sec. D. Mid. West Div. Joint grave 124.

Greenock Cemetery, Renfrewshire, Scotland

GILLIES, Leading Writer, WILLIAM, D/SR 16610, HMS *Dasher*, Royal Navy. 27 March 1943. Age 24. Son of William and Charlotte M. Gillies, of Edinburgh. Grave Ref. F. Recess. Queen Victoria Ground. Coll. Grave 32C.

HARPER, Able Seaman, HARRY, C/JX 260671, HMS *Dasher*, Royal Navy. 27 March 1943. Age 33. Son of Morris James Harper and Sarah Jane Harper; husband of Agnes E. Harper, of Bebington, Cheshire. Grave Ref. F. Recess. Queen Victoria Ground. Coll. grave 30A.

LIDDLE, Ordinary Seaman, RICHARD, C/JX 374403, HMS *Dasher*, Royal Navy. 27 March 1943. Age 27. Son of Richard and Margaret Ann Liddle, of Bedlington, Northumberland. Grave Ref. F. Recess. Queen Victoria Ground. Coll. grave 30A.

McFARLANE, Sub-lieutenant (E), JOHN LYLE, HMS *Dasher*, Royal Naval Volunteer Reserve. 27 March 1943. Age 21. Son of Angus and Jean McFarlane, of Greenock. Grave Ref. Sec. P.P.P. Grave 188.

NEATH, Leading Radio Mechanic, RONALD, P/MX 100601, HMS *Dasher*, Royal Navy. 27 March 1943. Age 20. Son of John Edward and Ethel Neath, of Heaton, Bradford, Yorkshire. Grave Ref. F. Recess. Queen Victoria Ground. Coll. grave 32C.

PERCIVAL, Ordinary Seaman, GEORGE HAROLD MORRIS, C/JX 359516, HMS *Dasher*, Royal Navy. 27 March 1943. Age 29. Son of George Henry and Anne Jane Percival, of Deptford, London. Grave Ref. F. Recess. Queen Victoria Ground. Coll. grave 32C.

PRICE, Lieutenant, FLEETWOOD ELWIN, HMS *Dasher*, Royal Naval Reserve. 27 March 1943. Age 42. Son of Charles Alfred and Eliza Jane Price; husband of Olive Norah Price, of Tunbridge Wells, Kent. Grave Ref. F. Recess. Queen Victoria Ground. Coll. grave 32C.

Mearns Cemetery, Eastwood, Glasgow, Scotland
WALKER, Sub-lieutenant (A), JOHN IAN RUSSELL, HMS *Dasher*, Royal Naval Volunteer Reserve. 27 March 1943. Age 21. Son of Ernest Gordon Walker and Margaret Boyd Walker, of Newton Mearns. Grave Ref. Sec. D. Joint grave 181.

Hawkhead Cemetery, Paisley, Scotland
CRAIG, Leading Seaman, ARCHIBALD, P/JX 212188, D S M, HMS *Dasher*, Royal Navy. 27 March 1943. Age 23. Son of Daniel and Jane Craig, of Paisley. Grave Ref. Sec. A. Grave 188.

Chatham Naval Memorial, Kent
ACOTT, Ordinary Seaman, FRANK ALFRED GEORGE, C/JX 376489, HMS *Dasher*, Royal Navy. 27 March 1943. Age 19. Son of Stephen George and Florence Annie Acott, of Bexley Heath, Kent. 70, 1.
ALLEN, Telegraphist, ARTHUR EDMOND, C/JX 149039, HMS *Dasher*, Royal Navy. 27 March 1943. 71,1.
ALLEN, Able Seaman, BERNARD, C/JX 301148, HMS *Dasher*, Royal Navy. 27 March 1943. Age 20. Son of John William and Elsie Allen, of East Kirkby, Nottinghamshire. 68, 2.
ANDERSON, Ordinary Seaman, ALEXANDER, C/JX 372884, HMS *Dasher*, Royal Navy. 27 March 1943. Age 18. Son of Alexander and Jane McColl Anderson, of Glasgow. 70, 1.
ATHERTON, Able Seaman, CHARLES EDWARD, C/JX 260436, HMS *Dasher*, Royal Navy. 27 March 1943. Age 39. Son of James and Edith Atherton; husband of Annie Atherton, of Harpurhey, Lancashire. 68, 2.
BAILEY, Signalman, JOHN WILLIAM, C/JX 309419, HMS *Dasher*, Royal Navy. 27 March 1943. 70, 3.
BAKER, Yeoman of Signals, VALENTINE JOHN, C/J 107758, HMS *Dasher*, Royal Navy. 27 March 1943. Age 35. Son of Thomas and Rose Baker; husband of Georgina Rose Baker, of Battersea, London. 70, 3.
BARNES, Able Seaman, WILLIAM, C/JX 238822, HMS *Dasher*, Royal Navy. 27 March 1943. Age 24. Son of Robert and Margaret J. Barnes; husband of Isabella Barnes, of Cleator Moor, Cumberland. 68, 2.
BARTLEY, Telegraphist, ERNEST STANLEY, C/JX 341560, HMS *Dasher*, Royal Navy. 27 March 1943. Age 19. Son of Archibald William Alfred and Lily Alexandria Elsie Bartley, of Feltham, Middlesex. 71, 1.
BARWISE, Able Seaman, JOHN HENRY, C/JX 259141, HMS *Dasher*, Royal

Navy. 27 March 1943. 68, 2.

BAYLIS, Signalman, MICHAEL VICTOR, C/JX 344709, HMS *Dasher*, Royal Navy. 27 March 1943. Age 20. Son of Francis Joseph and Ellen Baylis, of Blackpool, Lancashire. 70, 3.

BENNETT, Ordinary Seaman, JACK DIGHTON, C/JX 332202, HMS *Dasher*, Royal Navy. 27 March 1943. Age 27. Son of Ernest Dighton Bennett and Kate Ethel Bennett, of Woolwich, London. 70, 2.

BEVIN, Ordinary Coder, GORDON ARTHUR, C/JX 344942, HMS *Dasher*, Royal Navy. 27 March 1943. 71, 2.

BINGHAM, Able Seaman, GEORGE CORBETT, C/JX 319257, HMS *Dasher*, Royal Navy. 27 March 1943. Age 20. Son of George Corbett Bingham and Ada Bingham, of Sheffield. 68, 2.

BLAND, Ordinary Seaman, IVAN HENRY, C/JX 355221, HMS *Dasher*, Royal Navy. 27 March 1943. Age 19. Son of John Julian and Winifred Maud Bland, of Colchester. 70, 2.

BOND, Signalman, DOUGLAS ARTHUR, C/JX 344711, HMS *Dasher*, Royal Navy. 27 March 1943. Age 35. Son of Charles T. and Nellie Bond; husband of Beryl Elaine Bond, of Walton-on-Thames, Surrey. 70, 3.

BOTTON, Leading Stores Assistant, NORMAN DENIS, C/MX 69527, HMS *Dasher*, Royal Navy. 27 March 1943. Age 22. Son of William George and Violet May Botton, of Golders Green, Middlesex. 72, 3.

BOTTRILL, Able Seaman, CUTHBERT LESLIE, C/JX 303407, HMS *Dasher*, Royal Navy. 27 March 1943. 68, 2.

BOYLE, Able Seaman, FRANCIS, C/JX 312325, HMS *Dasher*, Royal Navy. 27 March 1943. Age 21. Son of James and Jean Boyle, of Paisley, Renfrewshire. 68, 2.

BRAMWELL, Ordinary Seaman, REGINALD RUSSELL, C/JX 351198, HMS *Dasher*, Royal Navy. 27 March 1943. Son of Thomas Lister Bramwell and May G. A. Bramwell, of St. Albans, Hertfordshire. 70, 2.

BRETHERTON, Able Seaman, THOMAS FRANK, C/SSX 36069, HMS *Dasher*, Royal Navy. 27 March 1943. Age 19. Son of Thomas and Violet Bretherton, of Acocks Green, Birmingham. 68, 2,.

BROWN, Ordinary Seaman, ALEXANDER MARTIN, C/JX 376796, HMS *Dasher*, Royal Navy. 27 March 1943. Age 26. Son of William and Isabella McGlone Brown; husband of Mary Steel Brown, of Bellshill, Lanarkshire. 70, 2.

BROWN, Leading Seaman, CLIFFORD THOMAS BOOKER, C/JX 151184, HMS *Dasher*, Royal Navy. 27 March 1943. 68, 1.

BRYANT, Leading Telegraphist, DANIEL WYATT KITCHENER, C/WRX 139, HMS *Dasher*, Royal Naval Volunteer (Wireless) Reserve. 27 March 1943. Age 29. Son of James Edwin and Florence Bryant; husband of Verna Elsie Bryant, of Edmonton, Middlesex. 74, 1.

BURLS, Able Seaman, FRANK CHARLES, C/JX 190291, HMS *Dasher*, Royal Navy. 27 March 1943. Age 23. Son of Alfred Charles and Mabel Amelia Burls, of Harrow, Middlesex. 68, 2.

BURNESS, Able Seaman, ALBERT EDWARD, C/SSX 34144, HMS *Dasher*, Royal Navy. 27 March 1943. Age 19. Son of Albert Edward and Dora Burness, of Birmingham. 68, 2.

BURSEY, Able Seaman, GRAHAM, C/JX 246665, HMS *Dasher*, Royal Navy. 27 March 1943. Age 21. Son of William and Bertha Bursey, of Old Perlican, Newfoundland. 73, 2.

BUSH, Leading Seaman, JOHN ROGER, C/JX 145580, HMS *Dasher*, Royal Navy. 27 March 1943. 68, 1.

BUTLER, Able Seaman, WILLIAM ALBERT, C/JX 277273, HMS *Dasher*, Royal Navy. 27 March 1943. Age 30. Son of Howard and Lily Butler, of Flat Islands, Newfoundland. 73, 2.

BUTTERFIELD, Able Seaman, JOSEPH NORMAN, C/JX 279269, HMS *Dasher*, Royal Navy. 27 March 1943. Age 38. Son of Frederick and Edith Butterfield; husband of Mary Butterfield, of Keighley, Yorkshire. 68, 2.

BYRNE, Able Seaman, DAVID ESAU, C/JX 225994, HMS *Dasher*, Royal Navy. 27 March 1943. Age 26. Son of David Patrick and Charlotte Byrne, of Hinckley, Leicestershire. 68, 3.

CALDOW, Ordinary Seaman, ROBERT, C/JX 352223, HMS *Dasher*, Royal Navy. 27 March 1943. Age 26. Son of William and Jane Muir Caldow, of Kirkcudbright. 70, 2.

CAMPBELL, Able Seaman, JOHN CAMERON, C/JX 262397, HMS *Dasher*, Royal Navy. 27 March 1943. 68, 3.

CANDLISH, Able Seaman, WILLIAM, C/JX 237543, HMS *Dasher*, Royal Navy. 27 March 1943. Age 33. Son of Henry and Jane Candlish; husband of Agnes S. Y. Candlish, of Crosshouse, Ayrshire. 68, 3.

CAPSTICK, Chief Petty Officer Telegraphist, JOSEPH AUBREY, C/J 46054, HMS *Dasher*, Royal Navy. 27 March 1943. Age 43. Son of Edward and Elizabeth Capstick; husband of Louisa Clara Frances Capstick, of Hitchin, Hertfordshire. 71, 1.

CARRATT, Able Seaman, WALTER, C/JX 199849, HMS *Dasher*, Royal Navy. 27 March 1943. Age 29. Son of Anthony and Ann Carratt; husband of Joyce Carratt, of Grimsby, Lincolnshire. 68, 3.

CARTER, Yeoman of Signals, HAROLD OSCAR, C/SSX 17317, HMS *Dasher*, Royal Navy. 27 March 1943. 70, 3.

CASSON, Able Seaman, WILLIAM EDWARD APPLEBY, C/JX 197543, HMS *Dasher*, Royal Navy. 27 March 1943. Age 23. Son of Edward and Margaret Isabel Casson, of Newcastle-on-Tyne, Northumberland. 68, 3.

CLARK, Leading Seaman, WILLIAM ERNEST, C/JX 160256, HMS *Dasher*,

Royal Navy. 27 March 1943. Age 20. Son of Henry H. and Agnes J. Clark, of Luton, Bedfordshire. 68, 1.

CLAUSON, Able Seaman, WILLIAM DAVID, C/SSX 23479, HMS *Dasher*, Royal Navy. 27 March 1943. Age 23. Son of James Philip and Ellen Elizabeth Clauson, of Tonbridge, Kent. 68, 3.

CLAYTON, Leading Seaman, JAMES, C/JX 142952, HMS *Dasher*, Royal Navy. 27 March 1943. Age 24. Son of Charles and Nora Clayton; husband of Greta Clayton, of Crawcrook, Co. Durham. 68, 1.

COCKERELL, Able Seaman, LESLIE HENRY, C/JX 248813, HMS *Dasher*, Royal Navy. 27 March 1943. Age 27. Son of Henry and Florence Cockerell; husband of Sarah Alice Cockerell, of Eltham, London. 68, 3.

CORRALL, Able Seaman, NOEL LUKE, C/JX 319290, HMS *Dasher*, Royal Navy. 27 March 1943. Age 37. Son of Henry and Annie Corrall, of Leyton, London; husband of Winifred Corrall. 68, 3.

COULSON, Able Seaman, GEORGE VINCENT THOMAS, C/JX 148891, HMS *Dasher*, Royal Navy. 27 March 1943. Age 22. Son of George Victor and Helen Gertrude Coulson, of East Barnet, Hertfordshire. 68, 3.

COWEN, Canteen Manager, DAVID, C/NX 2245, HMS *Dasher*, Royal Naval Canteen Service. 27 March 1943. 74, 1.

CROOKS, Ordinary Seaman, IVOR EDGAR, C/JX 379344, HMS *Dasher,* Royal Navy. 27 March 1943. Age 17. Son of George and Florence Grace Crooks, of Norwich. 70, 2.

CUNNINGHAM, Able Seaman, ALBERT, C/LD/X 2494, *HMS Dasher*, Royal Naval Volunteer Reserve. 27 March 1943. 73, 3.

CUTHBERT, Schoolmaster Warrant Officer, JOHN NICHOLAS, HMS *Dasher*, Royal Navy. 27 March 1943. Age 30. Son of Harcourt Cuthbert and Jemima Moir Cuthbert, of Haddington, East Lothian.M.A. 67. 3.

DAVIES, Lieutenant, KENNETH WILLIAM, HMS *Dasher*, Royal Naval Reserve. 27 March 1943. Age 29. Son of Charles George and Edith Rosaline Davies. 73, 2.

DAVIS, Leading Seaman, STANLEY, C/JX 225276, HMS *Dasher*, Royal Navy. 27 March 1943. Age 38. Son of Ester Davis; husband of Eva Davis, of Shepherd's Bush, London. 68, 1.

DAVISON, Able Seaman, EDWARD HEWITSON, C/JX 168959, HMS *Dasher*, Royal Navy. 27 March 1943. Age 22. Son of Thomas Alfred and Hannah Bell Davison, of Boldon Colliery, Co. Durham. 68, 3.

DAY, Able Seaman, FREDERICK GEORGE WILLIAM, C/LD/X 5093, HMS *Dasher*, Royal Naval Volunteer Reserve. 27 March 1943. Age 23. Son of Frederick James and Ellen Elizabeth Day, of Catford, London. 73, 3.

DIGGINS, Able Seaman, JOHN HENRY, C/JX 193568, HMS *Dasher*, Royal Navy. 27 March 1943. Son of George and Florence Diggins; husband of Sarah Diggins, of Luton, Bedfordshire. 68, 3.

DONOGHUE, Able Seaman, SYDNEY THOMAS, C/JX 224628, HMS *Dasher*, Royal Navy. 27 March 1943. Age 21. Son of Thomas and Sarah Ann Donoghue, of Stirchley, Birmingham. 68, 3.

DOWD, Petty Officer, THOMAS ALBERT, C/JX 147634, HMS *Dasher*, Royal Navy. 27 March 1943. 67, 3.

EDWARDS, Able Seaman, AUGUSTUS, C/JX 201321, HMS *Dasher*, Royal Navy. 27 March 1943. Age 26. Son of Augustus and Minnie Edwards; husband of Alice Edith Edwards, of Eltham Park, London. 68, 3.

FALLA, Telegraphist, LESLIE LE-NOURY, C/JX 271799, HMS *Dasher*, Royal Navy. 27 March 1943. Age 33. Son of Francis Arthur William and Ethel Agnes Falla; husband of Ethel Falla, of North Reddish, Cheshire. 71, 1.

FERNEYHOUGH, Able Seaman, WILFRED, C/JX 189663, HMS *Dasher*, Royal Navy. 27 March 1943. Age 22. Son of John William and Clara Alice Ferneyhough, of Fenton, Staffordshire. 68, 3.

FISHER, Electrical Artificer 3rd Class, ALBERT SIDNEY, C/SR 8276, HMS *Dasher*, Royal Navy. 27 March 1943. Age 24. Son of Albert and Frances Emma Fisher, of Brixton, London. 72, 3.

FITZGERALD, Able Seaman, ANTHONY, C/JX 220913, HMS *Dasher*, Royal Navy. 27 March 1943. Age 26. Son of Michael and Margaret Fitzgerald, of Bonavista, Newfoundland. 73, 2.

FRENCH, Stoker 1st Class, WILLIAM ERNEST PETER, C/KX 105295, HMS *Dasher*, Royal Navy. 27 March 1943. Age 22. Son of James and Grace E. F. French, of Wolverhampton, Staffordshire. 72, 1.

FURRELL, Petty Officer Supply, PATRICK ROY, C/MX 52485, HMS *Dasher*, Royal Navy. 27 March 1943. 72, 3.

GIBSON, Able Seaman, ROY, C/JX 316841, HMS *Dasher*, Royal Navy. 27 March 1943. Age 20. Son of Fred and Rosina Gibson, of Sowerby Bridge, Yorkshire. 69, 1.

GILBERT, Able Seaman, JAMES WILLIAM, C/JX 317966, HMS *Dasher*, Royal Navy. 27 March 1943. Age 20. Son of James and Clara E. Gilbert, of Leicester. 69, 1.

GILROY, Able Seaman, JAMES, C/JX 315140, HMS *Dasher*, Royal Navy. 27 March 1943. Age 20. Son of John and Emma Eliza Gilroy, of Renfrew, Scotland. 69, 1.

GOSWELL, Master at Arms, RICHARD FRANCIS, C/M 40032, HMS *Dasher*, Royal Navy. 27 March 1943. Age 34. Son of Frank and Elizabeth Goswell; husband of Ethel Louise Goswell, of Gillingham, Kent. 73, 1.

GUNNER, Able Seaman, FREDERICK JOSEPH, C/JX 195146, HMS *Dasher*, Royal Navy. 27 March 1943. Age 23. Son of Herbert James and Annie Gunner, of Vauxhall, London. 69, 1.

HAMBROOK, Chief Yeoman of Signals, ROBERT FITTALL, C/J 110579, HMS *Dasher*, Royal Navy. 27 March 1943. 70, 3.

HANDY, Petty Officer, ERNEST HENRY, C/JX 134868, HMS *Dasher*, Royal Navy. 27 March 1943. Age 27. Son of Edmund Henry and Beatrice Annie Handy. 67, 3.

HARVEY, Able Seaman, CLAYTON WILBENT ANDERSON, C/JX 316615, HMS *Dasher*, Royal Navy. 27 March 1943. 73, 2.

HARVEY, Able Seaman, WILLIAM JOHN, C/JX 279344, HMS *Dasher*, Royal Navy. 27 March 1943. Age 21. Son of John and Ellen Maria Harvey, of Bentley, Doncaster, Yorkshire. 69, 1.

HILL, Able Seaman, JAMES OLIVER TYNDAL, C/JX 316502, HMS *Dasher*, Royal Navy. 27 March 1943. Age 20. Son of James Simpson Hill and Williamina Hill. 69, 1.

HOBBS, Able Seaman, JOSEPH FREDERICK, C/JX 278289, HMS *Dasher*, Royal Navy. 27 March 1943. Age 34. Son of Joseph and Laura Hobbs; husband of Daisy Muriel Hobbs, of Chalfont St. Peter, Buckinghamshire. 69, 1.

HODKINSON, Telegraphist, PERCY CHARLES, C/JX 178427, HMS *Dasher*, Royal Navy. 27 March 1943. Age 24. Son of James and Rose Mary Hodkinson; husband of Annie Winifred Hodkinson, of Preston, Lancashire. 71, 1.

HORNE, Sick Berth Attendant, JOHN ROBERT, C/MX 85545, HMS *Dasher*, Royal Navy. 27 March 1943. 72, 3.

HUGHES, Lieutenant, JOHN, HMS *Dasher*, Royal Naval Volunteer Reserve. 27 March 1943. Age 36. Son of John and Alice Hughes. 73, 3.

HUMPHREYS, Leading Seaman, ALBERT, C/JX 127052, HMS *Dasher*, Royal Navy. 27 March 1943. Age 41. Husband of katherine M. Humphreys. 68, 1.

INGLESFIELD, Able Seaman, JOSEPH, C/JX 333162, HMS *Dasher*, Royal Navy. 27 March 1943. Age 32. Son of John and Mary Inglesfield, of Maryport, Cumberland. 69, 1.

JACKSON, Able Seaman, LEONARD, C/JX 315182, HMS *Dasher*, Royal Navy. 27 March 1943. Son of William Paul and Ethel Maud Jackson, of Hull, Yorkshire. 69, 1.

JENNINGS, Able Seaman, NELSON PATRICK, C/LD/X 4789, HMS *Dasher*, Royal Naval Volunteer Reserve. 27 March 1943. Age 23. Son of Ernest Patrick and Mary Jennings; husband of Winifred Lily Jennings, of Southall, Middlesex. 73, 3.

JOHNSON, Signalman, HAROLD WALTER, C/JX 298702, HMS *Dasher*, Royal Navy. 27 March 1943. Age 21. Son of Harold Douglas and Frances Johnson, of Fulham, London. 70, 3.

JOHNSTON, Sub-lieutenant, OWEN TEMPLE, HMS *Dasher*, Royal Navy. 27 March 1943. Age 19. Son of John Lawrence Johnston and Hilda Florence Johnston, of Felixstowe, Suffolk. 67, 3.

KEMP, Petty Officer, OSCAR COMPTON, C/JX 130904, HMS *Dasher*, Royal

Navy. 27 March 1943. Age 31. Son of Oscar Compton Kemp and Florence Emily Kemp; husband of Lucy Annie Kemp, of Bleadon, Somerset. 68, 1.

KENAH, Able Seaman, JOHN ERNEST, C/JX 279071, HMS *Dasher*, Royal Navy. 27 March 1943. Age 32. Son of John Ernest and Gladys Kenah; husband of Evelyn Louise Kenah, of Liverpool. 69, 1.

KENNEDY, Able Seaman, WILLIAM, C/JX 182786, HMS *Dasher*, Royal Navy. 27 March 1943. Age 23. Son of Mr. and Mrs. Thomas Kennedy, of Possilpark, Glasgow. 69, 1.

KNOWLES, Able Seaman, FRANK, C/JX 319685, HMS *Dasher*, Royal Navy. 27 March 1943. Age 20. Son of Reginald and Elizabeth Knowles, of Langley, Derbyshire. 69, 1.

KYLE, Able Seaman, CHARLES MCCLURE, C/JX 289245, HMS *Dasher*, Royal Navy. 27 March 1943. Age 37. Son of George and Sarah Ann McClure Kyle; husband of Annie Martin McAulay Kyle, of Dumfries, Scotland. 69, 2.

LANGLEY, Sub-lieutenant, JOHN ROBERT, HMS *Dasher*, Royal Naval Volunteer Reserve. 27 March 1943. Age 24. Son of John Basil Robert Langley, R.A.F., and Lorna Leslie Langley; husband of Susan Katharine Langley, of Amesbury, Wiltshire. B.A. (Cantab.). 73, 3.

LIGHTWING, Ordinary Seaman, JAMES ALAN, C/JX 374404, HMS *Dasher*, Royal Navy. 27 March 1943. Age 21. Son of John Robert and Ada May Lightwing, of Skelton-in-Cleveland, Yorkshire. 70, 2.

LINFIELD, Able Seaman, WILLIAM STEPHEN LLOYD, C/JX 247986, HMS *Dasher*, Royal Navy. 27 March 1943. Age 22. Son of Edward John and Hannah Pearce Linfield, of Twillingate, Newfoundland. 73, 2.

LUFFINGHAM, Able Seaman, ARTHUR, C/SSX 15239, HMS *Dasher*, Royal Navy. 27 March 1943. 69, 2.

MACAULAY, Ordinary Seaman, HUGH, C/JX 316449, HMS *Dasher*, Royal Navy. 27 March 1943. 70, 2.

MAHON, Able Seaman, JAMES THOMAS, C/JX 173315, HMS *Dasher*, Royal Navy. 27 March 1943. 73, 2.

MARSON, Able Seaman, WILLIAM, C/JX 316912, HMS *Dasher*, Royal Navy. 27 March 1943. Age 20. Son of George William and Doris Marson, of Hull, Yorkshire. 69, 2.

MARSTON, Able Seaman, HENRY CHARLES, C/JX 300111, HMS *Dasher*, Royal Navy. 27 March 1943. Age 23. Son of Charles and Sarah Marston; husband of Hilda Marston, of Brixton, London. 69, 2.

MASON, Telegraphist, HENRY SETCHFIELD, C/JX 250509, HMS *Dasher*, Royal Navy. 27 March 1943. Age 33. Son of Thomas Charles and Clara Lavina Mason, of Hull, Yorkshire. 71, 1.

MASON, Supply Assistant, WILLIAM CHARLES, C/MX 84090, HMS *Dasher*, Royal Navy. 27 March 1943. Age 39. Son of William Charles and Rosina Mason. 72, 3.

McCARTHY, Able Seaman, DANIEL, C/JX 201329, HMS *Dasher*, Royal Navy. 27 March 1943. Age 23. Son of Michael and Ellen McCarthy; husband of Rosina McCarthy, of Stepney, London. 69, 2.

McCARTHY, Able Seaman, VICTOR DINNEY, C/JX 195151, HMS *Dasher*, Royal Navy. 27 March 1943. Age 23. Son of Thomas and Ruth McCarthy. 69, 2.

McLEAN, Able Seaman, WALTER, C/JX 352453, HMS *Dasher*, Royal Navy. 27 March 1943. Age 20. Son of George Edward and Ethel Maud McLean, of Crookes, Sheffield. 69, 2.

MILSTED, Ordinary Seaman, WILLIAM HENRY, C/JX 331451, HMS *Dasher*, Royal Navy. 27 March 1943. Age 21. Son of Albert and Emily Bessie Milsted, of Shepherd's Well, Kent. 70, 2.

MITCHELL, Leading Supply Assistant, DAVID JOHN, C/MX 94654, HMS *Dasher*, Royal Navy. 27 March 1943. Age 20. Son of David Cross Mitchell and Agnes O'Neil Mitchell, of Glasgow. 72, 3.

MOLLETT, Ordinary Seaman, HENRY GEORGE, C/JX 353724, HMS *Dasher*, Royal Navy. 27 March 1943. Age 19. Son of Henry Alfred and Emmily Maud Mollett, of Walworth, London. 70, 2.

MOODY, Leading Seaman, GEORGE ERIC, C/JX 133401, HMS *Dasher*, Royal Navy. 27 March 1943. Age 30. Son of Mr. and Mrs. Charles John Moody; husband of Vera Elizabeth Sarah Moody, of Milton, Portsmouth. 68, 1.

MORGAN, Able Seaman, FREDERICK ARTHUR, C/JX 137744, HMS *Dasher*, Royal Navy. 27 March 1943. Age 26. Son of Isabella Morgan, of Hetton-le-Hole, Co. Durham. 69, 2.

MOSEY, Able Seaman, WALTER, C/SSX 25471, HMS *Dasher*, Royal Navy. 27 March 1943. Age 21. Son of Ralph and Alice Mosey; husband of Esther Mosey, of Greenock, Renfrewshire. 69, 2.

MURTON, Petty Officer Sick Berth, NORMAN, C/MX 49288, HMS *Dasher*, Royal Navy. 27 March 1943. 72, 3.

NEIGHBOUR, Able Seaman, THOMAS HENRY, C/JX 299146, HMS *Dasher*, Royal Navy. 27 March 1943. Age 21. Son of Thomas Henry and Gatherine Emma Neighbour, of Islington, London. 69, 2.

NICHOLSON, Able Seaman, ALBERT JOHN, C/JX 240864, HMS *Dasher*, Royal Navy. 27 March 1943. Age 27. Son of Albert and Emily Maud Nicholson; husband of Mary Rose Elizabeth Nicholson, of Romford, Essex. 69, 2.

NORTON, Leading Signalman, JOHN BOSWORTH, C/JX 148936, HMS *Dasher*, Royal Navy. 27 March 1943. Foster son of Mrs. H. Harvey, of Shotesham, Norfolk. 70, 3.

OAKMAN, Ordinary Seaman, STANLEY VICTOR, C/JX 315571, HMS *Dasher*, Royal Navy. 27 March 1943. Age 21. Son of Albert Victor and Ethel Edith Oakman, of Hockley, Essex. 70, 2.

O'BRIEN, Ordinary Seaman, ARNOLD, C/JX 353051, HMS *Dasher*, Royal

Navy. 27 March 1943. Age 19. Son of William and Elsie O'Brien, of New Whittington, Derbyshire. 70, 2.

O'CONNOR, Able Seaman, FRANCIS JAMES, C/JX 279101, HMS *Dasher*, Royal Navy. 27 March 1943. Age 21. Son of Andrew Patrick and Ida O'Connor, of Bromley, Kent. 69, 2.

PETTY, Able Seaman, CHARLES JAMES, C/JX 278463, HMS *Dasher*, Royal Navy. 27 March 1943. 69, 3.

PHILLIBROWN, Ordinary Seaman, HARRY CHARLES, C/JX 374889, HMS *Dasher*, Royal Navy. 27 March 1943. Age 18. Son of George William and Alice Maude Phillibrown, of Shirburn, Oxfordshire. 70, 2.

PIGDEN, Ordinary Seaman, CHARLES FREDERICK, C/JX 374891, HMS *Dasher*, Royal Navy. 27 March 1943. 70, 2.

PILE, Petty Officer, STEPHEN GEORGE, C/J 101696, HMS *Dasher*, Royal Navy. 27 March 1943. Age 38. Son of Walter Thomas and Sarah Pile; husband of Louisa Pile, of Chatham. 68, 1.

PLANT, Able Seaman, PERCY HOWARD, C/JX 283544, HMS *Dasher*, Royal Navy. 27 March 1943. Age 20. Son of Percy Howard and Clarice Mabel Plant, of Hanley, Staffordshire. 69, 3.

PLAYFORD, Able Seaman, CYRIL EDWARD, C/JX 160947, HMS *Dasher*, Royal Navy. 27 March 1943. 69, 3.

PRICE, Stoker 1st Class, PERCY DOUGLAS, C/KX 90532, HMS *Dasher*, Royal Navy. 27 March 1943. Age 23. Son off Florence Hilda A. Price, of Westgate-on-Sea, Kent. 72, 2.

REED, Ordinary Seaman, ROBERT, C/JX 352493, HMS *Dasher*, Royal Navy. 27 March 1943. 70, 2.

RICHARDSON, Able Seaman, HARRY, C/JX 171624, HMS *Dasher*, Royal Navy. 27 March 1943. Age 23. Son of Willis Richardson and Sarah Richardson, of Barkingside, Essex. 69. 3.

RIX, Able Seaman, RICHARD DAVID, C/JX 353084, HMS *Dasher*, Royal Navy. 27 March 1943. Age 19. Son of Richard Fredrick and May Rachel Rix, of Norwich, Norfolk. 69, 3.

ROBERTS, Leading Telegraphist, PETER, C/JX 143601, HMS *Dasher*, Royal Navy. 27 March 1943. 71, 1.

ROBSON, Able Seaman, JAMES, C/JX 314025, HMS *Dasher*, Royal Navy. 27 March 1943. Age 21. Son of John Thomas and Sarah Ann Robson, of Bradford, Manchester. 69, 3.

ROCKLIFF, Ordinary Seaman, JOHN, C/JX 354227, HMS *Dasher*, Royal Navy. 27 March 1943. Age 20. Son of Thomas and Mary Rockliff, of Barnsley, Yorkshire. 70, 2.

ROLPH, Stoker 1st Class, ALFRED JAMES, C/KX 104771, HMS *Dasher*, Royal Navy. 27 March 1943. Age 23. Son of William Thomas and Lilian Dixon Rolph, of Barking, Essex. 72, 2.

SCANLON, Able Seaman, THOMAS, C/JX 237014, HMS *Dasher*, Royal Navy. 27 March 1943. Age 27. Son of Edmond and Catherine Scanlon; husband of Mary Scanlon, of Woking, Surrey. 69, 3.

SCOTT, Able Seaman, WILLIAM HUGH, C/JX 172434, HMS *Dasher*, Royal Navy. 27 March 1943. Age 24. Son of Ronald and Margaret Scott, of Bampton, Westmorland. 69, 3.

SEWARD, Able Seaman, LESLIE ALFRED, C/JX 161731, HMS *Dasher*, Royal Navy. 27 March 1943. Age 20. Son of Alfred George and Elsie Alice Seward, of Upper Norwood, Surrey. 69, 3.

SHARPE, Able Seaman, WILLIAM CHARLES, C/JX 199851, HMS *Dasher*, Royal Navy. 27 March 1943. Age 29. Son of William Charles and Ada Sharpe; husband of Nellie Sharpe, of Grimsby, Lincolnshire. 69, 3.

SHEARER, Canteen Assistant, JAMES DOUGLAS, C/NX 2040, HMS *Dasher*, Royal Naval Canteen Service. 27 March 1943. Son of John William and Florence Helena Shearer, of Litherland, Liverpool. 74, 1.

SHELDON, Sick Berth Attendant, HORACE VICTOR, C/MX 94630, HMS *Dasher*, Royal Navy. 27 March 1943. Age 26. Son of Walter and Martha Louise Sheldon; husband of Janet Emily Sheldon, of Birmingham. 72, 3.

SHEPPARD, Ordinary Seaman, JOHN AMBROSE, C/JX 374470, HMS *Dasher*, Royal Navy. 27 March 1943. Age 27. Son of Herbert John and Violet Sheppard; husband of Barbara Sheppard, of Warblington, Hampshire. 70, 2.

SKINNER, Leading Telegraphist, LESLIE RAYMOND, C/SSX 16331, HMS *Dasher*, Royal Navy. 27 March 1943. Age 26. Son of Raymond and Alice Skinner; husband of Florence Ellen Skinner, of Eastney, Hampshire. 71, 1.

SMITH, Ordnance Artificer 4th Class, LESLIE DOUGLAS, C/MX 76076, HMS *Dasher*, Royal Navy. 27 March 1943. Age 22. Son of Joseph and Clare Frances Smith, of Leicester. 72, 3.

SPEIRS, Signalman, WILLIAM ALFRED, C/JX 309405, HMS *Dasher*, Royal Navy. 27 March 1943. Age 21. Son of William Alfred and May Speirs, of Dagenham, Essex. 70, 3.

SPENCE, Able Seaman, ALEXANDER CHARLES MACKIE, C/SSX 21966, HMS *Dasher*, Royal Navy. 27 March 1943. Age 22. 69, 3.

SPRATT, Able Seaman, RODNEY NEWTON, C/JX 199797, HMS *Dasher*, Royal Navy. 27 March 1943. 69. 3.

STAMP, Petty Officer, JOHN ALEXANDER, C/TD/X 909, HMS *Dasher*, Royal Naval Volunteer Reserve. 27 March 1943. Age 31. Son of John and Annie B. Stamp, of South Shields, Co. Durham. 73, 3.

STOREY, Surgeon Lieutenant, THOMAS POLLARD, D S C, HMS *Dasher*, Royal Naval Volunteer Reserve. 27 March 1943. Age 30. Son of Henry Morrison Pollard Storey and Mary Jane Storey, of Chadwell Heath, Essex. M.R.G.S., L.R.C.P. 73, 3.

SULLIVAN, Electrical Artificer 2nd Class, THOMAS, C/MX 46283, HMS

Dasher, Royal Navy. 27 March 1943. Age 41. Son of Phoebe Sullivan, of Bentley, Staffordshire. 72, 3.

TAYLOR, Ordinary Seaman, CYRIL GORDON, C/JX 327124, HMS *Dasher*, Royal Navy. 27 March 1943. Age 19. Son of Mr. and Mrs. A. Taylor, of Gravesend, Kent. 70, 3.

TERREY, Petty Officer Telegraphist, CYRIL JAMES, C/JX 134049, HMS *Dasher*, Royal Navy. 27 March 1943. 71, 1.

THISTLE, Able Seaman, CYRIL ROY, C/JX 315756, HMS *Dasher,* Royal Navy. 27 March 1943. Age 20. Son of Mr. and Mrs. W. J. Thistle, of St. John'S, Newfoundland. 73, 2.

THOMPSON, Able Seaman, JAMES, C/SSX 18878, HMS *Dasher*, Royal Navy. 27 March 1943. Age 24. Son of James and Annie Thompson; husband of Ruby Jessie Thompson, of New Brumby, Lincolnshire. 70. 1.

THORNHILL, Able Seaman, RAYMOND, C/JX 318466, HMS *Dasher*, Royal Navy. 27 March 1943. Age 19. Son of Ernest Wallace Thornhill and Kate Thornhill, of Leicester. 70, 1.

TICKNER, Petty Officer Regulating, WILLIAM THOMAS, C/J 109099, HMS *Dasher*, Royal Navy. 27 March 1943. Age 35. Son of Thomas James and Julia Tickner; husband of Sylvia Tickner, of Luton, Bedfordshire. Formerly Sgt. in Luton Borough Police Force. 73, 1.

TIMMIS, Able Seaman, ROBERT, C/SSX 24437, HMS *Dasher*, Royal Navy. 27 March 1943. Age 26. Son of John and Emily Timmis, of Hollinwood, Lancashire. 70, 1.

TOMBLIN, Coder, WILLIAM JAMES RICHARD, C/JX 293104, HMS *Dasher*, Royal Navy. 27 March 1943. Age 20. Son of William Samuel Robert and Elizabeth Rae Tomblin, of Frome, Somerset. 71, 2.

TURNER, Leading Seaman, FRANK OWEN, C/SSX 20187, HMS *Dasher*, Royal Navy. 27 March 1943. Age 22. Son of William and Lucy Turner; husband of Joyce Edith Turner, of Hull, Yorkshire. 68, 2.

WALKER, Able Seaman, JOHN CAMPBELL, C/JX 169472, HMS *Dasher*, Royal Navy. 27 March 1943. 70, 1.

WEBB, Leading Canteen Assistant, VICTOR LESLIE, C/NX 347, HMS *Dasher.*, Royal Naval Canteen Service. 27 March 1943. Age 22. Son of Albert and Annie Webb, of Cheltenham, Gloucestershire. 74, 1.

WHITTINGTON, Able Seaman, RICHARD ALBERT, C/JX 173033, HMS *Dasher*, Royal Navy. 27 March 1943. Age 23. Son of Thomas Richard and Beatrice Whittington, of Catford, London. 70, 1.

WOOLLEY, Chief Petty Officer, HENRY GEORGE, C/J 105610, HMS *Dasher*, Royal Navy. 27 March 1943. Age 38. Son of Emily Woolley, of New Cross, London. 67, 3.

WRATHALL, Lieutenant, JOHN SANDFORD, HMS *Dasher*, Royal Naval Volunteer Reserve. 27 March 1943. Age 27. Son of William Foster Wrathall and Marion Wrathall; husband of Margaret Wrathall, of Long Preston, Yorkshire. 73, 3.

YATES, Able Seaman, THOMAS, C/JX 168689, HMS *Dasher*, Royal Navy. 27 March 1943. Age 24. Son of Thomas and Mary Ann Yates, of Adswood, Cheshire; husband of Elsie Yates. 70, 1.

YOUNG, Able Seaman, CECIL AUGUSTUS, C/JX 316666, HMS *Dasher*, Royal Navy. 27 March 1943. 70, 1.

Lee-on-Solent Memorial, Hampshire

ABRAHAMS, Air Mechanic 2nd Class, CYRIL JAMES, FAA/FX. 83180, HMS. *Dasher,* Royal Navy. 27 March 1943. Bay 4, Panel 4.

ANDERSON, Air Mechanic 2nd Class, GEORGE SUTHERLAND, FAA/FX. 81026, HMS *Dasher*, Royal Navy. 27 March 1943. Age 22. Son of George Sutherland Anderson and Grace Ferguson Anderson, of Philpstoun, West Lothian. Bay 4, Panel 5.

ARSLETT, Air Mechanic 1st Class, FREDERICK JAMES, FAA/SFX. 2476, HMS *Dasher*, Royal Navy. 27 March 1943. Age 27. Son of Harry J. and Emily Arslett; husband of Margaret Elizabeth Arslett of Caversham, Reading. Bay 4, Panel 5.

BANISTER, Sub-lieutenant (A), MAURICE JAMES, HMS *Dasher*, Royal Naval Volunteer Reserve. 27 March 1943. Age 21. Son of the Revd. Marmaduke Haddon Banister and Beatrix Gwendoline Harriet Banister, of Greystoke Rectory, Cumberland. Bay 4, Panel 6.

BATCHELOR, Air Mechanic 1st Class, JACK HESKETH, FAA/SFX. 2517, HMS *Dasher*, Royal Navy. 27 March 1943. Age 21. Son of Walter William and Kate Gertrude Batchelor. Bay 4, Panel 5.

BLOOMFIELD, Leading Radio Mechanic, LEONARD WILLIAM, FAA/FX. 100747, HMS *Dasher*, Royal Navy. 27 March 1943. Age 20. Son of William and Gertrude Daisy Bloomfield, of Pinner, Middlesex. Bay 4, Panel 5.

BOAG-JONES, Air Mechanic 1st Class, DENNIS PAYTON, FAA/FX. 82212, HMS *Dasher*, Royal Navy. 27 March 1943. Age 20. Son of John Henry and Gwladys Helen Boag-Jones, of Langstone, Monmouthshire. Bay 4, Panel 5.

BOWMAN, Petty Officer (Radio Mechanic) HORACE EDWARD, FAA/FX. 82231, HMS *Dasher,* Royal Navy. 27 March 1943. Age 28. Son of Edward and Elizabeth Bowman; husband of Lily E. Bowman, of West Norwood, London. Bay 4, Panel 5.

BRETT, Air Mechanic 1st Class, DENNIS GORDON, FAA/SFX. 1499, HMS *Dasher*, Royal Navy. 27 March 1943. Age 22. Son of Norman James and Eith Elsie Brett; husband of Ethel Brett, of May Bank, Staffordshire. Bay 4, Panel 5.

BROWN, Air Fitter, JOHN HUDSON, FAA/FX. 77765, HMS *Dasher*, Royal Navy. 27 March 1943. Age 23. Son of Helena Brown, of Blyth,

Northumberland. Bay 4, Panel 4.

BUSWELL, Air Mechanic 1st Class, PETER ERNEST VICTOR, FAA/FX. 83909, HMS *Dasher*, Royal Navy. 27 March 1943. Age 21. Son of Edward Victor and Gertrude Agnes Buswell, of Caversham, Reading. Bay 4, Panel 5.

CHAPLIN, Chief Petty Officer (Air Fitter) GEORGE WILLIAM BARNARD, FAA/FX. 55010, HMS *Dasher*, Royal Navy. 27 March 1943. Age 35. Son of Samuel Joseph and Elsie Chaplin; husband of Harriet Ruby Chaplin, of Fatton, Portsmouth. Bay 4, Panel 4.

CLARK, Air Mechanic 1st Class, ARTHUR STANLEY, FAA/FX. 86308, HMS *Dasher*, Royal Navy. 27 March 1943. Age 20. Son of Mr. and Mrs. Eric Leonard Clark. Bay 4, Panel 5.

CLUETT, Air Mechanic 1st Class, WILLIAM GEORGE, FAA/FX. 86307, HMS *Dasher*, Royal Navy. 27 March 1943. Age 21. Son of Jesse and Sarah Elizabeth Cluett, of Portsmouth. Bay 4, Panel 5.

COOLEY, Leading Radio Mechanic, REGINALD DERRICK, FAA/FX. 87765, HMS *Dasher*, Royal Navy. 27 March 1943. Son of Harold George and Florence Jessie Cooley, of Wembley Park, Middlesex. Bay 4, Panel 5.

DANDO, Leading Airman, EDWIN JAMES, FAA/SFX. 2864, HMS *Dasher*, Royal Navy. 27 March 1943. Age 19. Son of Sidney Thomas and Kathleen Norah Dando, of Mill Hill, Middlesex. Bay 4, Panel 3.

DAWSON, Petty Officer (Air Mechanic) ALBERT JOSEPH BREDE, FAA/SFX. 628, HMS *Dasher*, Royal Navy. 27 March 1943. Age 24. Son of Mr. and Mrs. A. W. Dawson; husband of Mrs. L. E. Dawson, of Northampton. Bay 4, Panel 4.

FLOWER, Petty Officer (Air Mechanic) KENNETH HENRY, FAA/FX. 77086, HMS *Dasher*, Royal Navy. 27 March 1943. Age 22. Son of Mr. and Mrs. Thomas Henry Flower; husband of Jemima Flower, of Nether Scapa, Orkney. Bay 4, Panel 4.

FOX, Air Mechanic 1st Class, GEORGE EDWARD, FAA/FX. 79161, HMS *Dasher*, Royal Navy. 27 March 1943. Age 24. Son of George Edward and Cecilia Fox, of East Acton, London. Bay 4, Panel 5.

FULKER, Air Mechanic 1st Class, HENRY CHARLES, FAA/FX. 92524, HMS *Dasher*, Royal Navy. 27 March 1943. Age 22. Son of Alfred George and Edith Fulker, of South Bank, Yorkshire. Bay 4, Panel 5.

GAMBLE, Leading Radio Mechanic, JOHN MORRIS, FAA/FX. 88200, HMS *Dasher*, Royal Navy. 27 March 1943. Age 23. Son of John and Ellen Gamble, of Knock, Co. Down. Bay 4, Panel 5.

GRIFFITHS, Air Fitter, WILLIAM RALPH, FAA/SFX. 2042, HMS *Dasher*, Royal Navy. 27 March 1943. Age 21. Son of Charles and Louisa Griffiths. Bay 4, Panel 4.

HANDLEY, Leading Radio Mechanic, DONALD CHARLES, FAA/JX. 357091, HMS *Dasher*, Royal Navy. 27 March 1943. Age 21. Son of Jesse Allan

Handley and Minnie Elizabeth Handley, of Dagenham, Essex. Bay 4, Panel 6.

HANDLEY, Leading Air Mechanic, JOHN GREGORY, FAA/SFX. 264, HMS *Dasher*, Royal Navy. 27 March 1943. Age 22. Son of John Gregory Handley and Alice Handley, of Burslem, Stoke-on-Trent. Bay 4, Panel 4.

HARROP, Air Fitter, THOMAS, FAA/FX. 83023, HMS *Dasher*, Royal Navy. 27 March 1943. Age 20. Son of Lewis and Mary Harrop, of Coventry. Bay 4, Panel 4.

HARTILL, Naval Airman 2nd Class, HORACE, FAA/FX. 93960, HMS *Dasher*, Royal Navy. 27 March 1943. Age 20. Son of Herbert Parker Hartill and Elizabeth Hartill, of Upper Gornal, Staffordshire. Bay 4, Panel 4.

HASKAYNE, Petty Officer (Radio Mechanic) JAMES ALLAN, FAA/FX. 82981, HMS *Dasher*, Royal Navy. 27 March 1943. Age 31. Son of Richard and Agnes Haskayne; husband of Olive Haskayne, of Waterloo, Liverpool. Bay 4, Panel 5.

HAVERS, Lieut-Commander, PATRICK HOWARD, HMS *Dasher*, Royal Navy. 27 March 1943. Bay 4, Panel 3.

HICKS, Air Mechanic 1st Class, JOSEPH, FAA/FX. 84551, HMS *Dasher*, Royal Navy. 27 March 1943. Age 22. Son of Joseph and Sarah Jane Hicks, of Sheffield. Bay 4, Panel 5.

HIND, Air Mechanic 1st Class, BERT JOHN, FAA/FX. 92579, HMS *Dasher*, Royal Navy. 27 March 1943. Age 34. Son of Richard and Annie Hind; husband of Hilda Hind, of Slough, Buckinghamshire. Bay 4, Panel 5.

HORNE, Air Mechanic 1st Class, SYLVESTER RICHARD ANEURIN, FAA/FX. 83836, HMS *Dasher*, Royal Navy. 27 March 1943. Age 22. Son of Jesse and Alice May Horne, of Abertridwr, Glamorgan. Bay 4, Panel 5.

HOWSE, Photographer, LESLIE GEORGE THOMAS, FAA/MX. 101858, HMS *Dasher*, Royal Navy. 27 March 1943. Age 35. Son of George and Daisy Howse; husband of Edith May Howse, of Shepherd's Bush, London. Bay 4, Panel 6.

HOYLE, Leading Air Fitter, LAURENCE, FAA/SFX. 2913, HMS *Dasher*, Royal Navy. 27 March 1943. Age 20. Son of Harry P. and Margaret E. Hoyle, of Levenshulme, Manchester. Bay 4, Panel 4.

JACKSON, Leading Airman, HENRY RENSHAW, FAA/FX. 87319, HMS *Dasher*, Royal Navy. 27 March 1943. Age 21. Son of Mr. and Mrs. A. H. Jackson, of Alkrington, Lancashire. Bay 4, Panel 3.

JOY, Air Mechanic 1st Class, EDWIN GEORGE, FAA/FX. 84427, HMS *Dasher*, Royal Navy. 27 March 1943. Age 20. Son of Edward Ernest and Florence Lillian Joy; husband of Miriam Winifred Joy, of Chelsworth, Suffolk. Bay 4, Panel 5.

KEVERNE, Petty Officer Airman, RICHARD HENRY JAMES, FAA/FX. 77087, HMS *Dasher*, Royal Navy. 27 March 1943. Age 23. Son of Mr. and Mrs. C. Keverne; husband of Mrs. B. S. Keverne, of St. Thomas', Exeter. Bay 4, Panel 4.

LANGSTON, Air Mechanic 1st Class, ENOS JOHN, FAA/FX. 82213, HMS *Dasher*, Royal Navy. 27 March 1943. Age 21. Son of Edward and Rebecca Langstone, of Sedgley, Staffordshire. Bay 4, Panel 5.

LEVICK, Leading Air Mechanic, ROY ERIC, FAA/FX. 76058, HMS *Dasher*, Royal Navy. 27 March 1943. Age 23. Son of Fred and Edith Levick, of Retford, Nottinghamshire. Bay 4, Panel 4.

LOCKWOOD, Sub-lieutenant, WILLIAM KEITH, HMS *Dasher*, Royal Naval Volunteer Reserve. 27 March 1943. Age 20. Son of Cecil William and Mary Elizabeth Lckwood, of Linthwaite, Huddersfield. Bay 4, Panel 7.

LONSDALE, Air Mechanic 2nd Class, CYRIL, FAA/FX. 94533, HMS *Dasher*, Royal Navy. 27 March 1943. Age 19. Son of Lawrence and Mary Ellen Lonsdale, of Whickham, Co. Durham. Bay 4, Panel 5.

LUMBY, Petty Officer (Radio Mechanic) ARTHUR, FAA/FX. 87283, HMS *Dasher*, Royal Navy. 27 March 1943. Age 19. Son of Arthur and Annie V. Lumby, of Hull. Bay 4, Panel 5.

MAHON, Air Mechanic 1st Class, WILLIAM, FAA/FX. 84092, HMS *Dasher*, Royal Navy. 27 March 1943. Age 29. Son of William and Annie Mahon; husband of Clara Lucy Mahon, of Rosyth, Fife. Bay 4, Panel 5.

MAHONEY, Air Mechanic 1st Class, EDWARD JOSEPH, FAA/SFX. 2430, HMS *Dasher*, Royal Navy. 27 March 1943. Age 20. Son of Edward and Florence Mahoney, of Liverpool. Bay 4, Panel 5.

MAINLAND, Leading Air Mechanic, JAMES SINCLAIR, FAA/SFX. 612, HMS *Dasher*, Royal Navy. 27 March 1943. Age 24. Son of George and Violet Gibson Mainland, of Egilshay, Orkney. Bay 4, Panel 4.

MAXWELL, Leading Air Mechanic, ROBERT, FAA/FX. 80667, HMS *Dasher*, Royal Navy. 27 March 1943. Age 26. Son of John and Elizabeth Maxwell. Bay 4, Panel 4.

McCANN, Air Mechanic 1st Class, JOSEPH, FAA/SFX. 906, HMS *Dasher*, Royal Navy. 27 March 1943. Age 25. Son of Thomas and Catherine McCann. Bay 4, Panel 5.

McCRACKEN, Naval Airman 2nd Class, PETER WILSON, FAA/FX. 90055, HMS *Dasher*, Royal Navy. 27 March 1943. Age 23. Bay 4, Panel 4.

McLELLAN, Air Mechanic 2nd Class, JOHN, FAA/FX. 84560, HMS *Dasher*, Royal Navy. 27 March 1943. Age 21. Bay 4, Panel 5.

McMURRAY, Naval Airman 2nd Class, JOHN PATRICK, FAA/FX. 101282, HMS *Dasher*, Royal Navy. 27 March 1943. Age 22. Son of Rose McMurray, of Coventry. Bay 4, Panel 4.

MOODY, Leading Airman, JOSEPH HENRY, FAA/FX. 89609, HMS *Dasher*, Royal Navy. 27 March 1943. Age 21. Son of Joseph William and Jessamine Moody, of Skegness. Bay 4, Panel 3.

MOORE, Air Mechanic 2nd Class, JOHN ROY, FAA/SR. 317, HMS *Dasher*, Royal Navy. 27 March 1943. Age 25. Son of John Mitchell Moore and Elena

Moore; husband of Marie Moore, of Havant, Hampshire. Bay 4, Panel 5.

MOULAND, Leading Air Mechanic, JOHN HENRY LEWIS, FAA/SFX. 1242, HMS *Dasher*, Royal Navy. 27 March 1943. Age 25. Son of Henry and Ethel Mouland, of West Lulworth, Dorsetshire. Bay 4, Panel 4.

MULLINS, Air Mechanic 2nd Class, JAMES, FAA/FX. 89500, HMS *Dasher*, Royal Navy. 27 March 1943. Age 32. Son of Tomas and Joanna Mullins; husband of Lucy Mullins, of New Cross, London. Bay 4, Panel 5.

NORMAN, Air Mechanic 1st Class, FRANK, FAA/SFX. 2593, HMS *Dasher*, Royal Navy. 27 March 1943. Age 21. Son of Charles and Kathleen Norman, of Poplar, London. Bay 4, Panel 5.

NUNN, Air Mechanic 1st Class, ARTHUR DONALD, FAA/FX. 83693, HMS *Dasher*, Royal Navy. 27 March 1943. Age 19. Son of Frederick Donald and Gladys Estella Nunn, of Ardingly, Sussex. Bay 4, Panel 5.

PADEN, Sub-lieutenant (A), RICHARD, HMS *Dasher*, Royal Naval Volunteer Reserve. 27 March 1943. Age 22. Son of Richard and Mary Paden. Bay 4, Panel 7.

PAICE, Air Mechanic 2nd Class, REGINALD EDWARD, FAA/FX. 94546, HMS *Dasher*, Royal Navy. 27 March 1943. Age 19. Son of Henry George and Elizabeth Paice, of Moorfields, Bristol. Bay 4, Panel 5.

PARKINSON, Air Mechanic 1st Class, DONALD, FAA/SFX. 2616, HMS *Dasher*, Royal Navy. 27 March 1943. Age 19. Son of Edward and Mary Ellen Parkinson, of Thatto Heath, Lancashire. Bay 4, Panel 5.

PAXTON, Leading Air Fitter, GEORGE WILLIAM, FAA/FX. 83231, HMS *Dasher*, Royal Navy. 27 March 1943. Age 21. Son of George and Lottie Paxton, of Notting Hill, London. Bay 4, Panel 4.

PEET, Air Fitter, JOSEPH DOUGLAS OLDHAM, FAA/FX. 82416, HMS *Dasher*, Royal Navy. 27 March 1943. Age 25. Son of Joseph Oldham Peet and Harriet Annie Peet, of Caversham, Reading. Bay 4, Panel 4.

PELL, Leading Airman, FRED, FAA/JX. 193497, HMS *Dasher*, Royal Navy. 27 March 1943. Age 23. Son of Fred and Clara Pell, of Nottingham. Bay 4, Panel 3.

RAYWARD, Air Mechanic 1st Class, CLIFFORD, FAA/JX. 231349, HMS *Dasher*, Royal Navy. 27 March 1943. Age 20. Son of William Thomas and Winifred Maud Rayward. Bay 4, Panel 5.

REEVES, Petty Officer Air Fitter, JOHN, FAA/FX. 80136, HMS *Dasher*, Royal Navy. 27 March 1943. Age 32. Bay 4, Panel 4.

RICHARDSON, Petty Officer (Air Fitter) GEORGE THOMAS, FAA/FX. 79940, HMS *Dasher*, Royal Navy. 27 March 1943. Age 23. Bay 4, Panel 4.

ROBERTS, Air Fitter, GEOFFREY, FAA/FX. 86050, HMS *Dasher*, Royal Navy. 27 March 1943. Age 22. Son of Samuel and Dora Roberts, of Packington, Leicestershire. Bay 4, Panel 4.

RODWAY, Air Mechanic 2nd Class, HARRY, FAA/FX. 94665, HMS *Dasher*,

Royal Navy. 27 March 1943. Age 19. Son of Henry and Ethel Helen Rodway, of South Yardley, Birmingham. Bay 4, Panel 5.

ROGERSON, Air Mechanic 1st Class, NORMAN JOHN, FAA/FX. 82785, HMS *Dasher*, Royal Navy. 27 March 1943. Age 20. Son of Theodore Edward Rogerson and Louisa Florence Rogerson (nee Frost), of Craighall Park, Johannesburg, South Africa. Bay 4, Panel 5.

ROSS, Air Mechanic 1st Class, HENRY, FAA/FX. 83784, HMS *Dasher*, Royal Navy. 27 March 1943. Age 21. Son of Henry and Margaret Ross, of Byker, Newcastle-on-Tyne. Bay 4, Panel 5.

ROUTLEY, Petty Officer Airman, HAROLD GEORGE, FAA/FX. 76754, HMS *Dasher*, Royal Navy. 27 March 1943. Age 31. Son of Henry and Elizabeth Routley; husband of Joan Frances Routley. Bay 4, Panel 4.

SALTER, Air Mechanic 1st Class, SAMUEL JAMES, FAA/FX. 83109, HMS *Dasher*, Royal Navy. 27 March 1943. Age 29. Bay 4, Panel 5.

SCHOOLING, Leading Air Mechanic, JOSEPH ROWLAND, FAA/FX. 76644, HMS *Dasher*, Royal Navy. 27 March 1943. Age 21. Son of Joseph Rowland and Louisa Schooling, of Romford, Essex. Bay 4, Panel 4.

SCRAGG, Air Artificer 4th Class, FRANCIS HENRY, FAA/FX. 75576, HMS *Dasher*, Royal Navy. 27 March 1943. Age 21. Son of Charles and Gladys Scragg; husband of Sybil Scragg. Bay 4, Panel 4.

SHIRLEY, Leading Air Fitter, EDWARD WALTER, FAA/FX. 75535, HMS *Dasher*, Royal Navy. 27 March 1943. Age 19. Son of Walter and Caroline E. Shirley. Bay 4, Panel 4.

SHUTTLEWORTH, Air Mechanic 1st Class, GEORGE WALTER, FAA/SFX. 1037, HMS *Dasher*, Royal Navy. 27 March 1943. Age 22. Husband of Phyllis Alice Shuttleworth. Bay 4, Panel 5.

SIMMONDS, Leading Air Mechanic, ARTHUR STEPHEN, FAA/FX. 80985, HMS *Dasher*, Royal Navy. 27 March 1943. Age 22. Son of James and Maud Simmons, of Peckham, London. Bay 4, Panel 4.

SIMPSON, Air Mechanic 1st Class, DENNIS WILLIAM, FAA/FX. 84460, HMS *Dasher*, Royal Navy. 27 March 1943. Age 21. Bay 4, Panel 5.

SMITH, Photographer, ERNEST FREDERICK, FAA/MX. 93131, HMS *Dasher*, Royal Navy. 27 March 1943. Age 23. Son of Arthur and Dorothy Smith; husband of Amy Davies Smith, of Old Basford, Nottingham. Bay 4, Panel 6.

SNEDDON, Air Mechanic 1st Class, WILLIAM BLAIR, FAA/FX. 79517, HMS *Dasher*, Royal Navy. 27 March 1943. Bay 4, Panel 5.

SNELL, Air Mechanic 1st Class, IVAN, FAA/SFX. 2335, HMS *Dasher*, Royal Navy. 27 March 1943. Age 22. Son of Thomas H. and Mary A. Snell; husband of Annie Snell, of Nelson, Lancashire. Bay 4, Panel 5.

STEAD, Leading Radio Mechanic, WILFRED, FAA/FX. 88236, HMS *Dasher*, Royal Navy. 27 March 1943. Age 21. Son of Clifford Renton Stead and Doris Stead, of Harrogate. Bay 4, Panel 6.

STOCKFORD, Air Mechanic 1st Class, ALBERT JOHN, FAA/FX. 85689, HMS *Dasher*, Royal Navy. 27 March 1943. Age 21. Son of Spencer John and Harriet Elizabeth Sarah Stockford, of Grange Town, Cardiff. Bay 4, Panel 5.

TALLACK, Air Artificer 4th Class, RICHARD JOHN, FAA/SFX. 344, HMS *Dasher*, Royal Navy. 27 March 1943. Age 21. Son of Richard Charles and Grace Jane Tallack; husband of Dorothy May Tallack, of Fratton, Portsmouth. Bay 4, Panel 4.

THOMSON, Naval Airman 2nd Class, ALEXANDER MALCOLM ARTHUR, FAA/FX. 9233, HMS *Dasher*, Royal Navy. 27 March 1943. Age 20. Son of John W. and Sarah Jane Thomson, of Elie, Fife. Bay 4, Panel 4.

TURNER, Air Mechanic 2nd Class, ERIC RICHARD, FAA/FX. 94452, HMS *Dasher*, Royal Navy. 27 March 1943. Age 29. Son of Archie and Martha Turner. Bay 4, Panel 5.

VOICE, Leading Air Fitter, STANLEY CYRIL, FAA/FX. 81775, HMS *Dasher*, Royal Navy. 27 March 1943. Age 22. Son of Ernest William and Ellen Louisa Voice. Bay 4, Panel 4.

WAIN, Petty Officer (Air Mechanic) GEORGE WILLIAM, FAA/SFX. 144, HMS *Dasher*, Royal Navy. 27 March 1943. Age 25. Son of Mr. and Mrs. George Wain; husband of Lucy Victoria Wain. Bay 4, Panel 4.

WEBB, Naval Airman 2nd Class, JOSEPH HENRY, FAA/FX. 94804, HMS *Dasher*, Royal Navy. 27 March 1943. Age 21. Son of William and Mary Elizebeth Webb; husband of Mary Bridget Webb, of Harlesden, Middlesex. Bay 4, Panel 4.

WILLIAMS, Air Mechanic 1st Class, DENNIS RUSSELL, FAA/FX. 84125, HMS *Dasher*, Royal Navy. 27 March 1943. Age 21. Son of Harold Hancock Williams and Ellen Williams, of Ross-on-Wye, Herefordshire. Bay 4, Panel 5.

WILLIAMS, Air Mechanic 1st Class, ROBERT, FAA/FX. 90025, HMS *Dasher*, Royal Navy. 27 March 1943. Age 22. Son of William and Charity Williams, of Troon, Cornwall. Bay 4, Panel 5.

WILLIS, Air Mechanic 2nd Class, HOWARD, FAA/FX. 94483, HMS *Dasher*, Royal Navy. 27 March 1943. Son of John and Hilda Mary Willis. Bay 4, Panel 5.

WOODWARD, Air Mechanic 1st Class, CLAUDE, FAA/FX. 81670, HMS *Dasher*, Royal Navy. 27 March 1943. Age 22. Son of Harry and Isabella Woodward; husband of Connie Woodward. Bay 4, Panel 5.

YOUNG, Petty Officer Airman, ALBERT JOHN, FAA/F. 55142, HMS *Dasher*, Royal Navy. 27 March 1943. Age 44. Son of Alfred Harry and Mary Ann Young; husband of Lily Helena Young, of Cosham, Hampshire. Bay 4, Panel 3.

Liverpool Naval Memorial, Lancashire

ALLAN, Lieut-Commander (E), WILLIAM LOTHIAN, HMS *Dasher*, Royal Naval Reserve. 27 March 1943. Age 43. Son of William John and Jean Smith

Allan; husband of Margaret Ross Allan, of Bearsden, Dunbartonshire. M.I.Mar.E. Panel 1, Column 2.

AYERS, Carpenter's Mate, STANLEY, 164950, HMS *Dasher*, Naval Auxiliary Personnel (Merchant Navy). 27 March 1943. Panel 10, Column 2.

BARKER, Sub-lieutenant (E), FRANK ERNEST JOSEPH, HMS *Dasher*, Royal Naval Volunteer Reserve. 27 March 1943. Age 29. Son of Mr. and Mrs. E. L. Barker; husband of Hilda Barker of Wallasey, Cheshire. Panel 4, Column 1.

BOWLES, Scullion, GEORGE BENJAMIN, 235490, HMS *Dasher*, Naval Auxiliary Personnel (Merchant Navy). 27 March 1943. Age 22. Son of Benjamin George and Beatrice Mabel Bowles, of Poplar, London. Panel 10, Column 2.

BRAMHALL, Donkeyman, EDWARD LAMBERT, 105733, HMS *Dasher*, Naval Auxiliary Personnel (Merchant Navy). 27 March 1943. Age 35. Son of Randle and Edith Bramhall; husband of Ann Jane Bramhall, of Preston, Torquay, Devon. Panel 10, Column 2.

BRANDRETH, Assistant Cook, JAMES, 178419, HMS *Dasher*, Naval Auxiliary Personnel (Merchant Navy). 27 March 1943. Age 23. Son of Mr. and Mrs. T. H. Brandreth, of Bootle, Lancashire. Panel 10, Column 2.

CAMERON, Acting Sub-lieutenant (E), ANGUS, HMS *Dasher*, Royal Naval Volunteer Reserve. 27 March 1943. Age 24. Son of William and Isabella Cameron. Panel 4, Column 1.

CHAPPELL, Assistant Steward, RONALD ALBERT, 195980, HMS *Dasher*, Naval Auxiliary Personnel (Merchant Navy). 27 March 1943. Panel 10, Column 2.

CLEMENTS, Steward, KENNETH GEORGE, 126311, HMS *Dasher*, Naval Auxiliary Personnel (Merchant Navy). 27 March 1943. Age 25. Son of George and Elsie Clements; husband of Queenie M. Clements, of Fingringhoe, Essex. Panel 10, Column 2.

COX, Assistant Steward, FREDERICK JAMES, 144613, HMS *Dasher*, Naval Auxiliary Personnel (Merchant Navy). 27 March 1943. Age 23. Son of James and Beatrice Cox; husband of Patricia Jane Cox, of Wembley, Middlesex. Panel 10, Column 2.

DEVLIN, Carpenter's Mate, JOHN, 252419, HMS *Dasher*, Naval Auxiliary Personnel (Merchant Navy). 27 March 1943. Panel 10, Column 2.

DICKSON, Leading Steward, WILLIAM, 788938, HMS *Dasher*, Naval Auxiliary Personnel (Merchant Navy). 27 March 1943. Age 56. Son of Thomas and Matilda Campbell Dickson; husband of Kitty Dickson. Panel 10, Column 2.

FARLEY, Assistant Cook, WILLIAM GEORGE, 225185, HMS *Dasher*, Naval Auxiliary Personnel (Merchant Navy). 27 March 1943. Age 35. Son of James and Martha Farley; husband of Elizabeth Farley. Panel 10, Column 2.

FARTHING, Assistant Cook, RONALD ALAN, 235579, HMS *Dasher*, Naval Auxiliary Personnel (Merchant Navy). 27 March 1943. Age 20. Son of George

Charles William and Lily Louise Farthing, of Victoria Docks, Essex. Panel 10. Column 2.

FLANAGAN, Greaser, DENIS, 223846, HMS *Dasher*, Naval Auxiliary Personnel (Merchant Navy). 27 March 1943. Age 37. Son of William and Charlotte Flanagan, of Glasgow. Panel 10, Column 2.

GIBSON, Carpenter, JOHN ALEXANDER, 225451, HMS *Dasher*, Naval Auxiliary Personnel (Merchant Navy). 27 March 1943. Age 41. Panel 10, Column 2.

GRAY, Boatswain, ARCHIBALD, 39676, HMS *Dasher*, Naval Auxiliary Personnel (Merchant Navy). 27 March 1943. Age 34. Panel 10, Column 2.

GRIFFITHS, Greaser, CHARLES WILLIAM, 71047, HMS *Dasher*, Naval Auxiliary Personnel (Merchant Navy). 27 March 1943. Age 35. Son of Charles William and Louisa Griffiths; husband of Margaret Griffiths, of Birkenhead, Cheshire. Panel 10, Column 2.

HABGOOD, Butcher 1st Class, GEORGE ARTHUR, 225209, HMS *Dasher*, Naval Auxiliary Personnel (Merchant Navy). 27 March 1943. Age 32. Son of Arthur and Edith Habgood, of Liverpool. Panel 10, Column 2.

HART, Donkeyman, HENRY, 208840, HMS *Dasher*, Naval Auxiliary Personnel (Merchant Navy). 27 March 1943. Age 32. Son of William John and Annie Hart; husband of Winifred Hart, of Belfast. Panel 10, Column 2.

HILL, Ship's Cook, JOSEPH, 104467, HMS *Dasher*, Naval Auxiliary Personnel (Merchant Navy). 27 March 1943. Age 29. Panel 10, Column 2.

HURST, Ship's Cook, FREDERICK MARSH, 540000, HMS *Dasher*, Naval Auxiliary Personnel (Merchant Navy). 27 March 1943. Age 53. Son of William and Elizabeth Hurst; husband of Amelia Sarah Hurst. Panel 10, Column 2.

HUTCHINSON, Acting Sub-lieutenant (E), ROBERT, HMS *Dasher*, Royal Naval Volunteer Reserve. 27 March 1943. Age 38. Son of William and Hannah Hutchinson; husband of Mabel Hutchinson, of Sydenham, Belfast. Panel 4, Column 1.

INGRAM, Assistant Steward, DENNIS ALFRED, 268226, HMS *Dasher*, Naval Auxiliary Personnel (Merchant Navy). 27 March 1943. Age 19. Son of Alfred and Ethel Ingram. Panel 10, Column 2.

JACKSON, Baker, STEPHEN HOMER, 151555, HMS *Dasher*, Naval Auxiliary Personnel (Merchant Navy). 27 March 1943. Age 28. Son of Samuel and Mary Jackson, of Glasgow. Panel 10, Column 2.

JEFFERY, Greaser, ANDREW, 133626, HMS *Dasher*, Naval Auxiliary Personnel (Merchant Navy). 27 March 1943. Age 34. Husband of Ellen Jeffery, of North Shields, Northumberland. Panel 10, Column 2.

KILBURN, Chief Steward, WILLIAM, 979621, HMS *Dasher*, Naval Auxiliary Personnel (Merchant Navy). 27 March 1943. Age 39. Son of Adam and Dorothy Jane Louise Kilburn; husband of Annie Kilburn, of Liverpool. Panel 10, Column 2.

LEWIS, Assistant Steward, ALAN WILLIAM GEORGE, 179221, HMS *Dasher*, Naval Auxiliary Personnel (Merchant Navy). 27 March 1943. Age 21. Son of Lilian Lewis, of Robertsbridge, Sussex. Panel 10, Column 2.

LINCOLN, Lieutenant (E), ALBERT HARRY, HMS *Dasher*, Royal Naval Volunteer Reserve. 27 March 1943. Age 32. Son of William Francis and Ellen Louise Lincoln, of Norwich, Norfolk. Panel 3, Column 2.

MAXTED, Assistant Cook, JACK, 263390, HMS *Dasher*, Naval Auxiliary Personnel (Merchant Navy). 27 March 1943. Age 17. Son of Fredrick John and Rosemary Maxted. Panel 10, Column 2.

MONKS, Sub-lieutenant (S), NEWTON LEE PONTING, HMS *Dasher*, Royal Naval Reserve. 27 March 1943. Age 36. Son of Casswell Ponting Monks and Florence Monks; husband of Phyllis Emily Monks, of Slough, Buckinghamshire. Panel 3, Column 2.

MOORE, Sub-lieutenant (E), THOMAS JOHN ALEXANDER, HMS *Dasher*, Royal Naval Reserve. 27 March 1943. Age 38. Son of Mr. and Mrs. G. W. Moore; husband of Isabella M. Moore, of Plockton, Ross and Cromarty. Panel 3, Column 1.

MOSS, Steward, ALEXANDER MARSHALL, 59161, HMS *Dasher*, Naval Auxiliary Personnel (Merchant Navy). 27 March 1943. Age 28. Panel 10, Column 2.

NICHOL, Carpenter's Mate, WILFRED JAMES, 146170, HMS *Dasher*, Naval Auxiliary Personnel (Merchant Navy). 27 March 1943. Age 33. Son of Mrs. T. Nichol, of Tynemouth, Northumberland. His brother, William Henry, also died on service. Panel 10, Column 2.

O'DONNELL, Cleaner, JOHN, 228297, HMS *Dasher*, Naval Auxiliary Personnel (Merchant Navy). 27 March 1943. Age 27. Son of Patrick and Bridget O'Donnell; husband of Catherine O'Donnell, of Glasgow. Panel 10, Column 2.

O'MALLEY, Cleaner, CHARLES EDWARD, 200377, HMS *Dasher*, Naval Auxiliary Personnel (Merchant Navy). 27 March 1943. Age 33. Panel 10, Column 2.

O'NEIL, Fireman, JOHN, 199165, HMS *Dasher*, Naval Auxiliary Personnel (Merchant Navy). 27 March 1943. Age 41. Son of John and Flora O'Neil, of Glasgow. Panel 10, Column 2.

OXFORD, Fireman, WILLIAM ARTHUR, 229983, HMS *Dasher*, Naval Auxiliary Personnel (Merchant Navy). 27 March 1943. Age 22. Panel 10, Column 2.

PATERSON, Assistant Baker, JAMES REID, 223947, HMS *Dasher*, Naval Auxiliary Personnel (Merchant Navy). 27 March 1943. Age 21. Panel 10, Column 2.

PITMAN, Writer, PETER ERIC VICTOR, 224179, HMS *Dasher*, Naval Auxiliary Personnel (Merchant Navy). 27 March 1943. Age 22. Son of Donald

George Ernest and Florence Pitman, of Penarth, Glamorgan. Panel 10, Column 2.

POTTER, Assistant Steward, LAWRENCE, 202608, HMS *Dasher*, Naval Auxiliary Personnel (Merchant Navy). 27 March 1943. Age 18. Son of Benjamin William and Louisa Potter, of Chiswick, Middlesex. Panel 10, Column 2.

REID, Cleaner, ALLAN, 235015, HMS *Dasher*, Naval Auxiliary Personnel (Merchant Navy). 27 March 1943. Age 28. Panel 10. Column 2.

RICHARDSON, Storekeeper, WILLIAM, 227632, HMS *Dasher*, Naval Auxiliary Personnel (Merchant Navy). 27 March 1943. Age 26. Son of George Richardson, and of Mary McGeoch Bone Richardson, of Glasgow. Panel 11, Column 1.

ROBERTS, Cleaner, DENNIS NEAGLE, 230605, HMS *Dasher*, Naval Auxiliary Personnel (Merchant Navy). 27 March 1943. Age 20. Son of William Owen Roberts and Ethel Gertrude Roberts, of Llandudno, Caernarvonshire. Panel 11, Column 1.

ROBINSON, Steward, WILLIAM JAMES, 1072705, HMS *Dasher*, Naval Auxiliary Personnel (Merchant Navy). 27 March 1943. Age 39. Son of Edward and Mary Robinson; husband of Mary A. S. Robinson, of Downend, Gloucestershire. Panel 11, Column 1.

ROSS, Painter, HENRY, 215468, HMS *Dasher*, Naval Auxiliary Personnel (Merchant Navy). 27 March 1943. Age 33. Son of Matthew and Margaret Ross, of Ballymena, Co. Antrim. Panel 11, Column 1.

SCOTCHMOOR, Lieut-Commander (E), JOHN WILLIAM, HMS *Dasher*, Royal Naval Reserve. 27 March 1943. Age 33. Son of James and Grace Scotchmoor; husband of Irene Mildred Scotchmoor, of Sidcup, Kent. Panel 2, Column 1.

SWAN, Acting Sub-lieutenant (E), WILLIAM ARTHUR, HMS *Dasher*, Royal Naval Volunteer Reserve. 27 March 1943. Age 26. Son of William Samuel Swan, and of Harriet Rosina Swan, of Southampton. Panel 4, Column 2.

TAYLOR, Greaser, FREDERICK JOHN, 29325, HMS *Dasher*, Naval Auxiliary Personnel (Merchant Navy). 27 March 1943. Son of George Taylor; husband of Gladys Eva Taylor, of Woolston, Southampton. Panel 11, Column 1.

TENNANT, Assistant Storekeeper, HERBERT WILLIAM, 1071070, HMS *Dasher*, Naval Auxiliary Personnel (Merchant Navy). 27 March 1943. Age 38. Son of Herbert George and Mary Anne Tennant; husband of Florence Edyth Tennant. Panel 11, Column 1.

TETLOW, Acting Sub-lieutenant (E), FRANK, HMS *Dasher*, Royal Naval Volunteer Reserve. 27 March 1943. Age 28. Son of Florence May Tetlow. Panel 4, Column 2.

TINTO, Scullion, LESLIE GRAHAM, 151500, HMS *Dasher*, Naval Auxiliary Personnel (Merchant Navy). 27 March 1943. Age 31. Son of Alexander and

Georgina Chalmers Tinto, of Glasgow. Panel 11, Column 1.

TORDOFF, Carpenter's Mate, DENNIS ALBERT, 222857, HMS *Dasher*, Naval Auxiliary Personnel (Merchant Navy). 27 March 1943. Age 21. Son of Ben and Alice Maud Tordoff, of Halton, Yorkshire. Panel 11, Column 1.

TOSH, Assistant Steward, WILLIAM, 225175, HMS *Dasher*, Naval Auxiliary Personnel (Merchant Navy). 27 March 1943. Age 36. Panel 11, Column 1.

TRAVIS, Storekeeper, WILLIAM, 902499, Mentioned in Despatches, HMS *Dasher*, Naval Auxiliary Personnel (Merchant Navy). 27 March 1943. Age 53. Son of William and Effie Travis; husband of Ellen Travis, of Liverpool. Panel 11, Column 1.

VAUGHAN, Assistant Cook, GEORGE, 163431, HMS *Dasher*, Naval Auxiliary Personnel (Merchant Navy). 27 March 1943. Age 26. Panel 11, Column 1.

WALSH, Assistant Steward, THOMAS, 1102288, HMS *Dasher*, Naval Auxiliary Personnel (Merchant Navy). 27 March 1943. Age 38. Panel 11, Column 1.

WOOD, Fireman, GEORGE, 225337, HMS *Dasher*, Naval Auxiliary Personnel (Merchant Navy). 27 March 1943. Age 37. Son of Alexander and Mary Wood; husband of Elizabeth S. C. Wood, of Bridge of Weir, Renfrewshire. Panel 11, Column 1.

Plymouth Naval Memorial, Devon

ALLAN, Steward, WILLIAM FRANK, D/LX 26746, HMS *Dasher*, Royal Navy. 27 March 1943. Age 27. Son of Frank and Elizabeth Allan, of Latchford Without, Cheshire; husband of Iris Allan. Panel 83, Column 2.

ANSTRUTHER, Ordinary Seaman, DAVID RISK, D/JX 348819, HMS *Dasher*, Royal Navy. 27 March 1943. Age 19. Son of Robert and Janet Fortheringham Stevenson Anstruther, of Stirling. Panel 80. Column 2.

CASTLE, Steward, REX, D/LX 29115, HMS *Dasher*, Royal Navy. 27 March 1943. Age 24. Son of Fred and Annie Castle, of Dewsbury, Yorkshire. Panel 83, Column 2.

COMBSTOCK, Able Seaman, FREDERICK JAMES, D/JX 347470, HMS *Dasher*, Royal Navy. 27 March 1943. Son of Frederick George Combstock, and of Beatrice Anne Combstock, of Dawlish, Devon. Panel 79, Column 1.

HAMPTON, Able Seaman, THOMAS JOHN, D/SSX 13594, HMS *Dasher*, Royal Navy. 27 March 1943. Age 29. Son of Albert and Kathleen Hampton; husband of Bertha J. Hampton, of Cheltenham, Gloucestershire. Panel 79, Column 2.

LOADE, Steward, WILLIAMS, D/LX 26017, HMS *Dasher*, Royal Navy. 27 March 1943. Age 22. Son of Samuel and Ellen Loade, of Ledbury, Herefordshire. Panel 83, Column 2.

McSWAIN, Leading Seaman, JAMES MUNRO, D/J 27914, HMS *Dasher*, Royal Navy. 27 March 1943. Age 44. Son of Alexander Henderson McSwain and Isabella McSwain; husband of Amelia McSwain, of Edinburgh. Panel 78, Column 3.

NETHERCOTT, Steward, HENRY ELIAS, D/LX 26845, HMS *Dasher*, Royal Navy. 27 March 1943. Age 24. Son of Walter and Louisa Nethercott; husband of Ivy May Nethercott, of Cathays, Glamorgan. Panel 83, Column 3.

RICHER, Able Seaman, JACK, D/J 59908, HMS *Dasher*, Royal Navy. 27 March 1943. Age 43. Husband of Nellie Miles Richer, of Ellacombe, Devon. Panel 80, Column 1.

SALMONS, Leading Steward, JOHN THOMAS, D/LX 24940, HMS *Dasher*, Royal Navy. 27 March 1943. Age 35. Son of Isabella Salmons, of Litherland, Lancashire. Panel 83, Column 2.

SWEETNAM, Leading Supply Assistant, CUTHBERT BENJAMIN, D/MX 107019, HMS *Dasher*, Royal Navy. 27 March 1943. Age 34. Son of Augustus George and Mary Teresa Sweetnam, of Cardiff; husband of Margaret Maud Sweetnam, of Cardiff. Panel 83, Column 1.

VARCOE, Steward, JACK, D/LX 26736, HMS *Dasher*, Royal Navy. 27 March 1943. Age 28. Son of John Henry and Gladys Rose Varcoe, of Plymouth; husband of Vera Varcoe, of Plymouth. Panel 83, Column 2.

Portsmouth Naval Memorial, Hampshire

ALMOND, Ordinary Seaman, ERIC, P/JX 372307, HMS *Dasher*, Royal Navy. 27 March 1943. Age 19. Son of Robert Goodwin Almond and Drucilla Almond, of Kettering, Northamptonshire. Panel 76, Column 1.

BROWN, Able Seaman, ROBERT BURTON, P/JX 266654, HMS *Dasher*, Royal Navy. 27 March 1943. Son of Mary Elizabeth Brown, of Hounslow, Middlesex. Panel 74, Column 1.

COMBER, Able Seaman, ALFRED JOHN, P/J 94507, HMS *Dasher*, Royal Navy. 27 March 1943. Age 39. Son of Arthur William and Emma Jane Comber; husband of Cissie Comber, of Gosport, Hampshire. Panel 74, Column 1.

CONGDON, Ordinary Seaman, NOEL CHARLES EDWARD, P/JX 357886, HMS *Dasher*, Royal Navy. 27 March 1943. Age 40. Son of Charles Ernest and Priscilla Congdon; husband of Irene V. E. M. Congdon, of Catford, London. Panel 76, Column 2.

FAHEY, Able Seaman, JOHN THOMAS, P/JX 321159, HMS *Dasher*, Royal Navy. 27 March 1943. Age 17. Panel 74, Column 2.

GRIFFIN, Able Seaman, BERTIE WILFRED, P/JX 316118, HMS *Dasher*, Royal Navy. 27 March 1943. Age 29. Son of Bertie and Ada Griffin, of Chingford, Essex. Panel 74, Column 3.

HODKINSON, Leading Radio Mechanic, PETER, P/MX 84596, HMS *Dasher*, Royal Navy. 27 March 1943. Age 20. Son of John and Gertrude Dorothy Hodkinson, of Gloucester. Panel 79, Column 1.

IRVINE, Supply Assistant, GEORGE BRUCE, P/MX 82797, HMS *Dasher*,

Royal Navy. 27 March 1943. Age 29. Son of George G. T. and Helen J. S. Irvine; husband of Margaret Mary Irvine, of Lerwick, Zetland. Panel 79, Column 1.

KILPATRICK, Able Seaman, SAMUEL JAMES, P/JX 306997, HMS *Dasher*, Royal Navy. 27 March 1943. Age 19. Son of Samuel James Kilpatrick and Ann Jane Kilpatrick, of Belfast. Panel 75, Column 1.

MORGAN, Leading Seaman, JOHN JOSEPH, P/JX 186173, HMS *Dasher*, Royal Navy. 27 March 1943. Age 32. Son of Martin and Brigid Morgan; husband of Elsie Henrietta Morgan. Panel 73, Column 3.

MUDD, Able Seaman, HORACE HAROLD, P/JX 315913, HMS *Dasher*, Royal Navy. 27 March 1943. Age 29. Son of Henry and Elizabeth Mudd; husband of Adeline Mudd. Panel 75, Column 2.

SPORTON, Ordinary Seaman, ALBERT VICTOR HENRY, P/JX 324724, HMS *Dasher*, Royal Navy. 27 March 1943. Age 26. Son of Henry and Amy Sporton; husband of Elizabeth Emily Edith Sporton (nee Partridge), of Upminster, Essex. Panel 76, Column 3.

STANTON, Able Seaman, ROY LEWIS, P/JX 323583, HMS *Dasher*, Royal Navy. 27 March 1943. Age 19. Son of James Harold and Rosina May Stanton, of Worcester Park, Surrey. Panel 75, Column 3.

WORSDELL, Ordinary Seaman, ALBERT CYRIL, P/JX 345517, HMS *Dasher*, Royal Navy. 27 March 1943. Age 29. Son of Henry and Alice Worsdell, of Ludgershall, Wiltshire. Panel 76, Column 3.

Runnymede Memorial, Surrey

LEONARD, Sergeant, ROGER, 523319, Serving in HMS *Dasher*, Royal Air Force. 27 March 1943. Age 37. Son of William Thomas Leonard and Hester Maria Leonard, of Southampton; husband of Kathleen Mary Leonard, of Freemantle, Southampton. Panel 156.

PARKS, Corporal, STANLEY MUIRSON, 533572, Serving in HMS *Dasher*, Royal Air Force. 27 March 1943. Panel 171.

"When You Go Home, Tell Them Of Us And Say,
For Their Tomorrow, We Gave Our Today"

KOHIMA EPITAPH .

Above: Lieutenant Alan Kent Smith
Below: Sub-lieutenant Ernest Raymond Giles
Bottom: Sub-lieutenant Joe McEvoy (1st on left)

Chapter 12

Their Name Liveth Forever More

Fleet Air Arm Fighter Pilots

At the invasion of North Africa when Oran surrendered, the aircraft carrier HMS Avenger required fighter pilots. Four *Dasher* pilots were seconded to the aircraft carrier and all lost their lives when the ship was torpedoed on the 2nd day of the homeward voyage. Three of the fighter pilots were:

Lieutenant Alan Kent Smith was born on Stronsay, a small Orkney Island. His date of birth was 22nd January 1915, the son of Peter and Betsy.

He attended the local school and later graduated MA at Edinburgh University He then studied for another year at Edinburgh Provincial Training Centre to qualify as a teacher. He changed careers and went to Malaya where he became involved in rubber plantations. At the outbreak of WWII he joined the Fleet Air Arm, the aviation branch of the Royal Navy. On qualifying as a pilot he served in the Eastern Mediterranean then Scotland.

Just before the convoys departed for the Invasion of North Africa Alan (Kentie) enjoyed some leave at home on Stronsay. Sadly it was to be his last. Avenger was torpedoed and sunk within minutes. Alan died aged 27 and is remembered with honour on the Lee-on-Solent Memorial. Bay 3 Panel 7

Another of the *Dasher* pilots seconded to HMS *Avenger* was **Sub-lieutenant Ernest Raymond Giles** who was born to George and Irene Giles on the 7th February, 1921, at Dartford. Kent.

During his infancy the family doctor always passed comment on his peach complexion referring to him as "Young Peachy." Thereafter he was always affectionately known within the family as "Peach." He had a sister, Elaine and a half-sister Jose.

During his school days at Dartford Grammar School, the pupils were asked to choose a partner to enter the 3-legged race. On one of their sports days "Peach" chose a scholar with only one leg.

To win or lose did not matter to "Peach" as he always gave of his best and entered whatever the challenge was with a good spirit. On leaving school he was involved in the building industry as a surveyor's assistant.

After joining the Fleet Air Arm he commenced pilot training on the 16th June, 1942, and on qualifying he served at a number of Naval land bases and ships prior to flying on HMS *Dasher*. "Peach" died aged 21. Remembered with Honour on the Lee-on-Solent Memorial. Bay 4 Panel 1

Sub-lieutenant Joe McEvoy also lost his life on HMS *Avenger*.

Joe was the son of Joseph and Mary McEvoy. His father, a Company Sergeant Major was killed during WWI. After primary school, Joe attended St Bede's Grammar School from 1924-1932. He excelled academically and in sport he was House Captain. Joe enjoyed scouting, scout camps were an essential and enjoyable part of his education.

On deciding he would like to be a school teacher he attended St. Mary's College Twickenham. Once more his love of sport led to him being appointed Captain of the swimming team.

On completion of his teacher training he was successful at his first job interview and joined the staff at St. Ann's Primary School Bradford, Yorkshire. On the outbreak of war in September 1939, Joe volunteered for service. He was selected for aircrew training with the Fleet Air Arm and did his initial training at Lee-on-Solent and at HMS *St Vincent* training establishment Gosport.

Navy life suited him and he wrote enthusiastically from No.14 Elementary Flying Training School Elmdon:

> "I have been in the Fleet Air Arm now for three months and although dressed as a sailor, the only sailing I have done is to cross the ferry to the Isle of Wight. The first two months were spent at lectures, the most important one being air and sea navigation.
>
> "I was also taught various types of signalling where I had to revive my scout's semaphore, seamanship and wireless telegraphy. We also spent a lot of time on field training where as future possible officers we have to drill. The standard is one degree better than the Guards!
>
> "We had a pretty stiff exam at the end of the course and then moved to the Isle of Wight where we marked time until moving to this flying school. As yet I have had no leave but at the end of this course which lasts for another six weeks or so we hope to get quite a long one before embarking to the Colonies for further flying training. This is the life!"

It was a young adventurous Sub-lieutenant Joseph McEvoy, fully trained as a Hurricane fighter pilot who arrived at the Royal Naval Air Station Belfast, to join 804 Squadron. The date was Tuesday 17th March, 1942, St. Patrick's Day. Joseph remained with 804 Squadron and was with them onboard *Dasher* on the voyage to Oran.

The following 2 HMS *Dasher* Petty Officers were named in the Board of Enquiry report for their heroism. Both helped many young Ratings to safety but in doing so they lost their lives. The heroism of the 2 petty officers was never revealed to their families.

Petty Officer Telegraphist, Cyril James Terrey. Age 28, born to Louisa Rebecca Terrey in Clapton, London, in 1931. Cyril joined the Royal Navy and served on the light cruiser HMS *Durban*. During the next two years his ship sailed 48,000 miles through the Straights of Magellan, the most important natural passage between the Pacific Ocean and the Atlantic Ocean. He also sailed through the Patagonian Channel and all around South America.

He was stationed in Malta when he married Carmello Bartolo of Valetta. They moved to England and took up residence at 48 Leighton Road, West Ealing, London.

In 1937 their son James was born followed the next year by Leonard. Cyril served on two minesweepers, HMS *Holly* and HMS *St Anglo* before he joined the ill fated HMS *Dasher*. Cyril's heroism was recorded in the Board of Enquiry report.

Petty Officer John Alexander Stamp, age 31, son of John and Annie Stamp, South Shields, County Durham. He was a well built man with sandy coloured hair and blue eyes, the eldest son of caring loving parents, Annie and John. His three brothers were George, Harry and Alfred. His two sisters were Vera and Ann.

John was born and bred in South Shields where he attended Laygate Lane Baptist Church. He later joined the Boys Brigade and became an officer.

On joining the Royal Navy Volunteer Reserve, it became more than just a hobby to him. Before the start of WWII John was a crew member on coal ships that plied their trade from the River Tyne. He later served on a minesweeper then on the dangerous Russian convoys onboard HMS *Curlew* before joining *Dasher*.

John was the right-hand-man to *Dasher's* Chief Executive Commander Lane, who thought very highly of John. As a son and brother he was truly loved and respected. He was classed as an honest gentleman who was always willing to help anyone in need. His brother George lost his life at sea, four months before the *Dasher* tragedy, whilst serving on board *Wydestone*. John's heroism was recorded in the *Dasher* Board of Enquiry report.

Air Mechanic 1st Class George Edward Fox

Air Mechanic 1st Class George Edward Fox age 24, was the son of Edward and Cecilia Fox, East Acton, London. George was a very cheerful young man who never let things get him down. Nobody had a bad word to say about him. As a member of the Fleet Air Arm he worked on the aircraft ensuring they were ready for action and available to fly at a moments notice. His duties were carried out in the hangar where the horrendous explosion occurred.

George was engaged to be married. His father never really recovered from the loss of his only son, fuelled by the lack of information coming from the Admiralty, and the belief that perhaps his son's death was somehow suspicious or perhaps could have been avoided. George has his name engraved on the Lee-On-Solent Memorial, Hampshire.

Fleet Air Arm Air Mechanic (A) First Class Dennis William Simpson

Fleet Air Arm Air Mechanic (A) First Class Dennis William Simpson, age 21, was born on 15th February, 1922. Dennis's mother died in childbirth and he was brought up by his grandmother, whom he called Mum, and his four aunties; Ethel, Dorothy, Ivy and Marjorie. As he was the only boy amongst the ladies, they all greatly spoiled him.

Dennis volunteered on 23rd April, 1941, and was trained at HMS *Daedalus*. After further training at RAF *Locking*, HMS *Raven* and HMS *Condor* he joined 816 Squadron on 14th July, 1942, as an Air Mechanic. Seven months later on 2nd February, 1943, with 816 Squadron he joined *Dasher*. His service record states that his character was very good. Three days before the *Dasher* disaster Dennis wrote to his Mum enquiring about her cold and hoping she was much better. He also wrote:

"I have been on the move once again."

This was a reference to *Dasher* departing from Liverpool on voyage to the Clyde. The letter also makes reference to a girl named Doris. At the end of his letter he wrote:

"Cheerio for now. Your ever loving son, Dennis."

After the family received the dreadful telegram intimating that he was *"Missing On War Service,"* Dennis's letter arrived! When the family were unable to find out any information from the War Office about what had become of him, they contacted Dennis's best friend, survivor Petty Officer John Mann. The reply they received stated:

"I am afraid I am not allowed to say anything. I am of course bound by the Official Secrets Act. Dennis was my greatest friend and I am

deeply grieved as to his whereabouts. It would give me the greatest pleasure if you could let me have a photograph of Des. You can hardly know how much this means to me. Remember if there is anything I can do for you I should only be too pleased. Once again I offer you my deepest sympathy. I am your affectionate friend. John Mann."

On being reported *Missing on War Service,* it was more than three months before the family received confirmation of his death.

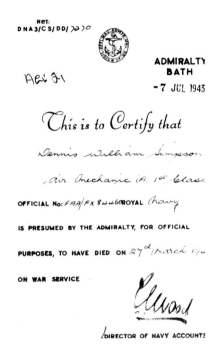

Ref:
DNA3/CS/DD/7070

AԲՆ ՅՆ

**ADMIRALTY
BATH**

-7 JUL 1943

This is to Certify that

Dennis William Simpson.

air Mechanic (A) 1st Class

OFFICIAL No: FAA/FX 84460 ROYAL Navy

IS PRESUMED BY THE ADMIRALTY, FOR OFFICIAL

PURPOSES, TO HAVE DIED ON 27d March 194-

ON WAR SERVICE

DIRECTOR OF NAVY ACCOUNTS

Henry (Harry) Hart

Henry (Harry) Hart was a 32 year old 'Donkey Man' on *Dasher*. His duties entailed operating all machinery involved in the emergency supply system, also the raising and lowering of the anchor and working the bilge pumps.

Harry was reared in Lisburn County Antrim. Northern Ireland. He worked in Glenmore Bleach Works. Prior to joining the Merchant Navy he served with three shipping companies, the Argentine Line; Port Lines, Liverpool; then with Lamport & Holt Line, Liverpool. On joining the Royal Navy he served on HMS *Rodney* before being transferred to HMS *Dasher*. His service number was 28840. Harry was the son of William John Hart and Annie Hart. He left behind his wife Winifred, who gave birth to a daughter six months later, on the 25th September, 1943. Winifred's dreams of their future together never materialised.

Petty Officer Kenneth Henry Flower

Petty Officer Kenneth Henry Flower, age 22, was the son of Thomas Flower. The Family home was in Yatton near Bristol. Shortly after leaving school Kenneth joined the Royal Navy and was stationed at the Training Ship HMS *Impregnable*. He was then transferred to HMS *St Vincent*, a Royal Navy establishment in Gosport, Portsmouth. This was followed by a posting to another shore base, HMS *Merlin* at Donibristle, Fife Scotland. 20 year old Kenneth married 18 year old Jemima Cook, in Weston Super Mare on 21st April, 1941.

Petty Officer Kenneth Henry Flower with wife, Jemima

The following year he joined HMS *Dasher*. The young couple were overjoyed when their first child, Valerie, was born in October 1942. The baby was only five months old when the dreadful telegram arrived with the devastating news that her husband was *"Missing On War Service."*

Every day the young mother waited anxiously, hoping upon hope that her husband would be found alive. Unfortunately it was not to be. Four long weeks after receiving the telegram, a letter dated 23rd April, 1943, arrived from Commodore E. Thornton stating:

"It has become necessary to presume your husband's death to have occurred on 27th March 1943."

A few days later, a letter of condolence arrived from Buckingham Palace. Due to the bewildering secrecy imposed, no further information was imparted to the bereaved families.

As Kenneth's wife, Jemima, found herself unable to cope with the loss of her husband and the complete lack of information from the Royal Navy, baby Valerie was brought up by her maternal grandparents. More than 50 years passed before Valerie found out about the tragic events surrounding the death of her father.

A few years later, reflecting on how *Dasher* events had impacted on her personally, Valerie wrote:

"As a child growing up all I was ever told was 'your father died during the war, he went down with his ship.' Nobody ever talked about what happened during the war years or what happened to my father's ship. I must have been about 8 or 9 years old when I was shown a

newspaper, The Scottish Daily Express dated 19th May 1945 which first reported the loss of the Dasher.

"I am now 64 years of age and have only over the last 10/12 years been finding out about the Dasher. I still have this newspaper together with the two telegrams 'Missing on War Service' and 'Presumed Dead.'

"I never really got over the sense of being 'abandoned' but began to understand how and why it happened after discovering a little of the story of the Dasher. I think we deserve to be told the whole true story of what happened. My mother died not knowing the truth and probably feeling guilty about abandoning me. The government should come clean and tell those of us who have been affected all our lives, what really happened!

"Maybe in our daughter's life time or even in my grandson's life time they will make public the secret information, but it will be far too late to mean anything to anyone and that is probably what the officials want. There must be many other 60-year-olds who have similar stories to mine. I think we deserve to know the whole true story of what really happened."

William (Bill) Gillies

William (Bill) Gillies, age 24, was the son of William and Charlotte Gillies, Edinburgh. Bill was born in Calgary, Canada. His family returned to Scotland when he was 4 years old. He attended Tynecastle School and attained his Higher Certificate. He worked for W. A. Gilbey and attended evening classes at Heriot Watt College. At the conclusion of the course he was awarded the bronze medal for economics, history and science.

When war was declared, Bill was called up to serve in the Fleet Air Arm as a Leading Writer with 816 Squadron. He was on duty on board HMS *Ark Royal* when it was torpedoed on 13th November, 1941. On his return to the UK, Bill was posted to Campbeltown, and he then joined HMS *Dasher* with 816 Squadron.

When the horrendous explosion occurred on *Dasher,* it caused devastation in the hangar area where the Pilots and their Air Mechanics were attending to their aircraft. 816 Squadron lost so many personnel the squadron was disbanded after this catastrophe on *Dasher.*

Bill's fiancée, Miss Helen Ramsey, wrote:

Bill's first aircraft carrier HMS Ark Royal was a very happy ship, but Dasher was 'awful.' When Dasher returned from the Russian convoy, most of the squadron were given leave. Dasher was a rotten, most unhappy ship. None of the boys wanted to go back on her.

"Unfortunately they returned on 15th March, 1943, and the next thing we received was a telegram saying Bill was 'missing.' Then a letter arrived declaring him to be dead. That was the last we heard. On writing to the Admiralty seeking more information, they replied that it was a War-time secret.

"On 27th March, 1943, one of Bill's pals had been on a course so he missed the sinking. He wrote to me, naturally he never told me what had happened. I understand that William was alive when he was picked up but died onboard the rescue ship.

"I travelled to Campbeltown, during July 1943, but nobody would talk about the sinking of HMS Dasher. After the war I wrote to the Admiralty and asked what had happened. They replied: 'it was a war-time secret which could not be released.' For the last 43 years I have tried to find out what happened. A friend in the Royal Bank of Scotland, who had served in the Royal Navy, told me a U-boat had torpedoed Dasher.

"I have also heard it was an internal explosion. Despite all my attempts, I have never got the right story; I shall not rest until I do so. I have found it all so frustrating and I felt the Admiralty could have done better over the whole affair and I don't think I will ever forgive them, but some day we might be given the answer.

"Bill's Petty Officer, Jock Addison, was a survivor. He met Bill's parents but he would not tell them anything. One thing I do know, the crew who were on leave, before the explosion, did not want to rejoin Dasher. It was an unhappy ship."

Able Seaman Charles Edward Atherton (39) is on the right wearing a boiler suit with Dasher crew members

Able Seaman Charles Edward Atherton, age 39, was born in Collyhurst, Manchester. He was the son of James and Edith Atherton. He worked locally and when he reached age 20, he joined the Royal Navy. During the next 19 years he enjoyed sailing all over the world on Royal Navy ships.

He married Annie, who resided in Harpurhey, Lancashire. They had two fine strapping sons, Norman Anthony (Tony) and Charles Edward. In 1942 he sailed out to Canada and travelled by train to New York where he was billeted in Flushing Barracks.

During the next few months he and his shipmates were allowed to visit Tietjen & Lang, Dry Dock Company, Hoboken, New York. It was in this shipyard that a merchant ship was being converted into an escort carrier.

On arrival in the UK Charles made his way home and was warmly greeted by his wife Annie and their two sons. After giving his sons some chocolate, he handed a small parcel to their mother. When the parcel was opened Annie was delighted to see a beautiful Mother of Pearl shell with a crucifix carved inside the shell. The next time all the family met was when *Dasher* arrived in Liverpool. This was after the ship took part in the invasion of North Africa.

Whilst the ship was in dock, Charles took his eldest son Tony to Liverpool, where they boarded HMS *Dasher*. Tony was thrilled to be taken on a tour of the aircraft carrier. The family had a dog as a family pet known as Willy. When Charles arrived home on leave he was always met by a warm welcome from his family and Willy. When the dreaded telegram arrived the family were simply devastated.

Some years later Annie remarried and gave birth to a daughter, Eileen.

Lieutenant Fleetwood (Fleet) Price at a gun station on board HMS *Dasher* scanning the sky with high powered binoculars.

Lieutenant Fleetwood (Fleet) Price, age 42, was born on 20th January, 1901, in the family home at Haringey Road, Tottenham, London, the son of Charles Alfred and Eliza Jane Price. His elder brother had been killed in the First World War. On leaving school he joined the Navy as a Midshipman and was posted in July, 1918, to HMS *Knight Templar,* an armed merchant ship. He was next posted to HMS *Sunhill* for 2 years and was then demobilised in 1920. In the early 1930s he married Olive and they had two daughters, Monica and Thelma.

In 1940 he volunteered once again for Navy service and on 12th August, 1941, was posted as gunnery officer to HMS *Montclare,* an armed merchant cruiser on convoy duty. His service on this ship lasted until May 1942. During this time the ship travelled in convoys between Bermuda, Nova Scotia and Reykjavik.

In June 1942, he was posted as gunnery officer to *Dasher*. He and other officers travelled to Brooklyn Navy Yard to await the completion of *Dasher* being converted from a cargo ship to an escort carrier. On arrival in America the Royal Navy officers were allocated private rooms in the plush Barbizon Plaza Hotel, New York.

Fleetwood served on the ship for all its short service life. During his service as *Dasher's* gunnery officer he was known as "Guns." He and his gunnery crew saw action on many occasions, including the invasion of Oran. On one occasion when he was on home leave, he told his sister:

"Dasher bounced around like a pea in a drum."

His family, including his sister, Primrose, never ever knew the circumstances surrounding the demise of HMS *Dasher*. The only information the family received was there had been an onboard explosion. Although Fleetwood was buried in Greenock Cemetery, Scotland, the family were never informed of this. His two daughters came to visit Scotland, one from Canada, after reading John Steele's book, *The Tragedy of HMS Dasher*. The author told them where their father was buried.

A letter of condolence received by Fleetwood's widow.

THE CONCERT ARTISTES' ASSOCIATION

ESTABLISHED 1897.

lephones :
OFFICE - TEMple Bar 3172.
CLUB - .. .. 2884/5.
heques to be made payable to
he Concert Artistes' Association.

20, CRANBOURN STREET,
LONDON . . W.C.2.

*All Communications to the
Secretary.*

Our Ref: 14th April, 1943.
RSR/FMG.

Mrs. F. Price,
C/o Messrs. Spicers Ltd:
Union Street,
S.E.1.

Dear Mrs. Fleetwood Price,

I am sorry not to have written you before but we didn't want to assume that your husband had been killed until we were fairly certain. We heard that some accident had happened and that he had gone, but had no details until now when we have received a press cutting with his photograph which seems to indicate that the news is unfortunately true. We have put the press cutting on our Roll of Honour board as many members will like to read it.

On behalf of my Committee, will you please accept our very deepest sympathy in your tragic loss. It seems such a short time since we saw your husband here. He was a very popular member and had a great many friends who will feel his loss very keenly. We saw him so recently that it was a great shock to hear the news.

Once again our very deep sympathy.   Yours sincerely,

Rose Smith-Ross

Able Seaman William (Bill) John Harvey, age 27

Able Seaman William (Bill) John Harvey, age 27, was born on the 19th December, 1921, son of John and Ellen Maria Harvey. He was the youngest of four children, two sisters Harriot and Nellie and one brother Harry. The family moved to Bentley, Doncaster, when Bill was two years old, this was to allow his father to seek work at the nearby colliery.

Bill attended local schools in Bentley and on leaving he worked in a local firewood business and later became a lorry driver. He was 6 feet in height and enjoyed playing football. At the outbreak of WWII he was called up to serve in the Royal Navy and on completing his basic training he was selected to become an asdic operator on anti-submarine detection.

Bill travelled to New York to await the completion of HMS *Dasher*. On arrival he met up with some family friends and then enjoyed the American hospitality. On one occasion he was with a group of his shipmates in a New York nightclub. Unknown to them a famous film star was enjoying a meal in the same club. The film star was James Cagney and when he saw the Royal Navy sailors entering the club, he sent a round of drinks over to their table.

When *Dasher* was completed Bill and his ship mates joined the ship to return to the UK. He was on home leave during December 1942 and his mother wanted to buy him a really good watch for his forthcoming 21st birthday. She had been saving a little money each week to pay for it. When Bill heard of her plans, he said he did not want a watch as it would be a waste of money because it would go down with him if anything hit *Dasher*. He maintained if with the condition of the ship, they simply would not stand a chance. (This was a belief shared by many of his shipmates.) Bill suggested that his mother give him some money to have a good time, but she was reluctant to do so.

Prior to returning to his ship he was going out with some of his mates. On this occasion his mother gave him some money to have a really good time. A decision she was never to regret.

After *Dasher* exploded and sank, his mother received a telegram saying that he was missing. She was devastated and refused to believe her son was dead. She wrote several times to find out what had happened but to no avail. This led her to believe there were no survivors, but that somehow her son was alive.

About 7 years later Bill's mother and her granddaughter Joan were on the way to the local cemetery when they passed a down-and-out looking man seated on a park bench with his head in his hands. Bill's mother asked the man if he was alright then gave him some money for a cup of tea. She then told the man that she had lost a son on HMS *Dasher* and that there were no survivors.

The man replied that he knew the ship and that there were survivors because he was one of them. He then said that there would have been more survivors but the sea had caught fire. He also said that as far as he knew, Bill did not get off the ship.

Bill's mother was so upset she told the man that he was lying. In tears she turned and walked away from the man. Unfortunately no further contact was made with the stranger.

George Benjamin Bowles, age 22

George Benjamin Bowles, age 22, was the son of Benjamin George Bowles and Beatrice Mabel Bowles, Poplar, London. George was born in East London and lived with his widowed mother, three brothers and three sisters. He left school and was employed at the Post Office as a messenger boy. He then moved on to a firm of cabinet makers in the City of London to learn the art of French polishing.

When war was declared the business closed and George commenced employment in the building trade helping to repair war damaged properties. He was a member of the Territorial Army and he was called-up for active service. At his medical he was declared unfit for the army. However, George was then encouraged to join the Auxiliary Fleet by two of his friends who were already in the service. He applied and was accepted. After initial training he joined HMS *Dasher*.

He was due on home leave when his mother received the telegram stating that he was missing presumed killed in an explosion. George's mother died at the age of 86, never knowing what happened to her eldest son.

Victor Leslie Webb, Canteen Assistant, age 22

Victor Leslie Webb, Canteen Assistant, age 22, was born on 10th March, 1921. He was a Leading Canteen Assistant with the Navy, Army and Airforce Institute (NAAFI). This organisation manages cafes, shops and bars on most British military bases and onboard Royal Navy ships. NAAFI personnel on Royal Navy ships are part of the Naval Canteen Service. They wear naval uniforms but remain civilians.

During war-time, although they were civilians, they were trained to take an active part when the enemy were engaged. Victor was one of 5 brothers actively involved in war service. Sadly, for 49 years, Victors name and the name of 2 other NAAFI personnel were not included in the list of *Dasher* casualties. However on the 2nd October, 1992, Mr JD Brown, Head of the Naval Historical Branch, recorded that all previous statements from the Ministry of Defence overlooked other casualties and the list should read:

"*346 Royal Navy personnel; 27 Merchant Navy Personnel (MNP);*
3 NAAFI personnel and 3 RAF personnel."

Able Seaman Frederick Arthur Morgan, age 26

Able Seaman Frederick Arthur Morgan, age 26, was born in 1917, son of Frederick and Isabella Morgan. The family home was at the pit village of Easington Lane, County Durham. Frederick had two sisters and four brothers, Elizabeth, Caroline, John, Robert, Harold and Donald.

His father worked at Elemore Colliery. Times were hard when his father died in 1923, but there was always roast in the oven and plenty of vegetables from the garden. There was no shortage of bread, as Frederick's mother always baked bread for her family. She also took in laundry and made all her children's clothes.

Frederick had a spaniel dog called 'Chocolate.' One evening a burglar tried to break into the family home and the dog set about the burglar who took to his heels. The house was never again bothered by intruders.

On joining the Royal Navy Frederick took up boxing and was selected for the Royal Navy boxing team. He served on the cruiser HMS *Achilles*, during the historic Battle of the River Plate, the first major sea battle in WWII. HMS *Achilles*, *Exeter* and *Ajax* engaged in a horrendous gun battle against the mighty German heavy cruiser *Admiral Graf Spee*. In the gun battle HMS *Exeter* was badly damaged and had to withdraw. The German heavy cruiser also withdrew and sailed for the sanctuary of neutral Montevideo.

In Berlin Hitler was concerned that his prize battle ship might have to surrender to HMS *Achilles* and *Ajax*. Rather than face this prospect, Hitler ordered the Captain to take the ship out to sea and scuttle it. The sinking of the dreaded German battle ship was a tremendous victory for the Royal Navy and in particular for the crew of the HMS *Achilles* and *Ajax*.

Over the years the family have been very proud of Frederick. His name is engraved on the Chatham Naval Memorial, Kent and on the village clock tower in Easington Lane.

Able Seaman Thomas Scanlon. Age 27. C/JX 237014

Able Seaman Thomas Scanlon was the son of Edmond and Catherine Scanlon. Thomas was born in Tralee, Waterford City, Ireland. He married Mary, of Woking Surrey, and they had one child Catherine. When Thomas was a young boy, it was recognised that he could turn his hand to almost anything. Prior to joining the navy he was employed by the railway maintaining the tracks. He was initially based at Chatham Naval Barracks then he joined HMS *Dasher*.

On his last leave his daughter Catherine was only 3 years old. Just before returning to his ship he told his wife Mary:

"If I don't come back look after Catherine."

This was something he had never said before. His niece Mary thought he had said this because he knew *Dasher* was in such a bad state and in need of repair. Thomas's name is engraved on the Naval Memorial at Chatham, Kent

Able Seaman Alfred John Comber age 39

Able Seaman Alfred John Comber, age 39, was born 28th August, 1903, the Son of William Arthur Comber and Eleanor Comber. As a boy Alfred joined the Royal Navy and served on numerous ships including *Iron Duke*, *Coventry* and *Orion*. After attending many courses he joined HMS *Furious* then HMS *Wishart*, *Courageous* and *Acheron*.

Whilst home on leave from HMS *Furious* he married Cissie Bourne at St Andrews Church, Paddock Wood, Kent. They had one son, Keith.

In 1942 Alfred joined 816 Squadron at HMS *Daedalus,* a Fleet Air Arm shore base at Lee-on-Solent. The squadron then joined the aircraft carrier HMS *Ark Royal.*

On the 13th November 1941 Alfred was onboard the mighty *Ark Royal* with 816 Squadron, in the Mediterranean, when it was torpedoed by the German U boat U-81. The *Ark Royal* was so badly damaged it had to be taken in tow. 13 hours after being torpedoed *Ark Royal* capsized and sank.

In February 1943 Alfred was with 816 Squadron when they were attached to the ill fated *Dasher*. All squadron personnel worked in the hangar and their sleeping quarters were adjacent to the hangar. On 27th March, 1943, only seven members of 816 Squadron survived the disaster. This terrible catastrophe resulted in the squadron being disbanded.

Alfred John Comber, service number P/J 94507, was known as a very jolly man who served his King and Country for more than 23 years. He lost all his personal belongings including his precious photographs at the sinking of *Ark Royal*. This was repeated when HMS *Dasher* sank.

Alfred's name is engraved on panel 74, column 1, at Portsmouth Naval Memorial. Hampshire.

Able Seaman James Robson C/JX 314025, age 21

Able Seaman James Robson, age 21, the son of John and Sarah Robson, of Cowper Street, Manchester, had 3 brothers and 2 sisters; William, Jack, Arthur, Edna and Bertha. They all attended Christchurch School.

James's father was a coal merchant. He fetched coal from Bradford Colliery for his delivery run. James was very close to his mother, father, brothers and sisters. His younger sister, Edna, died from pneumonia, age 21. James was very keen on photography and motorcycles. He particularly enjoyed the TT races on the Isle of Man His name is engraved on Chatham Naval Memorial, Kent. Bay 69. Panel 3

Howard Willis Air Mechanic 2nd class

Howard Willis, Air Mechanic 2nd class, son of John and Hilda Mary. His parents had a fish hook factory in Redditch. When Howard was 16 years of age he wanted to join the Royal Navy, but his parents steadfastly refused to sign the papers. He was employed in the office at Dixons, who were Coal and Wood Merchants. As soon as he was 18 years of age he joined the Royal Navy and was trained as an Air Mechanic. On completion of his training he was attached to the Fleet Air Arm. Remembered with Honour at Lee-on-Solent Memorial, Hampshire

Hugh MacAulay, Ordinary Seaman, C/JX.316449.

Hugh MacAulay, Ordinary Seaman, was born on 26th January, 1923, in Kirkibost House, on the island of Kirkibost. North Uist, Scotland. His parents were Norman and Ann MacAulay. His father died 4 months after the *Dasher* disaster. Hugh, known as Hughie, attended the local school Claddach, Kirkibost Primary on North Uist. On reaching age for secondary school he attended Inverness Royal Academy. Inverness was a long distance from Hugh's home on the little island of Kirkibost, North Uist.

As a teenager Hugh caught the girls' eye as he was very handsome. He excelled in sports and won a cup for best runner in a school competition.

During his last leave, 3 days before he was killed, Hugh visited his cousin Margaret at Shawlands Glasgow. That day Margaret was having her chimney swept and in preparation for this she had removed her ornaments and curtains. On the departure of the chimney sweep, Hugh hung the curtains and helped to get the house back into order.

On being home on his last visit Hugh attended a dance which was held in nearby Lochmaddy. When the sad news reached home, understandably parents, relatives and friends were devastated. His Uncle Roderick was like a an older brother to him and for the next 12 months he searched the local beach as he was of the belief that Hugh would return home by being washed onto the beach.

Hugh's friends placed a small plaque beside his parent's grave in nearby Kilmuir Cemetery.

Sub-lieutenant Newton Lee Ponting Monks

Sub-lieutenant Newton Lee Ponting Monks, age 36, was the eldest son of Son of Casswell and Florence. He married Phyllis and they settled in Slough, Buckinghamshire. He was educated at Bristol Grammar School and in 1927 joined the staff of Naylor Brothers Ltd. Two years later he obtained a position in the cash office at Horlicks. Newton was an outstanding hockey player and a valued officer in the Boys Brigade.

He was an accomplished musician and enjoyed playing the piano at the Sunday morning services. His close friends described him as a kind friend whose life was directed by high ideals in which faith, loyalty and honest endeavour were the principle forces. He was always pleasant company.

He was a member of the Royal Navy Volunteer Reserve and on departing to join *Dasher,* said:

"I am looking forward to this very much."

Whilst serving on *Dasher*, Newton wrote to his wife every day and always ordered roses for her birthday. Shortly before the dreadful explosion, Newton had ordered roses to be delivered to Phyllis.

When *Dasher* was in the throes of sinking, Newton managed to jump into the water. Luckily he swam over to a carley raft and was helped out of the water. When Newton saw a man struggling towards the carley raft, he hauled the man to safety out of the water. The man was John Mawhinney from Belfast.

He saw a small coastal vessel (either the *Cragsman* or the *Lithium*) about 100 yards away picking up survivors from the water.

Suddenly large flames skimmed over the water towards the carley raft. As the flames drew closer the majority of those in the carley raft, including Newton and John Mawhinney decided to attempt to swim to the coastal rescue vessel. John was hauled onboard the rescue vessel but unfortunately Newton was never seen again.

On the 28th March, the day before her birthday, Phyllis was notified that Newton was missing. The following day the roses from Newton arrived.

Newton's name is engraved on the Liverpool Naval Memorial. Panel 3. Column 2.

The ship was gone, the men were lost, and silence was ordered from high command. The great loss of life was to be covered up. But it seems compensation must be paid for the loss of wine and tobacco which went down with *Dasher*. The wine and spirit merchants had obviously been informed of the loss of the ship, unlike the mothers, who lost their husbands and the children their fathers.

Wine & Spirit Merchants & Shippers
Piccadilly
London

27th April 1943

Commander E.W.E. Lane
Admiralty
London SW1

Dear Sir,
We are advised by our Glasgow Branch for insurance purposes, that the ship
on which you have been serving has been lost. We gather there is some
doubt as to whether this was due to enemy action, and we propose to claim
the value of the goods on board in the usual manner. The total loss, according
to Glasgow books, was as follows;

Wine Account	£570 3 2
Mess Account	£59 13 6
Tobacco Account	£386 14 7
	£1,016 11 3

We shall be gratefully obliged if you will kindly arrange for any cash which
may be due to us for goods consumed to be remitted to us, as our claim will
naturally be affected by any such sums.

We understand from our Liverpool branch that Commander Thomas
suggested we should write to you in this connection, and we shall be grateful
for any assistance you may be able to give us in the matter.

Yours faithfully,

E. Williamson

Top: Liverpool February, 1943. Wrens accept an invitation to board Dasher. Happy
crewman with 12 Wrens. The crewman has his guitar on top of the wardrobe.
Bottom: A member of the Fleet Air Arm who managed to survive the catastrophe
found himself onboard a Royal Navy rescue ship. He was given some dry clothes and
when his own clothes were returned to him he found the keys to Dasher's Air Office.
Each key is stamped with the words – The Yale & Town Manufacturing Company New
Jersey. Remarkably almost 70 years later the survivor still has the keys!

Chapter 13

The Most Fiendish Plot Ever Conceived (Operation Mincemeat)

October 1942

After the successful invasion of North Africa in which HMS *Dasher* took part it became imperative that the allied forces should penetrate into Europe. The island of Sicily, being the closest part of Europe to North Africa, was the obvious choice.

Churchill himself famously remarked,

> *"Everyone but a bloody fool knows the next invasion will take place on Sicily"*

When the German Military Intelligence Service advised Adolph Hitler that the next invasion would be Sicily he ordered that the island was to be heavily fortified. More U-boats were re-positioned and additional fast torpedo boats were added to the fleet already there. Even though the number of enemy troops already on the island exceeded 100,000, more troops were landed to repel the invasion force. This fortification of Sicily would result in heavy losses of allied troops.

When Churchill asked of his advisers, *"What will our losses be at Sicily?"* the answer he received was 40,000! Churchill's response was to write a brief memo:

> *"Reduce the number of casualties at Sicily!"*

This memo was included in the minutes at the next meeting of *"The Twenty Committee"* a secret Military Intelligence inter-service team whose sole purpose was to hoax the enemy with false information. At that meeting they discussed ways of deceiving the enemy into deploying their troops away from Sicily thus leaving the island vulnerable to allied invasion.

Flight Lieutenant Charles Cholmondeley brought before the committee, the rudiments of a plan that his fellow committee members considered bizarre. He suggested planting false invasion documents on a dead body and letting it fall into German hands. He added ominously,

> *"Why shouldn't we get a body, disguise it as a staff officer, and give him really high level papers which will clearly show that we are*

going to attack somewhere other than Sicily. We could drop the body from an aircraft where it would float ashore. If we were to choose France or Spain the Germans wouldn't have much chance to examine the body."

The Twenty Committee was initially sceptical of the outlandish plan, but the more it was discussed, the more it seemed feasible. Lieutenant Commander Ewen Montagu, a brilliant barrister, took the lead in working out the details of the elaborate plan to hoodwink the Germans, deceiving them into believing the allies intended to invade Sardinia, Crete, Corsica and the Peleponnese, a large region in southern Greece.

Montagu's plan also included bogus information to the effect that a diversion invasion would take place on Sicily. He also intended to plant letters from the Vice Chief of the Imperial General Staff, General Sir Archibald Nye to General H.R.L.G. Alexander. Later Montague drafted out two more letters. One was to be signed by the Chief of Combined Operations Lord Mountbatten addressed to Sir A. B. Cunningham. Admiral of the Fleet, (Known as ABC).

Part of this letter included the following:

"Let me have him back please as soon as the assault is over. He might bring some sardines with him as they are 'on points' here."

The mention of sardines was included by Montagu in the hope German Intelligence would accept the sentence was referring to an invasion on Sardinia.

The 3rd letter was to be from Lord Louis Mountbatten, addressed to General Dwight Eisenhower. These letters would contain false information relating to the false invasion plans. The letters also included reference to a *"diversionary attack"* on Sicily.

For this plan to succeed one element was absolutely crucial. A body was required. How do we get one? At first it was thought that it would be an easy matter to obtain a body, after all the country was at war. A telephone call made to the Recorder of War Casualties received the reply:

"It had been a slack month; only 523 casualties had been recorded for the month of November 1942."

Montagu decided rather than go through official channels he would make a discreet approach to the coroner Mr Bentley Purchase, requesting he locate a suitable body, which had to be undamaged. The committee's confidence in Bentley Purchase was quickly rewarded. He located the body of an alcoholic tramp, a down and out with mental health problems and had died after drinking rat poison.

To confirm beyond doubt that the body was suitable, advice was sought from Sir Bernard Spilsbury, an eminent forensic pathologist. After receiving confirmation from Sir Bernard the body was put into cold storage in Hackney Mortuary London. At a Twenty Committee meeting held the following month

<u>Twenty Committee</u>

(215.)

THE HUNDRED & SECOND MEETING OF THIS COMMITTEE
WAS HELD AT 58, ST. JAMES'S STREET, S.W.1,
ON THURSDAY, 17th DECEMBER, 1942, AT 14.30 HOURS

Present:

Major J.C. Masterman	M.I.5 (Chairman).
Colonel S.D. Graham, M.C.	M.I.11.
Lieut. Colonel B.E.S. Mountain	G.H.Q., Home Forces.
Group Captain P.L. Plant	D.D.I.(S).
Lieut. Commander E.E.S. Montagu, R.N.V.R.	N.I.D.
Wing Commander C. Byron	A.I.S.(4).
Lieut. Colonel J.F. Cowgill, O.B.E.	M.I.6.
Major I.B. Greig, M.C.	G.H.Q., Home Forces.
Major E. Goudie	M.I.11.
Lieutenant Peer-Groves, R.N.V.R.	N.I.D.
Flight Lieut. C.C. Cholmondeley	A.I.S.(4).
Major T.A. Robertson	M.I.5.
Mr. J.H. Marriott	M.I.5 (Secretary).

1.   The Minutes were read and passed.

2.   <u>Arising out of the Minutes</u>.

   a) Commander Montagu reported that he had again seen
Mr. Bentley Purchase and that the latter had made arrangements
for getting hold of a suitable corpse, and for securing that
its disposal should be suitably accounted for. The latter
object would be achieved by Mr. Bentley Purchase issuing a
certificate that the corpse was to be buried outside the
country. It was <u>agreed</u> that no decision could be taken as
to the service to which the corpse should be supposed to
belong until M.I.5 had ascertained the position with regard
to whether officers travelling abroad carried their service
identity cards.

It was essential the plan had a code name. One name appealed to Montagu's sense of humour and that was the one he chose. The name *was 'Operation Mincemeat.'* Now that *'Operation Mincemeat'* was official, a plan of action had to be worked out in minute detail.

First, a new identity had to be created for the body, now held in cold storage. It was agreed by the Twenty Committee to invent *"Major William Martin, an officer in the Royal Marines."* He would be the courier who would "drown" while carrying Top Secret documents.

During the following months the Twenty Committee met on a very regular basis. All the details had to be worked out in meticulous fashion. Nothing could be left to chance. Thousands of lives were at stake. One flaw in the deceit would jeopardise the whole operation.

Initially the committee discussed dropping Major Martin into the sea from an aircraft. This suggestion was discounted as the body could be damaged on hitting the water. A damaged body might appear to be inconsistent with drowning. It was important that the body should be someone who had drowned. A Royal Navy submarine was the answer; it could surface undetected close to land. Major Martin could then be lowered from the open deck of the submarine into the water. If the tide and wind were calculated correctly he would be washed ashore at a selected area. When found it would appear to be an accidental drowning.

The next question discussed was to where should Major Martin be washed ashore? After a great deal of deliberation it was decided the best chance of success was Huelva in Southern Spain. It was well known in British Intelligence that a German spy was very active in Huelva. His name was Adolph Clauss. When the tide and current floated Major Martin towards land, it was hoped he would be "found" by local Spaniards, who would then hand him over to the Huelva town officials. When the story of the body reached the ears of the active German spy, he would be sure to play his part by procuring the briefcase and copying the contents. The copied documents would hopefully then be forwarded to Berlin.

If the documents were believed to be 100% authentic by Germany's Military Intelligence, they would believe that they had come into possession of a top secret military tactical plan, and hopefully order the relocation of thousands of troops and heavy armoured divisions, away from Sicily. It was also hoped that U-boats and torpedo boats would also be deployed to the Greek Islands.

Now that Ewen Montague, the mastermind of *"Operation Mincemeat,"* had everything in place, including a body, he had to approach the Chiefs of Staff for their approval. If granted, the Prime Minister then had to be approached for final consent.

On the 14th April, 1943, a memo classified as "Most Secret" was forwarded to Winston Churchill. It contained a request for an appointment.

OFFICE OF THE MINISTER OF DEFENCE

PRIME MINISTER

The Chiefs of Staff have approved, subject to
your consent, a somewhat startling cover plan in
connection with HUSKY.

2.	May the Controlling Officer (Colonel Bevan)
and I see you for five minutes, within the next day
or two, to explain what is proposed and take your
orders.

14th April, 1943.

The Prime Minister was impressed with the plan and had no hesitation in signing his approval. 'Operation Mincemeat' swung into action with the removal of the body from cold storage, to be suitably dressed as a Royal Marine officer. After being fully clothed a Mae-West life jacket was then fitted securely.

Around his neck was placed a silver crucifix on a silver chain. An identity disc was attached to his braces; the disc was engraved with the wording Major W. Martin, R.M. R/C. (RM signified Royal Marine. RC denoted Roman Catholic.) It was imperative Major Martin must be, or assumed to be a Roman Catholic as it was unlikely the Spanish pathologist would carry out a proper post mortem on a Roman Catholic. Hopefully only a medical examination would take place before burial.

In his possession were placed everything a man would normally carry such as loose change, a small bunch of keys, a box of matches, cigarettes and "letters" from his "Father" and his solicitor. To fabricate Major Martin's private life, an Admiralty secretary was instructed to write two very personal letters to him, as his fiancée. The final touch was a letter from Lloyds Bank, 731 Lombard Street, London, urging prompt payment regarding a £79 overdraft. In his wallet were personal papers identifying the body as 36 year old Major William Martin with military service number 148228, also a bill from the Navy and Military Club.

A locked diplomatic bag was chained to Major Martin's wrist, in the bag were the Top Secret documents indicating the invasion would take place on Sardinia and Greek islands, not Sicily. Also placed in the briefcase were the all important letters. The body was then placed in a tubular airtight container and packed with dry ice. Major Martin was ready to play his part in the biggest wartime deception ever known.

On April 17th 1943 the container was loaded onto an unmarked van to begin the long overnight journey from London to Greenock in Scotland. From there the canister was ferried a short distance across the Clyde to the Holy Loch where the HMS *Seraph*, a Royal Navy submarine, was waiting. The officer in command was Lieutenant L.N.A Jewell who, only two weeks previously, had been awarded the MBE for his successful involvement in many covert submarine operations.

At 5pm on 19th April Major Martin was taken onboard the Royal Navy submarine. One hour later the *Seraph* slipped her moorings and departed from the Holy Loch to begin her eleven day voyage to southern Spain.

As it was imperative that the British Consul and Vice Consul in Gibraltar and southern Spain were aware of the forthcoming operation, Montague sent a "Most Secret" message to the DSO in Gibraltar alerting him of *"Operation Mincemeat."* On receiving the message the DSO advised the British Consuls and Vice-Consuls.

On April 30th 1943, after an uneventful journey, the *Seraph* arrived offshore from Huelva. At periscope depth the officer in command, Lieutenant "Bill" Jewell, kept watch as the local fishermen loaded their nets into their small boats and set off for their usual fishing grounds.

When all was clear the submarine surfaced silently a mile offshore. The local time was 4 30am. Lieutenant "Bill" Jewell and three of his officers made their way to the open deck of the *Seraph*. The Lieutenant then explained the operation to his officers, after which the metal container was brought up through the deck hatch. After opening the container Major Martin was laid on the deck whilst Lieutenant Jewell said a few words of prayer.

After checking the briefcase was securely attached to the corpse and his Mae-West life jacket was inflated Major Martin was placed in the water and slowly started to drift inshore, aided by the swirl from the propellers of the submarine.

MOST SECRET

COPY   telegram to D.S.O. Gibraltar.

References: P.63/B.1.A   Date: 22.4.43

IMPORTANT

Following for K.G. to be deciphered by Spencer only:

1. In order deceive enemy following operation known as MINCEMEAT repeat MINCEMEAT has been mounted.

2. Dead body purporting to be Major W. MARTIN Royal Marines who does not in fact exist has been despatched by submarine which left Glasgow 20th April.

3. Body will be dropped overboard in position where it will be washed ashore about 28th April off HUELVA giving appearance of accidental death through crashed aircraft which also does not exist.

4. Body carrying important papers apparently compromising future operations in Mediterranean which it is hoped will fall into hands of Spaniards and consequently enemy.

5. Gomez BEARE has arranged matters with Consuls concerned. If body handed to Consul Gomez BEARE will be notified and matter will be dealt with satisfactorily.

6. Possibly Probably Spanish authorities will communicate with Gibraltar and send body there for burial.

7. Discuss with Governor and Codrington with view to action in Gibraltar as though this were a normal accident to aircraft. No repeat no message should be sent to anyone in England except by S.O.I. Gibraltar to D.N.I. personal or as in paras 8 and 9. Such action may include enquiries of Spanish authorities as to possibility of further survivors. No repeat no enquiries to be made regarding documents which may be missing. Press publicit must be stopped. Body should be buried anonymously if this will not raise comment.

The four officers then left the container open and pushed it overboard expecting it to sink. Unfortunately it remained afloat. They tried to push it under the water in an attempt to sink it but each time it bobbed back to the surface. There was nothing for it but to bring it back onboard. After safely securing it, the *Seraph* made its way further offshore. Once the submarine was well clear of land, the empty container was again pushed over the side. On showing no sign of submerging it was riddled with bullets from the Vickers gun. Mission accomplished, the submarine proceeded unnoticed to Gibraltar. En route, Bill Jewell dispatched a "Most Secret" message to the Naval Intelligence Department in London. It read:

From The Commanding Officer, H.M. Submarine "SERAPH".

Date: 30th April, 1943.

To Director of Naval Intelligence.

Copy to F.O.S.

(for Lt. Cdr. The Hon. E.E.S. Montagu,R.N.V.R.) personal.

OPERATION MINCEMEAT

Weather: The wind was variable altering between SW and SS. force 2.
It was expected that the sea breeze would spring up in the
morning, close inshore, as it had on the previous morning
in similar conditions.
Sea and swell - 2.0. - Sky overcast with very low clouds -
visibility was patchy, 1 to 2 miles - Barometer 1016.

2.**Fishing boats:** A large number of small fishing boats were working in
the bay. The closest was left, about a mile off,
and it is not thought that the submarine was observed
by them.

3.**Operation:** The time of 0430 was chosen as being the nearest to Low Water
Lisbon, (0731) which would allow the submarine to be well
clear by dawn. The Cannister was opened at 0415 and the body
extracted. The blanket was opened up and the body examined. The
brief case was found to be securely attached. The face was heavily
tanned and the whole of the lower half from the eyes down covered
with mould. The skin had started to break away on the nose and
cheek bones. The body was very high. The Mae West was blown up
very hard and no further air was needed. The body was placed in
the water at 0430 in a position 148° Portil Pillar 1.3 miles
approximately eight cables from the beach and started to drift
inshore. This was aided by the wash of the screws going full
speed astern. The rubber dinghy was placed in the water blown
up and upside down about half a mile further south of this
position. The submarine then withdrew to seaward and the
cannister, filled with water, and containing the blanket, tapes
and also the rubber dinghy's container was pushed over the side in
position 36°37'30 North 07°18'00 West in 310 fathoms of water by
sounding machine. The container would not at first submerge but
after being riddled by fire from Vickers gun and also .455 revolver
at very short range was seen to sink.
Signal reporting operation complete was passed at 0715.
A sample of the water close inshore is attached.

N. L. A. JEWELL.

Lieutenant-in-Command.

130

As the submarine continued on its voyage to Gibraltar, lone fisherman Jose Antonio Rey Maria was fishing close to Punta Beach Huelva. At 9.30am he spotted the body in the water and called out to some other fishermen to come and help him retrieve it. The other fishermen refused to assist with the body and left it to Jose to struggle and pull the heavy body half on to the stern of his small boat before slowly making his way to the beach.

At that time the local fishermen lived on the beach with their families in rows of little wooden shacks. As news of the drowned British officer spread the children and people came running to see. One local man, Antonio El Rafeno, remembers that he was 11 years old and saw the body lying on the sand. He recalls how one side of the man's face was black, as if burned. He also recalls looking with envy at the very expensive watch on the officer's wrist.

When news of the body reached the harbour authorities a Naval officer arrived on the scene. After taking charge of the briefcase, he authorised that the body be placed on a donkey and taken further along the beach where it could be transported by a canoa (small ferry) to Huelva and from there, to the local cemetery.

At the beach the Naval officer departed with the briefcase and made his way to the office of Judge Pascual de Pobil. After taking charge of the briefcase, the judge visited the British Embassy where he had an appointment with F.K. Haselden MBE, the British Vice Consul in Huelva. The purpose of the visit was to hand over the briefcase to the Vice Consul.

The British Vice Consul, however, had been advised of *"Operation Mincemeat"* and knew he could not accept the briefcase as it would put the operation in jeopardy. On arrival at the embassy the judge was told by the British Vice Consul that the proper procedure was to hand the briefcase over to the Spanish authorities. When it was handed over, the "neutral" Spanish officials immediately summoned the German spy, Adolph Clauss. On arrival he supervised the sealed envelopes being dried. They were then very carefully opened and the contents copied.

Meantime a post mortem was carried out by Spanish pathologist Eduardo Del Torno at Huelva Mortuary, adjacent to the cemetery. On completion the pathologist certified:

> *"The man had fallen into the sea whilst still alive and had no bruises, death was due to drowning. This body has been in the sea between 3 and 5 days."*

The next day a funeral service was held for Major Martin in Huelva Cemetery. When the Admiralty in London received the official report that Major Martin had "drowned" and been buried, Montagu sent a signal marked "Secret" to the British embassy in Madrid. It was marked for the attention of the Naval Attache.

The signal read as shown overleaf from the official record:

SPECIAL ROUTE.

Cypher or Confidential Code or
Non Confidential Code or Plain Language   } Delete as necessary.

My 181213. Bag arrived.

2.   Suggest unless unusual that a medium priced tombstone should

be erected on grave with inscription such as quote William Martin,

born 29th March 1907 died 24 repetition 24 April 1943 beloved son

of John Glyndwyr repetition Glyndwyr Martin and the late Antonia

Martin of Cardiff, Wales. Dulce et decorum est pro patria mori. R.I.P.

end quote. Order for this tombstone should be given at once.

3.   If currency restrictions would not make it unusual suggest

Consul places wreath now with card marked quote From Father and Pam

repetition Pam end quote.

211630 B   N.I.D.12.

D.N.I. only.   Ext. 193.

                        Approved D.D.N.I.

PASS BY HAND

132

So far all had gone according to plan. Major Martin had carried out his mission and was now buried far from home in a Spanish cemetery. In London the Twenty Committee could only wait anxiously to see if Hitler's military intelligence had fallen for the deceit. But on the instructions of German Military Intelligence, Major Martin's body was removed from the grave. The covert operation was carried out by German commandos in the early hours of the 4th day after burial. This was to allow a highly qualified German pathologist to carry out another post mortem. The German pathologist recorded:

"Death was by drowning and the body had been in the water between 5 and 8 days."

British agents in the area quickly found out about the clandestine operation and immediately advised Naval intelligence in London. Montagu wrote to Colonel Bevan, Controller of Deception, advising him that the body would have been, even within 3 or 4 days of interment, in a highly decomposed condition

On 10th May, 1943, a Spanish government official who had received a copy of the plans was the Spanish Foreign Minister, Count Jordana. He regarded the information as absolutely reliable and that the main attack would be against Corsica. He was so confident, he contacted the German Ambassador in Spain, Hans-Heinrich Dieckhoff, advising him that the invasion plans contained in the briefcase were "absolutely reliable."

After carefully studying all the documents, Dieckoff forwarded them to German Military Intelligence, Berlin. During the next nineteen days German Military Intelligence in Berlin received nineteen top secret signals, many of them involving Spanish government ministers. One signal from the Spanish Navy Minister, Moreno Fernandez, reported:

"Forthcoming allied action in south east Europe."

Two days later the Spanish Foreign Minister, Count Jordana, advised the German ambassador:

"Main attacks will be against Crete and the Peleponnese."

The Spanish waited until 15th May before they delivered the briefcase and content's intact to the British Vice Consul. On the same day the German Ambassador in Rome signalled Berlin, that he had received information from Mr Paolucci, the Italian Ambassador. The signal read:

"Based on absolutely trustworthy source, enemy landing in Greece is intended in the next few days."

German Military Intelligence meticulously recorded every signal they received regarding what they termed Engl. Kurierfund (English courier found). They also recorded who had been given access to the documents, including two Spanish government officials.

9 May:
[PG]

Signal from Abwehr I [Nr.2282/43] to WFSt passing on report from K.O. Spanien re letter to Alexander of 23 April found on the Kurier. Contents briefly described. Copies of the original to follow. (one page).

9 May:
[M.I.14]

Fremde Heere West appreciation [Nr.874/43] of the letter to Alexander. On balance thought to be genuine, not a plant. (four pages and map of Greece).

10 May:
[A.A.]

Brief sequel from Dieckhoff [Nr.2722] German Ambassador in Madrid, reporting usually reliable Spanish sources to the effect that an Anglo-American attack on Sardinia and Corsica must be expected.

12 May:
[A.A.]

From Dieckhoff to RAM (Ribbentrop) [Nr.2776] giving gist of the Alexander letter 'from absolutely reliable source'.

12 May:
[A.A.]

From Dieckhoff to RAM [Nr. 2777] referring to previous signal which is confirmed by confidential information from Jordana [Spanish Foreign Minister], which he regards as absolutely reliable. Main attacks against Crete and Peloponnese.

12 May:
[PG/M.I.14]

Further F.H.W. Report [Nr.27/43] after examination of the original of the letter. Contents described. (one page). [This signal was sent to Op.Abt. PG/32215 contains the same text sent to Seekriegsleitung. Both are in this

19 May:
[A.A.]

From Dieckhoff to RAM [Nr. 2922] reporting conversations with Moreno Fernandez and Jordana (Spanish Navy and Foreign Ministers) emphasising forthcoming Allied action in S.E. Europe.

19 May:
[A.A.]

Continuation of immediately preceding [no number] ref large convoy movement eastwards through Gibraltar Straits. Large scale undertaking in the Med expected shortly by the Spaniards.

20 May:
[A.A.]

From German Ambassador in Rome [Nr. 2365] to RAM reporting information from Italian Ambassador in Madrid (Paolucci), based on absolutely trustworthy source, that enemy landing in Greece is intended in the next few days.

26 May:
[A.A.]

Dieckhoff [Nr. 3066] transmits report from Consul General, Barcelona based on local British opinion. Attacks on Crete, Dodecanese and other Aegean islands: landings in South Italy, Sicily, and Sardinia provisionally suspended.

18 June:
[A.A.]

Dieckhoff [Nr. 3613] trustworthy report that Spanish General Staff have been informed that large U.S. attack probably against Sicily, is imminent from N.Africa.

24 June:
[A.A./RSHA]

From Schellenberg to Wagner [RSHA-HA VI Nr. 62/43], reporting from very trustworthy Spanish source, passage of very large convoy through the Straits. Franco anxious ref German preparations in southern France as in his view not only Sardinia and Corsica are threatened in western Med in the next few days.

Having carried out a comprehensive investigation and studied the top secret signals, German Military Intelligence issued a report stating:

"The authenticity of the captured documents is beyond doubt."

German High Command was also 100% convinced the documents were authentic. When their report reached Hitler, he accepted the documents as genuine and played his part perfectly. On 12th May, 1943, he issued an order summarising his estimate of the situation in the Mediterranean. The order concluded:

"Measures regarding Sardinia and the Peleponnese take precedence over everything else!"

The "measures" taken were what the Twenty Committee in London had been waiting for. They received reports that thousands of German troops including Panzer tank divisions, heavy artillery, Schnellboot Squadrons (torpedo boat units), U-boats and Luftwaffe aircraft were all being deployed away from Sicily to Sardinia, the Peleponnese, Crete and Corsica. German mine fields were also laid around the Greek islands.

Sardinia's defence was further increased by a battery of 10 centimetre guns, two batteries of 17 centimetre guns, one anti-tank company and 40 more tanks! The large area in southern Greece, known as the Peleponnese had been heavily reinforced as well as the islands of Sardinia, Crete, and Corsica. Thousands of enemy troops were now waiting for an invasion that, at that time, was not going to happen.

The Invasion of Sicily

On the evening of 9th July, 1943, an allied armada in excess of 2,000 vessels launched one of the largest combined operations of World War II, the invasion of Sicily. During the first 24 hours 150,000 troops landed on eight different beaches. Each landing site had a code name: *Joss, Dime, Cent, Bark West, Bark East, Bark South, Acid North and Acid South.*

The 51st Highland Division comprising of the Seaforth Highlanders, Cameron Highlanders, the Argyll and Sutherland Highlanders and the Black Watch, landed on the beachhead without a shot being fired. On a nearby beach, after a short gun battle, hundreds of the enemy troops surrendered to a Canadian regiment.

On landing at another invasion zone one of the allied soldiers spotted a lone enemy standing prominently on the horizon. On taking aim he fired several rounds of ammunition at the figure. After more rounds were fired and with still no movement from the figure, a 'platoon' then made their way up to "Take him out!" Much to the platoon's surprise, the lone figure was in fact a statue!

When the 154th Brigade made their landing, the enemy surrendered almost immediately. Similar reports were made with other landings.

The ruse devised by the Twenty Committee proved to be a resounding success. The first day of the assault however was marred when 31 gliders carrying troops to the war zone were released too early by their towing aircraft. Instead of landing safely on the beach the unpowered gliders crashed into the sea. With the heavy battle kit strapped onto their backs, the troops stood little chance of survival.

The day after the initial assault *"Friendly Fire"* caused a number of fatalities to the allied forces. This time the needless deaths were caused when allied aircraft were heading for the Sicilian airports where the enemy's armed forces had surrendered. The allied gunners mistakenly assumed the allied aircraft were enemy bombers and commenced firing at them. This grievous mistake caused numerous fatalities before the gunners were ordered to cease firing.

Within a few days of the invasion, a total of half a million allied troops had landed.

By now the enemy's commanding officer realised this was not a decoy assault and notified Berlin of the serious situation. On receipt of the latest information German intelligence agreed with their commanding officer on Sicily. However when they advised Hitler that the decoy invasion was in fact a full scale assault, he refused to believe them. His reply was:

"We will give the situation a total of ten days."

On the 9th day of the invasion allied troops had captured 120,000 Prisoners of War. The following day it was all too late for Hitler as the allies had taken control of half the island and were pushing on towards the Messina Straits, the stretch of water between Sicily and mainland Italy.

Over the next few weeks the enemy troops that were still on the island put up strong resistance. On Day 38 of the invasion the enemy surrendered.

The number of allied troops killed during the invasion was almost 10,000, well below the estimated number of 40,000. *"Operation Mincemeat"* was firmly recognised as being responsible for the saving of 30,000 Allied lives.

Chapter 14

The Body of a Homeless Alcoholic Tramp – Inconceivable

In the early 1950's Montagu was given special permission to write a book about Operation Mincemeat. He chose the title, *The Man Who Never Was*. The book was a best seller and many people became intrigued as to the true identity of Major Martin. Researchers scrutinised the pages searching for clues, trying to ascertain whose body had been used.

The identity of the body remained a secret until 1996 when the name was officially announced as Glyndwr Michael, an insane alcoholic tramp, from Aberbargoed, Wales, who had committed suicide by drinking rat poison in January 1943. Now that the name had been made public, it was only right that the name should be added to the headstone in Huelva Cemetery Southern Spain. In January 1998, Marmoles Toledano, a Spanish monumental sculptor, engraved the following:

Glyndwr Michael served as Major William Martin. R.M.

For *"Operation Mincemeat"* to be a 100% success Lieutenant Commander Ewen Montagu required a suitable body. It was imperative it had to be fresh and preferably recently drowned. If subjected to a medical examination or a post-mortem the report had to read *"death by drowning."* Another important factor recorded by Montagu was the body had to look like an officer. Montagu, the brilliant barrister, knew from his comprehensive legal background that he had to have possession of a body before he approached the British War Cabinet for approval. Prime Minister Winston Churchill would also have had to be approached for his personal approval.

In a letter to his own intelligence team, Montagu wrote:

"Everything will have to be in place before we seek approval for "Operation Mincemeat" otherwise the reply will be: 'What about this? What about that? Where will you get a body?'"

Montagu knew he had to be in possession of a body prior to seeking approval for *"Operation Mincemeat."* The body they took possession of was an insane homeless alcoholic tramp who had died on the 28th January 1943, at St Pancras Hospital, London. The death certificate states:

*"Male. Age 34 years. A labourer of no fixed abode. Cause of death
was phosphorous poisoning.*
Took rat poison. Did kill himself while of unsound mind."

The body was transported to Hackney Mortuary and placed in cold storage.
Montagu was now in a position to finalise his plans for Operation Mincemeat
including fictitious details regarding the body. The body of the tramp would
now be transformed into Major William Martin deceased.

Over the next two months Major Martin was removed from cold storage to be
measured for clothes and shoes. After the clothes were purchased, the body
was again removed from cold storage, thawed out, clothed, and then placed
back in cold storage.

Later the body was removed for a third time to have the shoes fitted. A small
electric fire was placed beside the frozen feet to thaw them out. The shoes
were fitted and once more the body was returned to cold storage. Montagu
wrote:

*"Even with the defrosting then freezing the body still looked quite
fresh, but it was accepted the internal organs would be 'mushy'."*

Many researchers were firmly of the opinion that a fresh body had been
procured prior to the submarine *Seraph* sailing. To investigate this theory, a
number of professionals were consulted, including Doctor James Grieve MB
ChB, RCPath, FFFLM, Senior Lecturer in Forensic Medicine, Forensic
Medicine Unit, University of Aberdeen.

Forensic Pathologist Doctor Grieve was of the opinion the Spanish and
German pathologists would have been advised the body was that of a British
Royal Marine Commando. On looking at the body of a tramp, they would have
taken note of the poor abdomen muscles and poor thigh muscles. They would
also have noted the body was neither athletic looking nor muscular. It would
also have wrinkled skin.

There would possibly have been froth around the mouth and nostril. After 3
months stored deep frozen, the body would also look wasted. During the
internal examination the German pathologist, due to being politically
motivated, would have carried out a more meticulous post mortem.

Depending on the amount of alcohol consumed, the liver would be fatty and
evidence of cirrhosis might be present. The phosphorous rat poison would
have changed the colour of the liver from brown to a bright yellow. This would
have been seen with the naked eye.

However, if they had the fresh body of a Royal Marine it would not have
wrinkles or a lot of fat. It would be muscular and athletic. During the internal
examination there would also be no expectation of finding fatty liver and there
would be no evidence of cirrhosis.

If the person had drowned in the sea, there might be water accumulated
around the lung, but not always. And there may or may not be water in the

stomach. Neither would there be signs of alcohol abuse. The most appropriate body would have been used in this operation, namely a fresh body. The other one would have been disposed of.

A second expert was also consulted. She was Evelyn C. Weir BSc Programme Leader, BSc Radiography/BSc Podiatry Conversion, Programme Leader BSc Physiotherapy Conversion/ BSc., Occupation Therapy Conversion, Lecturer- School of Health Sciences, Queen Margaret University, Edinburgh

Evelyn wrote:

"Depending on how long the body was in the water, what the footwear was, and the respective ages of the 'tramp' and the Royal Marine Officer, the presentation of the feet of an alcoholic tramp person was likely to have thickening of the toenails (Onychauxis) and fungal infection of the nails, thick, yellowish, crumbly. (Onychomycosis)

"It would generally have had poorly maintained foot care, cracks between toes, fissures, heel cracks, low grade skin infections. Lots of plantar callous (hard skin on weight bearing areas of sole of feet) The alcoholism would lead to poor circulation and neuropathy – so there would be a lack of hairs on the legs, feet and toes. There would also be discoloration (although again that depends on post mortem timings etc.) There could also be ulceration on the sole.

If you X-rayed the feet of the deceased, the joints of the tramp would be more likely to show osteoarthritic and osteoporotic changes. Additionally, by looking inside and outside of footwear, it is possible to tell from wear marks and comparing with the 'live' foot – if the footwear actually belonged to the deceased.

If the body of a Royal Marine officer had been used it would be less likely to have all of the above. It would more likely have hairs on his legs and feet. It would also be more likely to have well maintained toenails and the skin on the feet would be intact."

Warren Birnbaum is a Consultant with qualifications: BDS. FDS. RCS, Specialist in Restorative Dentistry, Acute Dental Care, Guy's and St Thomas's NHS Foundation Trust, London. As for the condition of a tramp person's teeth, he writes:

As this period was pre NHS and with no access to dental care, an alcoholic tramp would have terrible oral health including missing teeth, broken teeth, holes in teeth, decayed teeth, teeth not restored, stumps of teeth, exposed roots of teeth, very poor teeth. He would most likely have gum recession (shrunk gums). If he had false teeth they would be in poor condition."

John Steele also consulted Keith W Hobbs FIT FRSPH, Clinical Director, Governor and Fellow of the Institute of Trichologists, Fellow of the Royal Society of Public Health, Battersea Scalp & Hair Clinic, 108 St John's Hill, Battersea, London SW11 1SY, Tel: 0207 924 2195, www.scalp-hair.co.uk. Trichology is the study of Diseases of the Hair and Scalp. Regarding the hair and scalp of a homeless alcoholic tramp in the circumstances previously outlined, Keith Hobbs wrote:

"With the absence of modern pathology the man would likely have been of poor health and possibly suffering from infestations such as head and body lice, fleas, scabies and secondary infections from scratching the aforementioned infestations such as impetigo and boils.

"In contrast to the vagrant, a fit 36 year old Royal Navy sailor would most likely have a good head of hair, although both men could have suffered from inherited male pattern balding i.e. recession at both temples and/or thinning patch at the crown. He would be unlikely to have infestations such as lice, fleas, scabies or scalp infections. Both men, however, could have suffered from dandruff and seborrhoeic eczema, both of which are unrelated to cleanliness."

W M Haggarty BL. was a practising solicitor for 51 years and latterly a consultant with Mathie-Morton Black & Buchanan, Ayr. At Glasgow University he also studied forensic medicine under Professor John Glaister.
Mr Haggarty recorded:

"I am sure a tramp's body would bear no resemblance to that of an active Royal Marine officer of 36 years. A competent pathologist would remark on the state of nourishment for example and the state of the liver of an alcoholic.

"When Major Martin was slipped into the water offshore from Huelva, the body was found and removed shortly after. Had the body been that of a tramp that had never been previously immersed in water, I understand that the lungs would not have contained sufficient water to signify drowning. At the post mortem this is unlikely to have gone unnoticed."

Highly Esteemed Spanish researcher and author, Jesus Copeiro resides in Huelva, Spain. Jesus Copeiro's published books are: *Spies and Neutrals; Huelva During The Second World War; Valverde Through Photos; The English in Valverde; Target Africa* and *Lost Trains in Africa.*
Jesus Copeiro recorded:

"The planning of Operation Mincemeat was perfect. Major Martin was prepared in every detail with letters, bills, and photos of the fiancée, personal objects and theatre tickets.

"There would not have to be the slightest doubt concerning Major

Martin drowning. The body of a tramp that drank poison would not have been used. If it had, the Spanish pathologist would have found traces of the poison. Montagu would not have left the slightest doubt concerning the man's drowning, otherwise the whole carefully planned and vitally important operation would be ruined, so the body had to be that of a person who drowned at sea.

"The Germans must have been completely sure about Major Martin's whole authenticity. So sure, that two weeks after the allies had started the invasion of Sicily, Hitler still believed the main invasion would take place in Greece.

I do not believe the body of an alcoholic tramp could have been the person used for the operation."

Herbert Geoffrey Cameron served with the Metropolitan Police for 30 years. During his 28 years service with the CID he was attached to the Flying Squad, the Regional Crime Squad, the Organised Crime Squad, the Fraud Squad and other departments that must remain with him. In his capacity as officer in charge of a case, he had the task of presenting criminal cases before Magistrate's Courts or Crown Courts in the London area. On many occasions Detective Sergeant Geoff Cameron found himself presenting criminal cases before His Honour, Ewen Montagu, QC.

Geoffrey recorded:

"Judge Ewen Montagu was very much feared but highly respected by all court officials, police officers and young barristers. If his Lordship found you wanting, I am afraid you got the rough edge of his tongue.

You had to be exact, precise and know your particular case inside out, upside down and be prepared for the unexpected question to be thrown at you from him. Failure in any one of these aspects was not to be contemplated. You ignored Ewen Montagu at your peril. To sum up, he did not suffer fools gladly. As one of Her Majesty's Judges, he was very much respected by the vast majority of CID officers.

When the official papers, regarding "Operation Mincemeat," were released to the Public Record Office in London, I probed and asked questions, much as I did as a detective and I arrived at certain conclusions regarding "Operation Mincemeat." To help me in arriving at my conclusions I have communicated with: The Prime Ministers Office; The Commonwealth War Graves Commission; Jesus Copeiro, author of the official history of Huelva, during World War II; The British Consul, Malaga; Jeremy Montagu, son of the Right Honourable Ewen Montagu; The Imperial War Museum and the Ministry of Defence.

From all these communications, with those persons and organisations and arms of government, as a former trained investigator of crime, I have thought long and hard about all the facts at my disposal. My conclusions can be summarised as follows. The body of the tramp was kept in Hackney Mortuary for an extraordinary length of time. It begs the question; were the planners, in possession of a body, which had been damaged by rat poison, deliberately holding it back in reserve in the hope that a better candidate might come along.

To use the body contaminated with poison was a high risk. Glyndwyr Michael's poison riddled body was unsafe and does not fit in with the meticulous mind of a trained advocate such as Ewen Montagu. With such a risk at stake, why not use a body that had drowned in salt water? I have always felt uneasy about Glyndwyr Michael's role in this affair and the mere mention of his name raises my eyebrows a notch or two.

With all the Naval establishments on the south coast of England, including submarine depots, why take a body stored in London 500 miles by road, in war-time, to a submarine depot in Scotland. Why not transport the body by aeroplane, or better still, why not by road to a submarine depot in southern England where it could have been loaded onto the same submarine, HMS Seraph. Why the Holy Loch in Scotland?

Every aspect of his court cases was thoroughly researched. There is no doubt that Montagu planned 'The Man Who Never Was' operation with meticulous detail and that absolutely nothing would be left to chance."

Montagu had arranged a meeting in London with Norman Jewel, the captain of the submarine *Seraph*. The purpose was to advise the captain regarding the part he and his crew would play in the vital covert operation.

The date of the meeting between Montagu and the captain was 31st March, 1943, the date of the *Dasher* funerals.

Montagu had a pass printed for Major Martin. The pass was to help ensure the enemy would believe the body to be that of a Major. He had printed on the pass that it was expired. He could have selected any date between January and April 1943. The date Montagu chose was the 31st March. 1943. The date of the *Dasher* funerals!

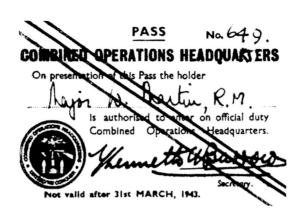

PASS No. 649.

COMBINED OPERATIONS HEADQUARTERS

On presentation of this Pass the holder

Major N. Martin, R.M.

Is authorised to enter on official duty
Combined Operations Headquarters.

Secretary.

Not valid after 31st MARCH, 1943.

Lieutenant Jewel reached the rank of Admiral. After retiring he stated in an interview to the Navy News, the Royal Navy newspaper:

> *"Regarding the body of a tramp being used in the covert operation, I met some members of the Twenty Committee because they needed me to know what was happening.*
>
> *No one in their right sense would use a body in which poison could be found.*
>
> *It had to look like the person had drowned.*
>
> *The people who were thinking these things were not fools. People like Sir Bernard Spilsbury would only have advised that it should be someone who perhaps died of pneumonia, so that the lungs could be washed out with salt water to make it seem genuine.*
>
> *From all the evidence in the press recently, it would be most unlikely that the body of a tramp and suicide by poison would have been used in this operation. I don't believe the claims about the body's identity being that of a man that killed himself with poison."*

Top: Laundry Room, four crewmen at work laundering with the American machinery. The laundry room was a smoking area.
Bottom: "Dasher" bodies being brought ashore and placed in the truck waiting alongside.

Chapter 15

A Body From HMS *Dasher*

It was well known in legal circles that Ewen Montagu was a perfectionist. His brilliance led to him becoming a King's Councillor, (Later a Queen's Councillor) He was also appointed Judge Advocate of the Royal Navy and later he became a High Court judge.

Montagu, the brilliant, meticulous barrister would most certainly not have used a body that would have raised suspicion, particularly when so many lives depended on the success of his planning. There is no doubt he would have used a fresh body that had drowned!

The use of a second body is referred to by a member of Montague's intelligence team who wrote:

"I am still bound by the official Secrets Act, however, I can tell you that more than one body was used in Operation Mincemeat."

Did the Royal Navy select another body from the *Dasher* casualties?

The day following the disaster, Sunday 28th March 1943, all bodies brought ashore were laid out on the ground of Castlecraigs tennis court, which was surrounded by a high wall. The Castlecraigs was a prominent Ardrossan building that had been requisitioned by the Royal Navy.

The following day the father of one of the deceased, John McFarlane, arrived in Ardrossan. He had travelled from Greenock to make arrangements regarding having his son's body taken home.

The family had a lair at Greenock Cemetery and it was here they wanted their son buried. The father, Angus McFarlane, was introduced to the Naval officer in charge of the *Dasher* burials. The meeting was held in the lounge of the Eglinton Hotel, Ardrossan, where the officers were billeted.

Surprisingly, the officer in charge of the burials refused to release the body. It would appear that a member of the services medical circle in Ardrossan had responded to Montagu's appeal for a body.

The father persisted with his request and this led to a heated argument. Other Navy officers in the lounge hearing the argument became so embarrassed they quietly left the room.

Meantime Angus McFarlane, in a loud angry voice, threatened to contact the *Daily Record* newspaper. It was only after the grieving father gave vent to his anger and threatened to contact the newspapers, that the Naval officer grudgingly gave permission for the father to take his son home.

That same day fifteen families received telegrams advising them that their loved one was being buried in Ardrossan cemetery on the 31st March. Five of the families responded immediately by forwarding a telegram stating that it was their wish to have their loved one returned to their home town for burial. Four of the requests were granted. Perversely, the young widow of John Melville, who resided in the town of Galashiels in the Scottish borders, was refused permission. She wanted to have her husband buried where she could visit his grave with her small daughter. This was not to be as she received a telegram stating:

"Regret unable to send body to Galashiels and that his funeral would take place in Ardrossan."

This young mother from the Scottish Borders was in no state of mind to question authority. When the Melville family arrived in Ardrossan for the funeral, they requested to view the body of their loved one. Cruelly, this request was refused with no logical explanation given. The Royal Navy officer even refused to open the coffin.

It seems more than likely that John Melville was chosen to be the body to be used in the ruse. Why was the body held in Ardrossan against the families wish? And why was the family's request to take John home denied? And why was the coffin not opened at the family's request?

Importantly, Montagu's request for a body included the criteria:

"It had to be fresh and recently drowned."

John Melville was a fine looking man in his late 30's, who had recently died of drowning in the Firth of Clyde. His body was in good condition and his lungs would contain salt water. This was exactly what Montagu was seeking.

Montagu later wrote:

"The right body was found at the right time!"

Esteemed Spanish researcher and author, Jesus Copeiro wrote:

"I believe one of the 355 bodies unaccounted for from HMS Dasher was used. The body was not given to the family; it was kidnapped, to be used in the war operation. It was a perfect body for Montagu's plan."

W. M. Haggarty. BL. Who was a practising solicitor wrote:

"The circumstances, particularly the time, points to HMS Dasher. Here they had the pick of the Dasher bodies from the Firth of Clyde and one closer in age and state of physical condition to Major Martin. In view of the foregoing I consider it very likely that the body used was that of one of the casualties from HMS Dasher."

Colin Gibbon, ex police officer and World War II historian, concluded:

"There would not have to be the slightest doubt concerning Major Martin's drowning. "Operation Mincemeat" was risking the lives of thousands of British and American soldiers who would storm

ashore onto the beaches of southern Sicily.
No small point would be overlooked and no risk could possibly have
been taken as this would have placed the Germans on a state of
alert. I have no doubt whatsoever that the body given the identity of
Major Martin came from HMS Dasher. The evidence is pointing
directly at a body from HMS Dasher being used."

Ten years after the war ended, retired Lieutenant Commander Montagu received permission from the War Office to write a book about Operation Mincemeat. In his manuscript, Montagu records seeking a suitable body from the Army, the Royal Navy and the Royal Air Force.

His manuscript reads:

we decided that we would have to play the game so far as we could. Very tentatively we to opened enquiries in Service medical circles. It was a very odd question we had to ask. Could we obtain possession of a body whose cause of death could be confused with shock or drowning or injury? We encountered deep suspicion but we kept An did not give up hope and We received various "offers" but for one reason or another they were not satisfactory. Finally when it looked as though our plot was likely to be still born a report came through about an officer of one of the services a men Someone who had just died from pneumonia, in a remote part of the country. Pathologically speaking it looked as though he would answer our requirements. Feverishly we searched through his personal records. He was an only son. His parents were still then alive and

Mrs J Harvey, who lost her brother on HMS *Dasher,* wrote to the Royal Navy Fleet Headquarters seeking assurance that her brother's body was not involved in operation Mincemeat. The reply received was contained in the letter dated 3rd April, 2006 confirming that the body that was used was indeed John Melville, a sailor serving on HMS *Dasher.*

From   S J Spear

ROYAL NAVY
FLEET HEADQUARTERS

Office of the Naval Secretary
Room G10 (MP G2)
Fleet Headquarters. West Battery
Portsmouth
Hampshire
PO2 8BY

Mrs J Harvey
9 Nicholson Gardens
Heeley
Sheffield
S8 9ST

3 APRIL 2006

Dear Mrs Harvey,
Thank you for your recent letter in which you refer to Operation Mincemeat. the deception operation that involved using the body of an unidentified man in a plan to mislead the axis powers about allied invasion plans in the Mediterranean.
Recent research has indicated that the body used was in fact John Melville, a sailor serving on HMS Dasher.

Thank you for writing

Yours sincerely

S J SPEAR

In early October 2004 Lieutenant Commander Mark Hill, Commanding Officer of the Naval Squadron in Cyprus, organised an at-sea memorial service. The Lieutenant Commander was based in the Mediterranean, where the service would take place. It was in honour of the late John Melville, Royal Navy, *"The Man Who Never Was"* and it took place on the 8th October, 2004.
The Royal Navy ship that would participate in the at-sea-service was a patrol vessel also named HMS *Dasher.* By a strange co-incidence, the Captain of the present HMS *Dasher* was Captain Boswell and the Captain on board *Dasher* in 1943 was also a Captain Boswell! Another coincidence was that the previous HMS *Dasher* was an Archer Class ship and the present *Dasher* a Royal Navy patrol vessel, is also Archer Class!
The programme organised by Lieutenant Commander Mark Hill read:

From: "Mark Hill" <spinnco@cytanet.com.cy>
To: <sandy@oz-arnold.com>
Cc: <derek@cytanet.com.cy>; "'Media Ops'" <mediaops@spidernet.com.cy>; "Buster Brov <buster_in_the_sun@hotmail.com>; <johnsteele.hmsdasher@ntlworld.com>
Sent: 03 October 2004 20:40
Subject: 'The Man who never was' Service of remembrance

Sandra,

Just touching base ahead of Friday – the plan is coming together nicely I feel, but it is probably timel engage Mrs. Mackay thoughts in order to ensure that her wishes, which we see as paramount, are n So here goes - the *DRAFT* plan is as follows:

SERVICE IN HONOUR OF THE LATE JOHN MELVILLE RN 'The Man who never was' Friday 8ᵗʰ 2004

Guest of honour Mrs. Isabelle Mackay (nee Melville)

Time	Event	Action
0900	Meet at Main-gate RAF AKROTIRI	COCS / Cox'ı
o/c	Escorted to AKROTIRI Mole	COCS / Cox'ı
0915	Meet CO HMS DASHER (Lt Danny Boswell)	CO
0915-0930	Brief tour of Ship	CO / XO
0930	Coordinated departure	CO's
0945	Anchor as req'd	CO's
0950 (start when HMS PURSUER is in position & ready)	Commence Service of remembrance; programme as follows: **Introduction** – Rev John Duncan Royal Highland Fusiliers **Reading** (Psalm 23) – Sandra (if happy to do so) **Tribute / Address** – CO HMS DASHER (to be confirmed) **RN Collect** (Naval prayer) - Member of HMS DASHER Ships Coy **Laying of Wreath** – Mrs. Mackay **Tryst** – COCS **The last post** – Waterloo Band Bugler **Piper's lament** – RHF Pipes & Drums **One minute's silence** – all **Reveille** – Waterloo Band Bugler **Prayer** – Rev John Duncan **Announcements** – Rev John (opportunity for Mrs. Mackay to speak – if she wishes) **Benediction** – Rev John	All
1030 (approx)	Weigh & Return to Harbour	CO's
o/c	Tea Coffee / Media interviews/photos as required	XO
1100	Depart	COCS / COX

Notes:
1. Timings are for guidance – we will not be using a stop-watch for this!
2. Guests and media are requested to dress in keeping with the solemnity of the occasion non-slip soles are recommended.
3. The level of media cover is as yet unconfirmed – HMS PURSUER will be standing by tc media and will be in position to film/photo the service from close range.
4. Weather permitting the service will take place on the forecastle HMS DASHER – in the foul weather we will use the flying bridge.
5. Guests are encouraged / invited to wear medals.
6. Cyprus Sqn will be dressed in whites & Rev John in RHF Tartan.

John Melville's daughter, Isobel, was invited to attend. She was very proud to be there with her son, Douglas. Her father had lost his life but in his death was the key part of a plan that had saved countless others

At the service Lieutenant Commander Mark Hill said:

"In his incarnation as Major Martin, John Melville's memory lives on in the film, The Man Who Never Was. But we are gathered here today to remember John Melville as the man who certainly was."

At the conclusion of the memorial service, Dennis Barnes, spokesman for the British Forces in Cyprus said:

"This was undoubtedly the first tribute by the Royal Navy to John Melville, The Man Who Never Was."

Chapter 16

The Mystery of the Missing Bodies

During the research for this book it became clear an anomaly had taken place. The number of bodies brought ashore at Ardrossan exceeded those who are listed as buried by the Commonwealth War Graves commission. It would appear that approximately 26 simply disappeared.

Another mystery regarding more missing bodies relates to Sunday 28th March, the day after the sinking, bodies were washed ashore at the North Beach, Ardrossan. They were collected and transported to the local Royal Navy base at Ardrossan Harbour. The lorry used was owned by a local contractor. The following day, more bodies were washed ashore and transported to the local Naval base. It soon became common knowledge in Ardrossan that bodies from *Dasher* were being washed ashore at the North Beach. The four Ardrossan schools were alerted and the headmaster of each school visited every class to warn the pupils that the North Shore was out of bounds.

Local man Roy Riddex recalled, as a ten year old, the headmaster visiting the classes telling the pupils that it was forbidden to walk anywhere near the North Beach of Ardrossan. Another local lad, 13 year old Sandy Brown, accompanied by his friend, Gilbert Hunter, walked to the North Beach even although they knew it was out of bounds to the public.

On seeing Royal Navy personnel patrolling the area the boys could go no further but they saw the beach covered with black oil and diesel. Later the beach was completely littered with fruit, debris, sailor's hats and uniforms.

For almost 3 weeks bodies were being washed ashore, during this period the public bus service which travels along the sea front between Ardrossan and Largs was cancelled due to the possibility of passengers witnessing bodies floating in the water or lying on the beach.

With the bus service temporary cancelled, Wrens who were billeted at the nearby requisitioned Glenfoot House situated by the coastal road, were transported to HMS *Fortitude* by Royal Navy trucks. When the bodies were washed ashore, the local contractor's lorry, accompanied by Royal Navy personnel, collected and transported them to the Royal Navy base. They were then laid out on the platform at Winton Pier railway station and individually covered with blankets. A high wall concealed the platform from the sight of anyone in the harbour area.

At the end of each working day the bodies were taken from the Naval base on the back of the contractor's lorry, covered with a tarpaulin, and driven away.

A number of locals witnessed the bodies including James Welsh. James was the Ardrossan Harbour joiner/diver and like other harbour workers, he had complete freedom to be in almost any part of the harbour. His family home was at Dock Road, beside the entrance to the harbour. (HMS *Fortitude*).

James and Mary Welsh had three sons and a daughter. Due to James's job within the Naval base, he frequently witnessed the sailor's bodies arriving and being placed on Winton Pier railway station platform, then being covered with blankets.

One day, Mary Welsh, the wife of the harbour joiner/diver, was standing outside the oil skin factory, where she worked as a seamstress, at the harbour entrance. Mary was having a chat with a few other workers when they spotted a lorry departing from HMS *Fortitude*.

The open lorry had a large canvas covering. As the lorry drove past the small group of women, they were shocked to see an arm sticking out from under the canvas. Fortunately the local police sergeant was walking past and he also noticed the arm dangling. The sergeant immediately waved at the driver to stop the vehicle. As soon as the lorry stopped the sergeant stepped forward and slipped the arm under the canvas sheet. The sergeant then waved the driver on.

Other locals have described the vehicles carrying bodies being driven from the base and along Glasgow Street, Ardrossan, the town's main thoroughfare. At the top of the street the vehicles were seen to turn to the right towards the cemetery. At the entrance to Ardrossan cemetery is a substantial detached house where the cemetery superintendent and his family reside. One of the rooms was used as an office where records were kept.

The cemetery has been in use since the mid 1800s and over the years each superintendent diligently recorded in ledgers, the details of each burial. The records were hand written and included the name, age, date of burial and lair number of each burial. After examining the records it was found that the 13 *Dasher* burials were not recorded! Remarkably, the local registrar's office has no documentation of these burials either.

During March 1999 John Steele visited the General Register Office for Scotland, at New Register house. Edinburgh. Every burial that takes place in Scotland has to be registered at the Edinburgh General Registrar Office. Incredibly the *Dasher* burials at Ardrossan had not been recorded!

A spokesperson at New Registrar Office stated:

> "I am appalled that unregistered burials have taken place in Scotland."

Over the next few weeks John and Noreen Steele visited registrar offices and cemeteries in the following districts, South Ayrshire, North Ayrshire, Inverclyde, and Renfrew. In each registrar office there were no records relating to the missing bodies. They checked the length and breadth of every cemetery looking for War Grave Commission headstones in the hope of finding some of the missing *Dasher* graves.

The diligent search proved negative. There were no memorial stones dedicated to the "missing" *Dasher* crew members. The disappearance of the 26 bodies still remains a mystery and a scandal which deserves to be resolved, irrespective of the embarrassment that may be caused to officialdom.

Regarding the number of bodies washed ashore and buried in unmarked graves, without viewing the classified records it is difficult to estimate the exact number of missing bodies. However, John Steele was alerted to 60 bodies being found in unmarked ground at Montfode Farm, Ardrossan. This was an area that was being excavated in preparation for a bypass being constructed at Ardrossan.

All work was stopped until the bodies were exhumed. However the sector of ground was discovered to be an ancient Roman Cemetery containing a mixture of long and short cists. Also unearthed were a number of simple basic graves, all dating circa 6th century.

The *Dasher* bodies are buried somewhere, and all the evidence points to unmarked graves, but where? The authors had compiled a vast amount of MoD documents marked "Top Secret." One of the documents was a report compiled by JAS Eccles, the Royal Navy Director of Operations Division. The report dated 6th April 1943 States:

"Bodies are being washed up, identified, buried etc., on the coast."

The meaning of "buried etc" has never been satisfactorily explained.

When Peter Cleminson, National Chairman of The Royal British Legion was advised of the missing *Dasher* bodies, he mentioned it to Admiral Lord Alan West, Government Minister for Security, and a former First Sea Lord.

Lord Alan voiced his opinion regarding the missing bodies and Peter Cleminson included Lord Alan's opinion in a powerful letter to the First Sea Lord.

The letter dated 17th December 2009 is shown overleaf.

Patron Her Majesty The Queen

FROM: NATIONAL CHAIRMAN'S OFFICE

The Royal British Legion
199 Borough High Street
London
SE1 1AA

T 020 3207 2100
F 020 3207 2276
E info@britishlegion.org.uk
W britishlegion.org.uk

Legionline 08457 725 725

Capt. Steve Murdock,
Executive Assistant to the First Sea Lord
Level 5, Zone K
MoD Main Building
London, SW1A 2HB

NC/Sec 1410/8

17th December 2008

Dear Lt.A. Steve (of ? ms)

I have been contacted by a member of The Royal British Legion whose father witnessed the sinking of HMS Dasher in The Firth of Clyde on March 27th 1943. He wishes to find out if there are any communal graves in the Ardrossan area that have not been marked, and if so, to erect a memorial to commemorate those so buried.

I sit on The Friends of Normandy Committee with Vice Admiral John McAnally and he suggested I write to you to so enquire. I do realise that at the time, and also thereafter, this tragedy was very carefully reported and, at times, treated as classified and I have no wish to open old issues that may be best left in peace. However, I was with Alan West last week and mentioned this matter to him. He felt that it may be in order for me to enquire, although he confirmed it was a delicate issue at the time but after 65 years, possibly less so now.

I do hope you can help and put this before those concerned but I will understand if it is felt best not to.

Very kind wishes,

The reply received was:

154

Captain S J Murdoch MBA Royal Navy
Secretary and Executive Assistant to First Sea Lord and Chief of Naval Staff

Ministry of Defence
5th Floor, Section K
Main Building
Whitehall
London
SW1A 2HB
Telephone: 02072 18 2214
Fax: 020 7218 4702

CNS/6/5

.OG No. 049/09

ACTION: A2C

24/1

Mr Peter Cleminson
National Chairman's Office
The Royal British Legion
199 Borough High Street
London
SE1 1AA

20 Jan 2009

Dear Peter

Thank you for your letter NC/Sec 1410/8 dated 17 December 2008 about possible unmarked graves in the Ardrossan area of casualties from HMS DASHER, lost to an internal petrol explosion on 27 March 1943.

Neither the Ministry of Defence nor the Commonwealth War Graves Commission has any records, information or knowledge on the existence of any such graves. Although the assumption that some must exist is not new and surfaces from time to time. However, none of those proposing their existence has produced any evidence beyond conjecture that "surely there must be some", given that the loss of life was so high (over 300) and the number of known named graves so few. I understand only 23, thirteen of which are actually in Ardrossan Cemetery and in the care of the CWGC.

In addition to those who have known graves, the remainder, officially listed as 'Missing Presumed Killed', are commemorated on the appropriate Memorials maintained by the CWGC. You will also be aware that there is a memorial stone and plaque in the Sunken Gardens, South Bank, Ardrossan. The wreck of HMS DASHER is, in itself, a controlled site under the Protection of Military Remains Act 1986; importantly there is also a memorial plaque on the wreck.

The loss of HMS DASHER was only secret for the duration of the War in Europe, the policy of the time being that we did not release information on losses that were not due to enemy action – and, therefore, probably unknown to them. There is nothing secret about the loss now and all the relevant records are in the National Archive.

Should any real evidence emerge to support claims that there are unmarked graves of personnel lost in the HMS DASHER incident in existence in the Ardrossan area, then the matter would be addressed again. But so far that has not been the case and so, neither the MOD nor the CWGC are contemplating any further action.

I hope this is useful

Yours sincerely

Steve

155

The Royal Naval Association was responsible for placing the HMS *Dasher* memorial stone and plaque at Ardrossan. The authors, along with the European Technical Dive Centre, from Kirkwall Orkney Isles, were responsible for placing the memorial plaque on *Dasher*. The MoD had no involvement in either.

The Breakthrough

During the summer of 1997, John Steele received an emotional telephone call from Tony Atherton. Tony, who lives in England, had just finished reading John's and Noreen's book "They Were Never Told." Tony had lost his father on HMS *Dasher* and had always been bewildered by the lack of information given to the bereaved families.

The *Dasher* book spurred him on to find out what had happened to his father and more specifically, the location of his last resting place. After he contacted his Member of Parliament the wheels were set in motion for the MP's Parliamentary Aid (PA) to visit the National Archives to research the files relating to the loss of HMS *Dasher*.

The MP's PA made contact with John Steele to inform him of his intention to search the classified files. It was arranged that the result of the search would be relayed to the author on the condition the PA's name and the Member of Parliament's name would not be revealed.

After a time lapse of 3 weeks the author was informed, via a phone call, that the PA had been allowed to view the classified files on condition that nothing could be copied and no notes were to be taken. The information reported back to the author was as follows:

> 26 Dasher bodies were buried in 2 unmarked graves. Some of them
> were unidentified. The identity of the others will never be revealed.

Over a period of almost 2 months another 7 telephone conversations took place. During them the PA emphasised the burial of 26 *Dasher* bodies in 2 unmarked graves. He also mentioned, on a number of occasions, that he had also read minutes of a meeting between Prime Minister Winston Churchill and his Chiefs of Staff. The date of the meeting was the 15th April, 1943. The PA said the minutes of the meeting included reference to the unmarked graves of 26 *Dasher* fatalities. Also, specific instructions that the name of the body involved in *"Operation Mincemeat"* must never be revealed.

The PA was very friendly at all times and during one of the conversations, he gave the author his mobile telephone number, his home phone number, his home address, including his post code and the date of his annual forthcoming holiday with his family. The PA explained that John Steele should not hesitate in contacting him at his home or if the family were on holiday, John Steele should contact him on his mobile phone.

During his many visits to the constituency office, Tony Atherton was meeting the MP and the PA and being advised of the same information that John Steele was being told!

On one of his many visits to his MP's constituency office, Tony Atherton, asked the PA to confirm the date of the all important meeting between the Prime Minister and his Chiefs of Staff, the PA wrote the date on House of Commons headed note paper and handed it to Tony Atherton!

HOUSE OF COMMONS
LONDON SW1A 0AA

Dockyards ref : Graves Commission

Micro fish : 15th April 1943
Church meeting with Chiefs
& staff-

A few months after his visit to the National Archives, the PA arranged to pay a return visit. To assist him he had invited another MP's Parliamentary Aid to join him. Their objective was to view the *Dasher* files in an attempt to find more information regarding the bodies, the sinking of HMS *Dasher* and *"Operation Mincemeat."*

On the appointed day, 27th March 2006, the two men arrived at the National Archives and commenced searching the records. When searching the Chiefs of Staff files, the minutes described a note appertaining to *"Operation Mincemeat"* which had been circulated to each of the Chiefs of Staff. Upon further enquiries, it was established that the "Note" was not held at the Archives.

The two PA's spent two days searching the records in vain, and interestingly they were even unable to view the files that the PA had viewed on his first visit. It would appear that they had been "removed." John Steele wondered why the valuable information was forthcoming from an MP's constituency office, especially when John had never met the MP, or any of his staff.

Indeed, John had never even heard of them yet a senior member of staff in the MP's office was freely passing information to him! Unable to comprehend the incident, the author spoke to a Scottish MP whom he knew. After relating his story, John said:

"Why are they telling me?"

The Scottish MP replied with a smile:

"John, This is a breakthrough, they have information they cannot make public, but they can relate it to you, and you can make it public!"

The Search at Ardrossan Cemetery

The authors have always been of the opinion that the missing bodies might very well be buried at Ardrossan Cemetery, in the 13 empty lairs beside the *Dasher* graves. Their opinion was included in their book, *"They Were Never Told: The Tragedy of HMS Dasher"* which was published in 1997. They also published their opinion in the sequel *"The Secrets of HMS Dasher."* Both books contained a photograph of the lairs where they suspected the bodies were buried.

How, then, could it be ascertained if bodies from *Dasher*, were located in the unmarked graves? The possibility of bodies being found would need to be carried out in 3 stages. Stage 1 would be a low level radar scan of the identified area at Ardrossan cemetery. Stage 2 would involve an investigative dig to confirm the presence of bodies and the number of burials. Should Stage 3 be implemented, it would involve the commissioning of all remains being removed, subjected to DNA testing and the remains being given a dignified burial.

John Steele contacted Doctor Tony Pollard, Director of Battlefield Archaeology. Glasgow University, Archaeological Research Division.

The doctor is well known for his success in locating hundreds of bodies in World War One battlefields. When John related his research regarding the missing *Dasher* bodies, Doctor Pollard wrote:

"The presence of unmarked mass graves should be known about and marked accordingly."

Paul Stevenson, local funeral director from Saltcoats, wrote a letter dated 11th July 2010 supporting the call for the unmarked graves to be examined.

The Scan at Ardrossan Cemetery

In early April 2010, at a meeting between John Steele and David O'Neill, Leader of North Ayrshire Council, John sought support from the council to have the 13 empty lairs surveyed with the use of state of the art ground penetrating radar. Without disturbing the ground the sophisticated machine can determine if the ground had ever been disturbed, in other words if burials have taken place. This equipment is used by police forces throughout the world and can detect bodies up to a depth of 8 metres.

Shortly after the meeting the council appointed Glasgow University Archaeological Division (GUARD). The geological survey was carried out on the 30th April, 2010 by Doctor Ian Banks and the Project Manager was Doctor Tony Pollard.

When archaeologist, Doctor Ian Banks arrived at the cemetery he set up his ground penetrating equipment at the 13 empty lairs. This was the small area of ground identified by John Steele. The object of the survey was to determine if intentionally unregistered burials had taken place in the 13 lairs which are officially empty. After scanning the area of ground 3 times, Doctor Ian Banks returned to Glasgow University to download the results of the scan. The results were analysed and recorded! Two months later North Ayrshire Council received a comprehensive report from Glasgow University. Of particular interest was an area of ground comprising of 5 "empty" lairs

The report, compiled by Doctor Ian Banks stated:

> *"The survey suggests that there is some disturbance to the ground on the western side of the gravestones, albeit very different to the disturbance on the eastern side (where the known graves lie) or in the control transects (again an area of known burials).*
>
> ***The survey does not rule out the possibility that there might be a large pit containing numerous bodies without coffins on the western side of the gravestones.***

(Doctor Banks refers to the 13 empty lairs as "The west side")

> *An alternative interpretation is that the survey data reveal the layers of soil with only geological features creating the anomalies in the data. The conclusions of the survey will require ground-truthing to become certain. This would be done through trial trenching to confirm or disprove the presence of a feature on the western side of the gravestones."*

Local witnesses reported bodies being transported from HMS Fortitude (Ardrossan Harbour) without coffins, John Steele did not advise Doctor Ian Banks that the bodies, possibly buried in Ardrossan Cemetery, were not in coffins. It is interesting to note the university survey report includes:

"There might be a large pit containing numerous bodies without coffins."

Regarding funerals for British service personnel the regulations state;

Military funerals are to be carried out in a dignified manner. Coffins are to be draped in the union Flag.

When John Steele contacted the Commonwealth War Graves Commission regarding investigating the result of the scan a spokesman stated:

This does not come under our remit. If it did, due to the financial climate, we could not fund this project!

On the 23rd August, 2010, the following written quotation was received by John Steele, from Glasgow University to carry out the necessary investigative work:

As requested I am pleased to provide a costing for the evaluation of the site in Ardrossan cemetery. The figure is based on a three day exercise, involving a small team of specialists (all of whom were members of the team which carried out the evaluation of the WWI mass graves at Fromelles in France). The project would be directed by me.

The aim of the exercise would, in the first instance, be to demonstrate the presence or absence of multiple burials related to the sinking of the Dasher. Should burials be present other aims would be to establish as accurately as possible the number of burials, the condition of the remains and the feasibility of body recovery (no remains would be removed during the evaluation). The price is an all in cost including staff costs, report production, project management, mechanical excavator hire, site screening etc.

The task could be carried out on a cheaper basis should the council be willing to provide mechanical excavator, screening etc. Additional savings could also be made if no remains are found to be present (i.e. the full three days would not be required). We would be happy to discuss options here but for the present we have provided a full costing for all elements.

Cost of Evaluation at Ardrossan Cemetery £7,270 (excl. VAT).
Best Regards
Tony
Dr Tony Pollard, Director
Centre for Battlefield Archaeology, University of Glasgow

North Ayrshire Council

North Ayrshire Council's legal department advised that the council cannot progress any work at Ardrossan Cemetery.

The reason is that although North Ayrshire council is responsible for anything inside the cemetery, they cannot progress further work, unless there was a specific individual (named) who is believed to be there, and is not on the previous records, of those interred there.

The legal department believes it will remain a mystery, as the criteria cannot be met, especially since the "papers" pertaining to the *Dasher* incident, will remain sealed.

Paul Stevenson is the managing director and owner of **Paul Stevenson Funeral Directors.** The company have offices in Saltcoats and Largs, North Ayrshire. www.funeral-scotland.co.uk
Regarding the missing *Dasher* bodies Paul Stevenson wrote:

29 Chapelwell Street | Saltcoats | KA21 5EB
tel: 01294 607001 | fax: 01294 606407

3 Lade Street | Largs | KA30 8AZ
tel: 01475 670555

FUNERAL DIRECTORS
email: info@funeral-scotland.co.uk
www.funeral-scotland.co.uk

Mr & Mrs J Steele
104 Eglinton Road
ARDROSSAN
Ayrshire

11th July 2010

Dear John and Noreen

Due to the sinking of HMS Dasher a high number of lives were lost but why are there only 24 registered graves?

This brings my thoughts to the missing graves. Bodies have been buried unregistered and I am convinced there must be records to show this. It is now 2010 and I think it is time to recognise that it is only fair and just for them to at least located and marked appropriately, not only for the deceased but for their loved ones and surviving relatives. Whatever the reasons were in March 1943, be it security, publicity or even identification.

No longer should relatives have to live with "Missing presumed Killed" but now know that they where found and laid to rest somewhere.

Yours sincerely

1O DOWNING STREET
LONDON SW1A 2AA

THE PRIME MINISTER

Dear Mr. Terrey,

As you may be aware, I have been approached in connection with a campaign seeking recognition for the bravery of your late father, Petty Officer Telegraphist Cyril Terrey, who died saving the lives of his comrades in a fire on board his ship, HMS Dasher, in 1943.

I am afraid that, at this late stage, it is not possible to make gallantry awards for acts of bravery dating back to World War II, however outstanding they may be. I note, however, that he has been commemorated on the Commonwealth War Graves Naval Memorial at Chatham.

The report of the events leading to the loss of HMS Dasher would leave no doubt that your father gave his life in bravely assisting many young ratings to safety. The fact that your father did not receive a posthumous award in 1943 does not in any way detract from his act of heroism.

You may be sure that the memory of your father, and the many other gallant servicemen and women who gave their lives in the service of their country so that others might live, will never be forgotten.

Yours sincerely,

Tony Blair

Mr Leonard Terrey

Recognition for heroism 67 years after the disaster

Isobel MacKay with photo of her father
John Melville.
(The Man who Never Was)

John Melville with his wife and daughter
in March 1943, 15 days before disaster

HMS Dasher Memorial Day. Ardrossan. Royal British Legion Parade.

Royal Marine Band leading the Memorial Service parade

Jack Dempsey's lounge bar.
Jack Dempsey was an American boxer who held the world heavyweight title from
1919 until 1926. His Broadway Bar and Cocktail Lounge in Broadway New York was
very popular with Dasher's crew.

HMS Dasher Memorial Garden Ardrossan

Mrs Boswell and Captain Boswell, DSC,
Officer in Command of HMS Dasher on that fateful day.

Attending Memorial Service
on board Caledonian Isles.
(Ship stopped directly above
Dasher)
From Left:
Donny Grier, Ardrossan;
Piper Sandy Gauld, Arran;
Noreen Steele;
John Steele;
Robbie Brown,
Area Manager CalMac;
Ted Godfrey,
Shiskine Isle of Arran

North Shore Ardrossan. The beach where the bodies were washed ashore. Dasher lies to the right of the small island almost mid-way to Arran. (6.8 miles from Ardrossan)

HMS Dasher 1943 Association members paying their respects at the 13 Dasher graves. Behind the headstones the plot of ground is believed to hold numerous unnamed bodies from Dasher.

First day cover of Rio de Janeiro before being converted to HMS Dasher.

HMS Dasher (1943) Association members onboard Caledonian Isles holding an at-sea memorial service above Dasher.

HMS Dasher (1943) Association members attending the annual memorial service at Brodick, Isle of Arran

Chapter 17

Dives on *Dasher*

Dive Party 1007

The Wrecks Section of the Royal Navy Hydrographical Office appear to have had a particular interest in the wreck of HMS *Dasher* as the Royal Navy have located the wreck on eight occasions. The 1st survey over *Dasher* was carried out on the 12th January 1944, 10 months after the disaster. This was followed by 6 more surveys which were carried out on: 8th May, 1956; 25th February, 1976; 19th-29th January, 1982; 16th April, 1982; 17th April, 1984; and 13th May 1985.

May 2007

The most recent survey operation was during May 2007, by HMS *Echo*. Some of the surveys involved closed circuit technology which allowed those on the survey vessel to look at their onboard monitor and study the wreck on the seabed. On each occasion the outline of *Dasher* was upright on the sea bed and intact.

Regarding the dives which took place between the 19th and 29th January 1982 the survey/dive vessel was the *Seaforth Clansman,* a civilian ship that the Royal Navy had on a long term charter. The officer in command of the *Seaforth Clansman* was Lieutenant Duncan Bridge, a mine warfare and clearance diving officer. The officer and crew were Royal Navy personnel. Their hazardous mission was to locate and recover drifting mines, torpedoes and depth charges, unpredictable and highly dangerous remnants of World War II.

The ship sailed from Greenock on 18th January 1982, to investigate a report of a torpedo offshore from Troon, South Ayrshire. After locating and recovering the torpedo, Lieutenant Bridge received a report from the hydrographic officer in London. The report stated there were 2 ships lying on the seabed close to each other. One was HMS *Dasher,* the other was a large trawler. Of the 2 wrecks the Hydrographer was unsure which was HMS *Dasher.*

Lieutenant Duncan Bridge was tasked with identifying the wreck, HMS *Dasher.* The dive ship was in position above *Dasher* on the 19th January and the survey training operation took 10 days. Although the Master Dive Log is still subject to "official secrecy," the following is known about events.

DEPTH	PLACE	DURATION	TABLES	REMARKS
S4T 35				
SURFACE				L/T MARSH
DEPTH	CLYDE	Total Time	SEAFORTH	L/D WIGGINS
60m		9 days 15hrs		L/D HAMMOND
excursion		36 hours	CLANSMAN	L/D PRICHARD.
to 80m.				
back to 55m		total mins		bot dive 35 on Hms
+ then down				dasher surveying
to a new		13895mins		+ framing
depth of				
110m Short				
age excur				
sion to 130m		...		

Four highly experienced Royal Navy divers were involved in locating *Dasher*. The operation was also to be a training exercise for the 4 divers. Before moving onto the aircraft carrier, the dive team had been working at shallower depths on mine and torpedo locating tasks.

The 4 divers were Lieutenant Marsh, Leading Diver Neal Wiggins (Wiggy), Leading Diver Phil Hammond (Ozzie) and Leading Diver Prichard. Working in pairs they spent a total of 2 days on the bottom and 7.5 days decompressing. They commenced diving to a depth of 60 metres then 80 metres. On being acclimatised they descended to 110 metres and finally 130 metres onto the flight deck of *Dasher*.

The climax of the operation came at 10pm on 23rd January, when 3 of the dive team entered the dive bell. One of the men was the operator-in-charge of the dive. On reaching *Dasher's* flight deck the other 2 men would depart from the dive bell and carry out a close examination of *Dasher*. Once the bell was sealed, it was lowered over the side of the ship, and commenced its descent. At all times the deep dive operation was being closely monitored, via the underwater closed circuit TV system, by Lieutenant Duncan Bridge on the dive ship.

For de-compression purposes the bell was lowered very slowly, deeper and deeper. On reaching a depth of 100 metres the divers were now breathing a tightly controlled mixture of around 7% oxygen and 93% helium. As the dive bell pushed past the 100 metres mark both divers stood up and shook hands. They were celebrating because at this deep depth their salary was enhanced. After dropping ever deeper the bell came to a gentle stop, all inside thought they were on the flight deck of *Dasher* but they had just missed the flight deck and had landed on the muddy seabed. There were mounds of debris lying near *Dasher,* which was perfectly upright. The rubble had been parts of the ship which had been blown off when she exploded and sank.

The bell was then raised up off the seabed until it was level with the flight deck. When their position was relayed to Lieutenant Duncan Bridge on the *Seaforth Clansman* the lieutenant moved his ship slightly until the bell was in the correct location to land on the flight deck of the aircraft carrier. Once in position the divers connected the speaker system to their 30 metre umbilical cord. Leading Diver "Ozzie" Hammond and Leading Diver "Paddy" Prichard swam out connected to their umbilical cords. As they made their way along the flight deck they were unsure which part of the flight deck they were on. Their biggest concern was the sharp twisted and corroded arrester wires. An encounter with a broken arrester wire would pose serious problems for the Royal Navy divers.

On the surface Lieutenant Duncan Bridge inched the *Seaforth Clansman* up on her mooring pulling the dive bell along the shipwreck. This allowed the divers to extend their survey of the aircraft carrier. Lieutenant Bridge watched on his monitor as the divers walked along the flight deck. As they were able to communicate with the lieutenant on the dive ship, the divers reported that there was a lot of cable lying about the flight deck. They were unsure if they were heading towards the stern or the bow until they came across the aircraft lift shaft on the flight deck.

Leading Diver "Ozzie" Hammond dropped into the lift shaft and with the aid of his powerful torch could see completely distorted aircraft that had been parked in the hangar, all those years ago. Within a few minutes of the horrendous explosion the intense heat from the raging flames had completely mangled the propellers, wheels, engines, aircraft machine guns and fuselage.

To "Ozzie" the first aircraft looked like the remains of a Swordfish, it was very difficult to identify it now but he recognised the under carriage of a Swordfish. In the hangar "Ozzie" passed lots of wood that had collapsed and metal wreckage. At this point he wisely decided to go no further into the hangar for fear of his umbilical cord being cut by the sharp pieces of metal. As their air gauges were now showing 10 minutes of air left, the divers made their way back to the safety of the diving bell.

As they approached the bell they heard what they thought was the noise of a generator. When the noise became louder they realised it was the sound of a ship's engine. As this made the divers very wary, they contacted Lieutenant Bridge to confirm that a ship was passing. On being advised there were no ships in the vicinity they became concerned as it now appeared to be the engine noise of a submarine. When the noise grew louder it could only mean the submarine was sailing ever closer to them, and more importantly to the dive bell.

If the submarine caught the wire which attached the dive bell to the *Seaforth Clansman* the ramifications would not bear thinking about.

Fortunately the engine noise became fainter until it could be heard no more. The divers would never know if the submarine was American, British or Russian.

After the 2 divers entered the dive bell it was slowly raised to the surface. Seven hours and 35 minutes had passed since they had commenced their dive.

The tour of duty for the officers and crew of the *Seaforth Clansman* had commenced on the 4th January 1982 and finished on the 22 March. During that period they had located and recovered a number of mines, depth charges and torpedoes. The officers involved in the dive on HMS *Dasher* were recorded as being *Dive Party 1007*.

It is recorded they spent more than 23 hours diving on the aircraft carrier. Lieutenant Duncan Bridge was of a mind to recover one of the aircraft in the hangar. He had all he required onboard the *Seaforth Clansman* to complete the task, including a crane and highly experienced divers.

Unfortunately the *Seaforth Clansman* was called away on an emergency, the Lieutenant having received a report of a dangerous torpedo in a nearby loch.

At the conclusion of the torpedo mission the lieutenant submitted his report to the Hydrographer at the Hydrographic Office, Taunton. The report read:

> *Wreck number 06300194 in position 55 37 54 North. 004 56 53 west is that of a fast decomposing trawler.*
>
> *Wreck number 06201489 in position 55 37 37 North.W005 00 49 west is that of HMS Dasher, lying perfectly upright in 170 metres with her flight deck intact at 140 metres."*

When the Master Dive Log relating to the dives on *Dasher* was received in London, it was immediately classified and subjected to 30 years of secrecy. The files will remain closed until February 2012! It would appear the carnage in the hangar, witnessed by the divers was deemed to be of a sensitive nature, too sensitive to be released to the public.

(A member of Dive Party 1007 Neil Wiggins (Wiggy) left the Royal Navy one year after the *Dasher* dive. Whilst working offshore on an oil rig he rescued a fellow diver who appeared to be unconsious in very deep water.

Without hesitation "Wiggy" entered a dive bell and was lowered to the sea bed. "Wiggy" immediately swam over to the unconscious diver and dragged him inside the dive bell. On returning to the surface the diver regained consiousness. His life was saved by the quick thinking and bravery of Wiggy.)

Eighteen Years Later

In the early summer of 2000 John and Noreen Steele discussed the possibility of a memorial plaque being laid on *Dasher's* flight deck. This was intended as a mark of respect on the sunken aircraft carrier, making it not just another wreck on the seabed, bearing in mind the horrendous loss of life suffered on *Dasher*.

By co-incidence 2 divers were discussing the possibility of diving on HMS *Dasher*. The 2 men were part of the European Technical Dive Centre based in Orkney. They were Mark Reeves, Technical Director of the company and a diving instructor, the other was Kevin Heath, a very experienced diver who specialised in locating U boats.

The owner of the company, Alex Deas, contacted the authors and agreed that if the dive went ahead a memorial plaque would be placed on the flight deck. A few weeks later it was decided this very dangerous dive would definitely take place. On being told the good news John Steele, Noreen Steele and Alex Deas funded the purchase of a Brass plaque and had the plaque engraved with the words:

> "Dedicated to the memory of the 379 men who died when HMS
> Dasher blew up and sank on the 27th March 1943. R.I.P."

Within weeks the dive had been meticulously planned and on 27th June, 2000, the dive ship, *Loyal Mediator,* an ex Royal Navy vessel arrived in Ardrossan Harbour. The next morning a memorial and dedication service was held onboard. The service was conducted by the Reverend Jim Smith of the EU Church, Ardrossan. After the service the rest of the day was spent checking and rechecking all the dive equipment, such was the importance of safety of all the divers.

The next morning, 29th June, the minister returned to the harbour side to wish the divers every success. The weather was perfect for the dive, the sun was shining and the Firth of Clyde was flat calm.

On departing from Ardrossan Harbour, the dive ship headed across the Firth of Clyde, to the *Dasher* site. On arrival, whilst the divers Mark Reeves and Gary Allison were preparing for the dive, there was an air of excitement onboard as the vessel went round and round in a small circle. This was to allow the skipper to plot the exact position when he would call for the shot line to be thrown overboard. The shot line was a stout rope with a heavy weight tied to one end and a small mooring buoy attached to the other end.

The rope was almost 200 metres in length, more than adequate to reach down to *Dasher*. As the ship circled slowly the skipper was carefully watching his sonar display monitor in the wheel house. A transducer fixed to the outside of the hull was sending out high pitch sound waves to the seabed. The sound waves were bouncing off the sea bed and returning to the monitor showing the complete outline of *Dasher* lying upright.

Suddenly the skipper shouted "Now!" and the heavy shot line was immediately thrown overboard. As Noreen and John Steele focused keenly on the monitor in the bridge, eyes glued to the heavy weight with the rope attached falling quickly, deeper and deeper down towards *Dasher*. It landed on the flight deck, near the bow on the right hand (starboard) side. With incredible accuracy, the heavy weight landed exactly where the skipper had calculated.

On the surface the other end of the buoy bobbed about keeping the heavy rope straight from top to bottom. When the diver was in the water he would hold on to the shot line as he descended, taking him direct to the aircraft carrier's flight deck. On his return journey he would ascend beside the shot-line to ensure he reached the surface, close to the dive boat.

Mark wrote his personal account of his record-breaking deepest dive in Europe.

"I stepped from the dive boat and in a split second I was surrounded by the effervescence of the plunge, slowly I surfaced and glanced towards the vessel and signalled okay. I made my way to the shot line and began my descent. At 30 metres I switched to my bottom gas. Jelly fish of every shape, size and description passed by majestically in this twilight green soup. My descent accelerated with each passing metre.

Until now I had felt strangely calm, now my thoughts wandered, I switched on my torch, the plaque I held started to spin and cause me problems as I plunged through the water column to the depths below. Around 85 metres, just for a moment I doubted myself, I became very aware of my own mortality and my thoughts turned to my family. 'Don't be stupid,' I told myself, 'You can do this,' and it was down and down.

Suddenly a Lion's Main jelly fish leapt out of the blackness, wrapping itself around my face. It was so fast I couldn't avoid it. I brushed it aside but it was too late, it had stung my lips. As I winced at the scalding feeling, I realised I had lost control of my breathing and buoyancy. On regaining my composure I added gas and took some deep breaths.

Suddenly I could see the wreck below, so I slowed down and landed gently. Standing for a moment in the silence, the only disturbance was my breathing and the sediment I had disturbed which was a good 4 inches deep. Beneath the sediment I could feel the hard structure of the flight deck.

On moving along, as I could not find a place to hang the memorial plaque, I disconnected it and laid it on the flight deck. I then read the words for the last time!

'Dedicated to the memory of the 379 men who died when HMS Dasher blew up and sank on the 27th march 1943 R. I. P.'

In the darkness I could almost see the faces of all the young lads who had lost their lives. I remembered the photograph I had seen of them in the mess room enjoying their lunch. My thoughts then turned to my own family, it was time to go. As I ascended my temperature gauge showed 5 degrees centigrade.

My first stop was at 75 metres; my next at 55 metres. My last stop before reaching the surface was at 30 metres depth. I had to remain at this stop for just over one hour before making my way to the surface. Three hours and eight minutes after stepping of the dive ship I wearily ascended the deck ladder.

Everybody was excited and relieved. The whole dive had been executed to perfection and I had dived the deepest dive in Europe. The immensity of what I had achieved sunk in. With only a small team of dedicated professionals, we had overcome countless obstacles, the hazard of cold, low visibility and extreme depth had been overcome. This was cutting edge extreme technical diving, yet the only thing that mattered to me was laying the memorial plaque on the flight deck."

As Mark was preparing to surface, the support team cleared a bench for him to rest on, to recover his strength. Once Mark was helped on board, his mask was quickly removed to reveal a huge grin on his face as he said: "I did it; give me a phone to speak to my wife."

The authors, John and Noreen Steele, were on the dive ship and prior to departing, each laid a rose at the site in remembrance of the 379 men who had died.

Later That Same Year

The Northern Gas Team, a group of 14 divers from the north of England meticulously planned a dive on *Dasher*. They had a spent years diving as a group and had great deal of experience. After obtaining permission from the Ministry of Defence, the team arranged to complete the dive on 21st September, 2000.

The dive vessel departed from its Clyde base at Inverkip at 8am. Unfortunately the sea was choppy and on reaching the dive site the weather had deteriorated. Conditions became so bad that after plotting *Dasher,* the dive operation was postponed.

The following day conditions had improved slightly and the team again set off. As the dive ship made its way down the Clyde towards the east coast of Arran the first team kitted up ready for the dive. They were Ziad Al-Obaidi, Ric Waring, Mark Elliot and Richi Stevenson. Approaching their destination, they were all huddled round the radio listening intently to the weather forecast.

Their support vessel *Predator 11* followed them out. Onboard were Bill Smith and 2 deep support divers.

Prior to the dive the final checks were made and on arrival the first team of 4 divers entered the Clyde. Richi Stevenson was carrying a Nikonos 4 camera. It was his job to take photographs from various angles of *Dasher*. The first to reach the flight deck was Ziad taking only 5 minutes to descend 140 metres.

On landing on the flight deck he walked along the deck to explore the large wreck.

Within 2 minutes Richi Stevenson landed near the same spot. He looked along the flight deck and saw the muddy deck had been disturbed by Ziad as he made his way to explore the huge wreck. As Richi swam along the side of the ship he saw a number of broken and twisted portholes. As he thought they would make interesting photographs the diver lined up his camera to take photographs. However, he was dismayed to see that the camera had imploded at a depth of 141 metres and was completely useless.

By now the other 2 divers from the first team had landed on the flight deck. They were Ric Waring and Mark Elliot. The time on the ship went past all too soon and on checking his gauges, Richi saw that it was time for him to make his way to the surface. As he reached halfway up, the other dive team went zinging past him on their way down to the aircraft carrier. It was now their turn to experience extreme diving. This team comprised of Phil Cheetham, Tony Harris and Mike Langbourg. They all landed on the flight deck then swam along the side of the ship towards the stern.

All the divers had landed on the flight deck within 5 minutes of departing from their dive ship, but to reach the surface they had to make decompression stops. The time taken for each of them to reach the surface was approximately 2 hours. The dive team complied with the Ministry of Defence on all guidelines At the end of the day all the divers spoke about landing on the flight deck at between 140 and 144 metres as this was the team's deepest dive. Little did they know they would be the very last divers to land on the aircraft carrier as the ship is now an official war grave.

THE BALLAD OF HMS *DASHER* R. I. P.

Written by Corrie Primary School pupils, Corrie, Island of Arran

Down, down, down went the *Dasher* down to the bottom of the sea
Burned into her sunken hull the letters R. I. P.

An ordinary seaman in the Royal Navy, back on board the *Dasher*
On the Firth of Clyde
He had time to call his sister - got a message to his mother
'Cause when he left this morning, how she cried

The *Rio de Janeiro*, converted in a hurry
War time requisition, like the boys on board
So many young lives - children and young wives
And the ship they called unlucky - bound to die

Down, down, down went the *Dasher* down to the bottom of the sea
In the freezing waters of the Firth of Clyde in 1943

Taking off and landing, ordinary training
Lining up for pay, they've got some leave tonight
Had time to take a shower - had at least an hour
Never thinking for a minute he'd be swimming for his life
The ship beneath him shuddered, descended into darkness
Hell let loose and all the lights went out
Never heard such a big bang - a deafening bell rang
They were running for the bulkheads, towards the light

Down, down, down went the *Dasher* down to the bottom of the sea
And their families were never told
Official secrecy

Sinking by the minute she went down by the stern
All around were sailors leaping overboard
Like hitting concrete - lucky to have bare feet
Strike out for the life rafts, going numb

Then a boiling in the water, fire all around them
Panic and confusion in the smoke and flames
And the boats that came to save them
There were never men as brave then
As the crew of the *Cragsman* and the *Lithium*

Down, down, down went the *Dasher* down to the bottom of the sea
In the freezing water of the Firth of Clyde in 1943
Down, down, down went the *Dasher* down to the bottom of the sea
Burned into her sunken hull the letters R. I. P.

Children's Thoughts

"I like the " song because it is like a story. It is interesting and I really like the tune. The Dasher sank just in front of our school. We were doing a World War 2 topic. I think the song is quite sad but the real thing would be VERY sad."
A sailor's body from this ship was used in "The Man Who Never Was" ruse which persuaded the Germans to move some of their defences to Greece before the invasion of Europe.

Each of the seven primary schools on Arran composed two songs that were contained in the booklet, *Songs of Arran Life*. Published June 2006.
The seven primary schools are: Brodick Primary School, Corrie Primary School, Pirnmill Primary School, Kilmory Primary School, Lamlash Primary School, Shiskine Primary School and Whiting Bay Primary School.

HMS *Dasher*
Health and Safety

Solicitors
Estate Agents
Financial Advisers
www.taylorandhenderson.co.uk

Our Ref: ANG/PS/STEELE   Your Ref: 22 September 2010
Please reply to: Saltcoats   Direct Dial 01294 606726   Fax No. 01294 464827
E-Mail agreen@taylorandhenderson.co.uk

Mr & Mrs John Steele
104 Eglinton Road
ARDROSSAN
KA22 8NN

Dear Mr and Mrs Steele

Taylor & Henderson is North Ayrshire's largest legal firm established for more than 50 years. Their head office is in Saltcoats and they have three other offices strategically situated in North Ayrshire. The Company deals with a wide range of legal matters.

<u>HMS Dasher 1943</u>

Clearly there were serious breaches of health and safety in the design of the ship.

Although the families of those who died may feel distressed that with proper observance of health and safety procedures the tragedy could have been avoided, John Steele and Noreen Steele have done an excellent job of highlighting the tragedy of HMS Dasher in their books and relatives of those lost will be grateful for the extensive research they have done.

It is hoped that, as a result of John and Noreen's hard work, the unfortunate situation where numerous bodies appear to be buried in an unmarked grave can now be put right. If not by a proper military burial at least by commemoration by a plaque and an appropriate memorial service.

Yours sincerely

<u>Alistair N Green</u>

SALTCOATS : TEL : 01294 464341   51 Hamilton St Saltcoats Ayrshire KA21 5DX FAX : 01294 464827 LP3 Saltcoats   IRVINE : TEL : 01294 278300 65 High St Irvine Ayrshire KA12 0AL FAX : 01294 272886 LP6 Irvine
KILWINNING : TEL : 01294 557506   83 Main St Kilwinning Ayrshire KA13 6AN   FAX : 01294 558552 LP2 Kilwinning   WEST KILBRIDE : TEL : 01294 823888 27 Ritchie St West Kilbride Ayrshire KA23 9AL FAX : 01294 829903 LP1 West Kilbride
PARTNERS :   ALISTAIR N GREEN LL.B.   MARTIN J McALLISTER LL.B.   ASSOCIATES : JACQUI TAYLOR LL.B. Hons Dip.LP M.B.A. T.E.P. SHEILA J McCOSH LL.B.   ALISON MURPHY LL.B. Dip. LP
BARBARA BLACK LL.B. Dip. LP   FINANCIAL SERVICES : MALCOLM GIBSON Dip. PFS.   PRACTICE MANAGER : YVONNE COOK S.L.A.   PROPERTY MANAGER : JACKIE KEAN

AUTHORISED AND REGULATED BY THE FINANCIAL SERVICES AUTHORITY
INCORPORATING : DUNNANS, MCALLISTER & CO, ALISON SMERTON, GILMOUR & O'HARE AND LAMBDENS, SOLICITORS

CDM Scotland is one of Britain's foremost providers of health and safety services. John Cowan Technical Director operates from:
Suite 1, Beresford Court. 6-8 Beresford Lane. Ayr. www.cdmscotland.co.uk.
The Technical director compiled a health and safety report regarding the sinking of HMS *Dasher*. The report read;
On hand-over the Archer Class escort carriers did not meet Royal Navy standards and required major alterations to make them fit for purpose. The required alterations would take a number of weeks.
However these ships had already been incorporated within the plans of the Royal Navy and were crucial to have in place as soon as possible. This meant the required upgrading works were not carried out.
Officers and pilots complained of an overpowering smell on board their Archer Class aircraft carrier and some ratings feared for their safety.
As to the sinking of HMS *Dasher* there seemed little doubt the explosion was a petrol one.
From the damage sustained it was evident the cause of the explosion was a large one consistent to a partial filling of at least the petrol compartment with vapour.
The causes of the presence and ignition of the vapour are not apparent but due to the inadequate safety arrangements in this class of ship may have been many.
Safeguards against accidents of this nature are, by Royal Navy standards practically non existent in the petrol arrangements and hangars of these American converted aircraft carriers.
The indirect causes were;
Adequate time was not allowed to undertake the works to a satisfactory standard, resulting in sub standard work that had to be rectified.
Poor communication between the Royal Navy and the USA regarding the scope of works to be undertaken to the ships, to bring them up to the quality required for war-time operational duty.
Cost implications, the cheapest option was the only option due to the financial constraints at the time.
Poor communication by the person taking possession of the converted ships and the department within the Royal Navy that was incorporating the converted ships within strategic battles.
Insufficient time allowed for sea trials not taking into account the remediation works that had to be undertaken in the UK once the supposed completed ships had arrived from the USA.
Conversion work was to a poor standard and not fit for purpose, the works did not conform to the standards required by the Royal Navy.
No health and safety audits had been carried out to identify hazards associated with the alteration works and implemented measures to reduce

any residual risk.

Health and safety concerns raised by Captain Boswell were not heeded by the management.

No new procedures were drawn up to take account of changes to the design of the ship and the amount of fuel stored onboard.

As a result of the sinking of HMS *Dasher* the petrol system on her sister ships required modification in accordance with normal Royal Navy practice.

Numerous alterations were instructed to the sister ships, the first measure to be undertaken was to reduce the amount of petrol carried from 75,000 gallons to 36,000 gallons.

Regarding the cause of the persistent petrol fumes, for greater safety later escort carriers had their petrol system modified in America prior to being handed-over to the Royal Navy.

HMS Dasher (1943) Association

The Association was formed in 2000 to maintain contact between members of the ship's company, the Fleet Air Arm personnel who served on *Dasher* and their relatives, also those involved in the rescue operation, after care and those who helped the bereaved and the survivors.

The bereaved and survivors meet and derive the maximum benefit from mutual support and understanding.

Members receive regular newsletters and meet in Ardrossan each year on the weekend nearest the 27th March to participate in memorial events to remember the 379 lives lost with the sinking of HMS *Dasher*

For further information contact:

John Steele

Founder Member.

j.steele2@talktalk.net

or

davidhodkinson@btinternet.com

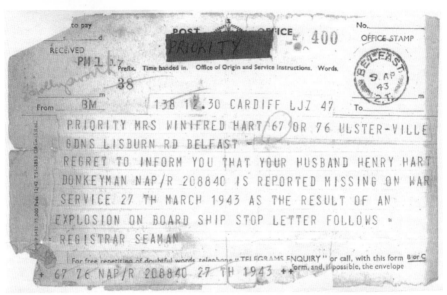

Top: Telegram stating explosion on board ship. Note no mention of ship sinking.
Bottom: Survivors meeting up in Ardrossan after 60 years.

History and Timeline of HMS *Dasher*

Archer Class Escort Aircraft Carrier

1941

12 April: Launching of American merchant vessel *Rio de Janeiro*. Built by Sun Shipbuilding & Dry Dock Company, Chester, USA.

22 November: *Rio de Janeiro* taken over by U.S. Navy for conversion as Archer Class Aircraft Carrier. Given the code letters BAVG-4. Pendant D 37.

1942

1 July: Conversion completed at Tietjen & Lang, Dry Dock Company, Hoboken, New York. Handed-over to US Navy.

2 July: Official hand-over ceremony from US Navy to Royal Navy. Ship named HMS *Dasher*. Captain Richard Bell Davies in command. Due to adverse weather conditions, the handover ceremony took place in HMS *Dasher's* hangar.

3 July: Brooklyn Navy Yard. 9am engine trials. 1.30pm, both bow anchors dropped. 2.30pm engine trials complete.

4 July: 11.30am first aircraft lands on *Dasher*. 12.41pm aircraft crashes whilst landing on *Dasher's* deck. Pilot unhurt. 2.10pm Aircraft attempting to land fails to connect with arrester wire and careers over bow into sea. Aircraft sinks, pilot picked up by rescue boat unhurt.

5 July / 29 August: Engine trials and rectification of defects. Fire broke out onboard. Further repairs carried out. HMS *Dasher* prepares for convoy duty.

Armament taken onboard. Three single 4inch American Mark 9 Anti Aircraft Guns; Ten single Oerlikon 20mm Anti-Aircraft Guns; Three 40mm Anti-Aircraft Guns; 80 Mark 7 Depth Charges; 500lb Semi Armour Piercing Bombs; Anti U-Boat 250lb Semi Armour Piercing Bombs; Anti U-Boat 250lb General-Purpose Bombs; Torpedoes; Thousands of rounds for Aircraft machine guns; Flares; Pyrotechnics.

6 August: As Captain Bell Davies is required for other duties, Captain C.N. Lentaignes takes command of HMS *Dasher*

24 August: 837 Squadron lands on.

30 August: *Dasher* part of Convoy HX 205 from Halifax, Canada, to the Clyde, Scotland.

September: Arrived in the Firth of Clyde. 837 Squadron disembarks to Royal Naval Air Station, Machrihanish. *Dasher* docked in Clyde shipyard. Modifications required to bring the ship up to Royal Navy standards.

27 October: Ship required for convoy duty. Modifications postponed. All dockyard workmen left ship. 3.20pm *Dasher* slipped mooring. Boom net lowered. Sailed for lower Clyde past Cumbrae. 5.10pm Swordfish aircraft landed onboard. Passed Pladda and Ailsa Craig. Anchor at Holy Isle.

28 October: At Sea. 6.45am sighted HMS *Argus* & HMS *Jamaica*. Squadron of aircraft land on *Dasher*.

29 October: *Dasher* returns to the Clyde.

30 October: In company with HMS *Argus*, HMS *Jamaica*, HMS *Delhi* and 4 escorts. Depart Clyde with convoy. Code name, Force LX. Forming part of Eastern Naval Task Force. Operation Torch. Invasion of North Africa. Six UK convoys departed from UK. Total number of ships involved = 215.

A US convoy, with 99 ships departed from America. All ships bound for North Africa. 2.45pm HMS *Zetland* radar operator makes contact with enemy submarine. Emergency turn to port. 2.48pm HMS *Zetland* making depth charge attack. No further contact with enemy submarine.

31 October: At sea. Convoy bound for Oran, North Africa.

1 November: Pass 5 miles off Lisbon, South West Spain. Aircraft sighted. Identified as friendly.

8 November: Off Oran. North Africa. Action stations. In position with HMS *Rodney*, HMS *Furious*, HMS *Biter*, HMS *Delhi* and nine Royal Navy destroyers. 5am. Heavy gunfire bombardment commences from all HM ships. Return gunfire from Oran. Heavy bombardment sustained. All aircraft flew off *Dasher* to provide escorts for bombing raids, secure air cover at Oran and to drop propaganda leaflets.

9 November: All aircraft flew off. Enemy submarine contact. Royal Navy ships carry out depth charge attack. Due to U-boat contact HMS *Dasher* was ordered to re-position further off-shore.

10 November: At Sea. Destination Gibraltar. 11.24am submarine contact. Emergency turn to port. Resumed course. Arrive at Gibraltar.

11 November: 11am Armistice day observed. 11.20am two Ratings arrive from HMS *Biter*.

12 November: Secure for sea. In escort with convoy MFK1 from Gibraltar to UK.

November 13: Commence zigzag course. Convoy time advanced one hour.

November 14: 1.00 pm aircraft sighted. Commence zigzag course. Aircraft friendly. Cease zigzag course. Arrive at Liverpool for repairs and fitting of Air Defence Room. HMS *Dasher* allocated to Home Fleet.

December: Wrens invited onboard for tea.

1943

27 January: Depart Liverpool for Clyde.

28 January: Arrive at Clyde. A Vice-Admiral was onboard during flying trials.

29 January: Arrived at Greenock.

January 31: Arrive at Rothesay Bay, Clyde. Depart for Scapa Flow.

February 1: Arrived at Scapa Flow for work-up.

February: Take part in royal visit. HM King George VI inspects Fleet. Excess of 200 vessels in Scapa Flow.

15 February: Sailed in convoy JW53 bound for Murmansk. Squadrons 816, 837 and 891 onboard. Aircraft, Swordfish & Hurricanes.

17 February: HMS *Dasher* and convoy encounters storm force winds, snow squalls and severe icing conditions. Port side lifeboats and Carley Floats whipped from their davits and stowage positions. Three Swordfish aircraft lashed to flight deck of *Dasher* washed overboard. Weather is extremely savage. Speed maintained. *Dasher* suffers from severe weather damage. American welding of hull splits apart. Ship ordered to depart from convoy, proceed to Seydisfjordur, north east Iceland.

18 February: 9am arrive off Seydisfjordur. 3.30pm. Enter Seydisfjordur in company with HMS *Belfast*, *Cumberland* and *Scylla*. *Dasher* at anchor. Review of damage. Refuelled Ship. Proceed to Eyjafjordur, north Iceland. Anchor at Akureyri. Ship careened (turned on one side for repair). Temporary repairs carried out. Proceed to Caledon Shipyard, Dundee. Permanent repairs took 3 weeks to complete. Sail to Rosyth Royal Navy dry dock. Hull inspected and found to be sound.

Mid March: Proceed to Clyde. Anchor at Tail O' The Bank. Greenock

24 March: Commenced work-up in Clyde area.

26 March: Boom net lowered at Lamlash Bay. Arran. Ship enters Lamlash Bay. Anchor dropped

27 March: (Day of the tragedy – sinking of HMS *Dasher*)

9 am. Depart Lamlash Bay. Involved in aircraft landing exercises. 12 depth charges removed from forward bomb room and 12 removed from after depth charge magazine. Stowed in the port and starboard side of hanger. 12 feet (3 metres) from aircraft lift. All for ready use. 68 depth charges left in depth charge magazine. Removed from stowage, 9 torpedoes with warheads and primers inserted. Stowed in hanger. 3 on either side of lift well. 3 on a rack port side. **4.35pm** Last signal from *Dasher* to Lamlash Signal Station, Arran. *"Will arrive Greenock at 1800 hours."* **4.40pm.** Dull thud heard throughout ship, not unlike backfire from engine. Followed immediately by a horrendous explosion. Many large fires broke out in hanger area. Aircraft machine gun ammunition exploding. **4.42pm.** Ship commences to sink at the stern. **4.45pm.** Ship's bow rises slowly out of the water almost vertical pointing to the sky. **4.48pm.** HMS *Dasher* sinks stern first to170 metres to rest upright on seabed

Battle Honours.

Atlantic, North Africa and Arctic.

Carrier Specifications

Overall length: 494 feet (145 Metres)
Beam: 70 feet. (20 metres)
Speed: 16 knots
Fuel stowage: 75,000 gallons. (337,500 Litres)
Displacement: 8,200 tons.
Aircraft: Sea Hurricanes and Swordfish. Between 12 and 16 at any one time.
Catapult: Aircraft catapulted off ship by means of a hook attached to a steel cable driven by compressed air. The cable ran along a 35 metre (100yard) groove on the flight deck. As hook disengaged it flung the aircraft at high speed off the ship into the air.

Top: Crew off duty posing in gun turret beside wooden flight deck.
Bottom: Sub-lieutenant Lionel Godfrey preparing to fly off at sunrise. Royal Navy roundel has been replaced with American star.